LIFE CHANGING
TESTIMONIES
of the
LORD JESUS CHRIST

LIFE CHANGING
TESTIMONIES
of the
LORD JESUS CHRIST

Compiled by
MARLENA TANYA MUCHNICK

Marlena Tanya Yambra
myambra@hotmail.com
jewishconvert-lds.com

Photo Credits

Cover picture: Rembrandt Harmensz van Rijn: The Ascension of Christ. In the Alte Pinakothek, Munich, Germany. Used with permission from Scala/Art Resource, New York.

Black and white reproduction of etching by Rembrandt Harmensz van Rijn: Detail of Christ with the sick around him, receiving little children. (The Hundred Guilder print) Used with permission of Metropolitan Museum of Art, New York, NY 10028

Copyright TXu865-066

ISBN 1-55517-394-2

v.6

Cover design: David Marty Designs
Page layout: Corinne A. Bischoff

Publisher: Bonneville Books
             P.O. Box 531
             Springville, UT 84663
             801-489-4084

Manufactured in the United States of America

Also by the same author:
Notes of a Jewish Convert to the LDS Church:
Conversion of a Soul

For God so loved the world,
that he gave his only begotten Son,
that whosoever believeth in him should not perish,
but have everlasting life.

John 3:16

For God hath not given us the spirit of fear;
but of power, and of love, and of a sound mind.

Be not thou therefore ashamed of the testimony
of our Lord, nor of me his prisoner:
but be thou partaker of the afflictions of the gospel
According to the power of God;

2 Timothy 1:7-8

INTRODUCTION

The sun shall be no more thy light by day; neither for brightness
shall the moon give light unto thee: but the Lord shall be unto thee
an everlasting light, and thy God thy glory.

Isa 60:19

I think there are times in an author's life when a book seems to need writing, when an idea will not go away but tags along behind daily problems and family concerns, waiting patiently just outside of consciousness, but still it is there, wanting that audience. I know then it is only a matter of time until it challenges me for attention. A really good idea will always come forward...

Such was the occasion for the onset of this collection. I simply could not avoid its inception. Since becoming a Christian a decade ago I have felt it increasingly necessary that a few of those faithful who love the Lord Jesus Christ somehow leave a legacy of him as he is experienced in our hearts. It seemed that a chorus of voices raised in written praise could do much to uplift, edify and hopefully be of significant value to many lives. A book of testimonies of Jesus Christ becomes an act of faith for each contributor willing to share his or her very private story of conversion and growth in and because of the Gospel of Jesus Christ.

In writing the several chapters that follow I endeavored to appeal to anyone who is searching for knowledge of the Savior and his teachings. I believe greater missionary work is possible if done in this way. It is important, therefore, to honor the various spiritual levels and the separate, intensely personal beliefs of each person who contributed testimonies to this book. To that end I have taken the quotations from the King James Version of the Holy Bible, with some latter-day scripture references, as The Book of Mormon and other latter day scriptures are companions to the Bible. Rather than produce a work which centers exclusively upon any one lifestyle (other than mentioned in individual testimony) I have chosen to focus upon major Christian themes and history found in the Old and New Testaments. Those several participants represented herein whose testimonies are not LDS-inspired have been assured that church affiliation was not of primary significance, though in the introductory chapters the principles embedded in the Plan of Salvation which Christ taught are presented in the light of latter day revelation.

The foremost thrust of this book is to tell of the marvelous ways of God and Jesus Christ in our lives, to share with as many readers as possible some of the deepest convictions of our Christianity and especially to tell how we have been enlightened by our faith. Each testimony, with the exception of my own, has been gathered on that basis. As a Jewish convert, my story must be taken in its entirety as the deepest expression of my particular persuasion as well as the propelling impetus behind the making of this book.

Each person I approached warmed to the concept. Each earnestly prayed to know of the rightness of this book and his or her place in it. They then came forward and gave freely of their most deeply held spiritual beliefs, relishing this new opportunity to share testimonies with others, to hopefully touch many people through a solemn declaration of love for their Heavenly Father and for Jesus Christ.

The interviews themselves were exciting. We began them with prayer, in hope of companionship with the Spirit. Each time we were given that wonderful feeling of peace and love which assured us that the Spirit was with us and that our mission is indeed an important one.

Each interview was recorded and transcribed as spoken and then edited. Great effort has been made to retain each speaker's ideas and story content, their level of understanding, their personality, grammatical style and rhythm of speech. The result is thirteen beautiful, uplifting and touching stories that offer to the fortunate reader a wide spectrum of personal knowledge, cumulative life experience and spiritual food for thought.

The confessions of faith gathered herein are as precious gems that I doubt could ever again emerge with the beauty of expression found in these stories. In compiling them I gained a special insight into the spirits which God has placed in each of us. The beauty I glimpsed within each soul really touched me and I know that our Father loves us for that innocence and humility that is within all of His children.

What is a testimony? How does it come about and what does it mean to the bearer? In 1Cor 12:3 the Apostle Paul, teaching of the gifts of the Spirit said "...no man can say that Jesus is the Lord, but by the Holy Ghost." John the Baptist gave a perfect testimony to the Jews and priests: "And I saw, and bare record that this is the Son of God." (John 1:32) It is also true, I believe, that a young boy named Joseph Smith asked his Heavenly Father to direct him to the correct church one fateful day in 1827, and that as a result of his ensuing testimony he endured from that time forward naught but hardship, persecution and eventually murder, finally sealing with his own blood his testimony of what he heard and saw that day in the grove near his father's farm.

Like a court witness who gives affirmation of fact, a testimony is actual evidence of an event. It does not come simply, in most cases. If it is a spiritual affirmation, it comes by the power of the Holy Ghost to one who has dutifully studied, prayed and perhaps fasted in faith to know for certain some great point of eternal truth. The Holy Ghost (or Holy Spirit) then gives its revelation. But this sacred prompting must be received as truth when revealed, for that holy messenger of the Lord will not linger with unbelievers. Those who deny what they have felt or who look to intellectualize or criticize it will find the prompting slipping away and their inspiration lost in confusion.

A testimony, then, is a witness of things which are true, constituting a knowledge that cannot be denied by the believer, who feels the impressions made by the Holy Ghost become indelible upon his enlightened soul. How many mortals have willingly given their lives because they could not deny the knowledge so convincingly given them by the Holy Ghost? It is the same with those who have contributed to this book, and through their inspirational stories and special affirmations all who partake of their great faith can be uplifted.

When this compilation of testimonies of Jesus Christ was begun, there was one strongly held goal in everyone's mind. Every contributor wanted to tell the salient events of their life; how they had changed, especially after their conversion to the Gospel of Christ, much as one who has discovered great wealth wants to share that special story with others who also seek precious treasure. Each person felt prompted to relate to me some of their most private beliefs concerning the one we call our Savior and Redeemer, and our Heavenly Father. They felt the need to express their gratitude for the Christ who has risen from the dead to save us all that we need not fear death or torment and each one gained great satisfaction in expressing in this way their love of the Savior, regardless of the scope of their knowledge, the complexity of their background, their station in life or the color of their skin.

No one asked for or received compensation of any kind. All interviewees were chosen as a result of spiritual prompting. Scriptural knowledge was not a prerequisite for an interview. These wonderful people believe that testimonies of Christ are an ark of truth and hope which can bring all weary passengers safely across their troubled waters to the peace and good news of the Gospel, which always awaits those who earnestly seek it in humility.

I believe the central themes in the following testimonies are four-fold. Before knowledge can begin there must be a desire to know the truth about our existence: Where did we come from? Why are we here? Where are we going? What can we do to better ourselves and better serve others?

The first theme, therefore, is search and discovery. Heavenly Father always rewards those who seek Him with great blessings of knowledge. In Chuck's story we learn of his lean childhood years, accompany him through years of searching for life's greatest gifts, led always forward by strong impressions of spiritual needs. His discoveries have led him to Christ and to a life of devoted service.

Dana's background was filled with deep unhappiness and drug problems. Her courageous attempts to change became centered upon Christ and his Church. As she felt the pure love of her Savior she followed the prompting of the Spirit toward that saving light. Self-dislike turned to self-esteem. She discovered the beauty of her own spirit and became a bright, guiding light for her family.

My testimony (Marlena's Story) is also the history of an intense search to find answers. My quest has taken me across age-old religious boundaries to find Christ and to love him. My passionate need to know more of God's kingdom was the force that led me from the synagogue and the Old Testament into the light of full truth.

Prayer is another theme that runs throughout these stories. Praying for enlightenment, for spiritual strength and discernment directs our quest for solutions to the most crucial problems we face. Chris fell to his knees when his cousin was injured and slipped into a coma. Through communication with the Almighty he came to understand that his cousin would be healed, and more, he received answers to basic questions of faith. Through constant and fervent prayer, Chris learned to rely upon his Savior and found peace and happiness in his life.

Sylvia's Story is a beautiful lesson in how to constantly keep in touch with the Holy Spirit through prayer. She lives in the light of Christ, basking in his love for her. Though handicapped by an emotionally damaging childhood she reached out to God in prayer and found that He lifted her above her problems. He directed her toward rewarding missionary work in a trouble-filled country.

Heartfelt, humble prayer leads to affirmation of faith, and faith grows in direct proportion to the intensity of the need to know. Faith is more than a word. It is the essence of life and without it we cannot live and we cannot prosper. When Bill felt the affirmation of the Holy Spirit in his busy professional life he chose to serve others through outreach projects. Tested in poverty and trials of the spirit, he triumphed, learning to depend wholly upon his Heavenly Father. He is a living testimony to the joy that commitment to the Lord and perseverance to his cause brings. That faith and prayer bring great change and growth is the theme of Fred's story, a beautiful, uplifting testimony of a lifelong Mormon who found that living our lives within the bound the Lord sets is the only way to happiness.

When John and his wife lost their son to illness their faith was greatly tested. John's grief became so great he began to turn away from his life and work, but he was shown a marvelous manifestation which strengthened and renewed him. Through this miracle he understood the mercy of God and learned forever to have greater faith in his Father in Heaven.

Greg's life-changing experience came subtly, through faith, prayer, service and heartfelt reliance upon the love and mercy of his

Father in Heaven. How earnestly he prayed to be strengthened and relieved of his shyness that he might better serve God. His prayers were abundantly answered in a way that later blessed his wife and children as well.

The testimony of John T. is one of confirmation of truth through faith and study. His unwavering allegiance to all the saving principles of the Gospel of Christ helped John to cope with his father's addiction and to firmly plant his own soul on the path of righteousness. Today he and his family serve the Lord in many capacities; their home is based upon the standards Christ has set for us all.

The Gospel of Jesus Christ is based upon love and service, its corollary: the divine love of God for his creatures, the love we are endowed with in our own and our children's lives, the charity we give to others, our concerns for the earth and its creatures, and especially the special feeling of oneness we can have with our Heavenly Father and His Son. Susan's sweet story of feeling filled with intense light—the love of God for her—is tender and uplifting. She has, through her great faith, been given knowledge of the unconditional love that God has for all of us, how we must seek and acknowledge Him. Her story tells of the compassion of Christ for all of mankind. Our direct challenge is to show by the way we live, work and serve our Heavenly Father and each other that sweet, strong testimony we all have of Him, and of our Savior.

Again, Gloria's story is one of the wonderment of knowing and longing to receive the love and guidance our Heavenly Father has for us, as expressed through the Savior. The calmness and peace she experiences as a result of knowing Christ is a testimony to what we can all feel in the presence of the Holy One of Israel, even Jesus Christ.

David's story is another that is filled with the love of Christ and service to others in an institutional setting. The leadership and guidance he provides those who are ill and downtrodden occupies most of his time. His life is an inspiring lesson in charity and missionary work. His scholarly approach to religious themes are rooted in a humble love for his Heavenly Father and His Begotten Son who brought to all of us the perfect example of selfless ministry.

It is a common belief of those whose lives have been given over to the ministrations of the kingdom of God that His Word be spread as seeds among the fields of mankind, seeking their burrow in the fertile soil of grateful hearts. That is the spirit in which the following stories were given. Regardless of differing faiths and church affiliations the common bonds that unite these testimonies are disarmingly simple: they share a great faith in Christianity, a faith born of intense spiritual testing. Each voice that speaks from these pages rings, too, of learned obedience to biblical commandments that demands a lifestyle which shuns the common ways of the world in favor of the self-effacing teachings of Christ. Each person represented here joins me in making a fervent plea for a return to righteousness by living a Christlike life, turning from selfish and destructive preoccupations toward service to humanity. It is in this spirit that these stories should be read.

Everyone involved in this project believes that their story is special and that it will benefit from the telling as I have recorded it, sensing as we did that we were guided toward one another by those holy messengers who are always figuring in our lives for good.

This book has been written, too, as a warning voice. Jesus Christ is our Savior. He "died to make men holy" (from Battle Hymn of the Republic). He came to save this world before it drowns in iniquity. There are many signs of the times that tell us that the wickedness now upon the earth must be purged. Many scriptural prophecies point to the knowledge that in these final years before the Lord's Second Coming the world will be cleansed spiritually and physically. The time is short. It is vitally necessary that our world's societies turn toward the gospel as Jesus taught us. Let us heed the call to come unto Christ, to learn his ways and grow in our faith that we may speedily and lovingly clear the path for his return.

"And after that he came men also were saved by faith in his name; and by faith, they became the sons of God. And as surely as Christ liveth he spake these words unto our fathers, saying: 'Whatsoever thing which is good, in faith believing that ye shall receive, behold, it shall be done unto you.'" (Moroni 7:26 Book of Mormon)

Love from God is the polestar, the guiding light in everyone's life, the source of even the breath we take. Faith is the conduit that puts us upon the path homeward and prompts blessings from above. Our Heavenly Father and His Son, through the teachings and ministrations of the Holy Ghost, are the master architects of existence. How important it is to know them and to build a life dedicated to sharing their care for us with all who we meet! In the short time we have left to us to repent of our worldly attitudes, let us look toward those things we have been commanded to focus upon and put our lives in order. Let us leave our personal legacy of Christ. Let us take up our cross and with great works and wonder walk in his footsteps until he lifts us up and we can, with him, reach again toward our eternal home that lovingly awaits us.

With the gracious consent of the contributors to this book I invite you to partake of the feast!

Marlena Tanya Muchnick
Seattle, Washington
1998

And after him was Shamgar the son of Anath,
which slew of the Philistines six hundred men
with an ox goad:
and he also delivered Israel.

Judges 3:31

CHAPTER ONE

PALESTINE AT THE NEW ERA

For God doth not walk in crooked paths, neither doth he turn to the
right hand nor to the left, neither doth he vary from that which he
hath said, therefore his paths are straight, and his course is one
eternal round.

Doctrine and Covenants 3:2

JESUS CHRIST IS OUR SAVIOR. HE CAME to this earth to save our souls
from certain death at the hands of the Adversary of the world. He
came to cleanse this world of its sinfulness, to soothe and teach us in
our pain and sadness and sorrows. He came to show us the fount of
true joy and fulfillment. He came to teach us of his Heavenly Father
who is also our Creator. Corollary to that lesson, Jesus taught brotherly love as an eternal principle of living, presenting the hearers of
his Word with many examples from his private and public life.

Jesus Christ gave the earth and all people on it an unprecedented
opportunity: eternal life with God in Heaven who reigns supreme in
the cosmos and Who is the Judge of all things. Jesus came to save us
from the wages of sin we create by our disobedience and our
maligning. He came, he taught, he conquered death and sin for us all
through his infinite and eternal Atonement. Though we can never
fully understand the magnificent gift we have been given, the
Atonement is a reality and the only way to our salvation. It is a
terrible thing to contemplate that if no Messiah had come to us,
God's immeasurable gift of eternal life could never be bestowed
upon the race of men. Through five saving principles of God: propi-
tiation, reconciliation, mediation, intercession and advocacy, Christ
appeased the demands of divine justice by which all who desire to

1

again dwell in their Father's presence may do so. Because of Jesus Christ we are redeemed from death and sin.

> ...*even so ye must be born again into the kingdom of heaven, of water and of the Spirit, and be cleansed by blood, even the blood of mine Only Begotten; that ye might be sanctified from all sin, and enjoy the words of eternal life in this world, and eternal life in the world to come, even immortal glory. For by the water ye keep the commandment, by the Spirit ye are justified, and by the blood ye are sanctified.*

Moses 6:59-60, Pearl of Great Price

The Plan of Redemption, also called the Plan of Happiness or the Plan of Salvation, is based upon a dual foundation: the Fall of Adam and the divine Sonship of Jesus Christ. Man cannot resurrect or save himself. It had to be done by an infinite being—God Himself, manifested through His only begotten Son in the flesh, Jesus Christ. The Atonement satisfied two necessary requirements; temporal (body) and spiritual. Jesus Christ voluntarily shed his blood to atone for Adam's transgression, a condition which changed his and Eve's deathless and holy state to a mortal one through their expulsion from the Garden (shut out from the presence of God) bringing upon them physical changes (their bodies became subject to death).

But our Heavenly Father does not want any of His children to perish. Through his mercy our first parents could be reconciled again to Him through faith, repentance and obedience to the commandments. Because they reconciled themselves to the will of God their trials helped to prepare the way for all of us to experience the same trials and blessings, the same gift of mortal life and the priceless opportunity if we are worthy to return to live with God after death.

> *Therefore remember, O man, for all thy doings thou shalt be brought into judgment. Wherefore, if you have sought to do wickedly in the day of your probation, then ye are found unclean before the judgment-seat of God; and no unclean thing can dwell with God...*

1Ne 10:20-21 Book of Mormon

Because of the intercession of Jesus Christ mankind does not carry Adam's transgression, but each of us are answerable to God for our sins. Very briefly stated, we are redeemed from physical death as a gift. In keeping with the principle just stated, redemption from spiritual death is a lifelong process which we participate in through faith, our solemn and constant repentance, righteous longsuffering, taking upon us the name, i.e. the character of Christ in baptism by one having proper authority, and the bestowal of the gift of the Holy Ghost. Then we are saved by grace after all we can do. This is the central principle of the divine Plan whereby we may, except for the sons of perdition—those who fight against God—be cleansed of sin and renewed of body and spirit in this world and in our lives to come.

Jesus Christ was and is today the greatest of heroes, a masterpiece of creation by his immortal Father, our Supreme God. We need to learn of him, of his ways in the world, his trials, his purpose here among our ancestors, his true feelings as he walked gently, bravely and so boldly through his short but matchlessly powerful life. This is Jesus Christ—the risen, the perfect, the only Begotten Son of the Father. This is a bit of his story.

Jesus came to earth as a babe in Bethlehem, born to a woman named Mary and her husband Joseph, his stepfather. These two raised him. In his lifetime, Jesus was sought after by kings who wanted him destroyed. He was attacked many times by men who would have him lose his way, his life, his holy name and divine purpose. But Jesus never ran from his trouble—he never gave less than his all to the people who crowded around him and he never complained when they took his precious life and spilt his blood. Instead, he willingly offered himself to show us the way, conquering life and death forever through his resurrection. In forgiving us our sins, his Atonement makes possible our eternal life, with him, for every worthy soul.

Jesus the Christ is the royal king of all who have and who will live on this earth in any age. In all ways the Savior Jesus Christ is a miracle among mankind—an everlasting symbol of all we can be to each other. We sing his praises. He is beloved by those in Heaven who attend him, as well as those mortals who serve him on earth. He belongs to the ages.

The four gospels, unfortunately, are protracted in their reports of the life of Jesus. They present few comments on his childhood and early life as a young Jewish man, working for his father as a carpenter and learning the ways of men. Even the records of his short ministry are void of any long narratives or time lines. The result of this dearth of material has been that most of the mortal life of Christ, Son of God and son of Man, is unavailable to us. Or is it?

From those several narratives, prophecies and insights from the Old Testament and a close attention to those eternal principles which Jesus taught us, it is possible to come to a fuller understanding of the way our Master perceived himself and his mission among the Hebrews and Romans he met and influenced for good. Though little of what he said is recorded, it is obvious that he spoke a great deal to multitudes of people in his travels. Greater insight can be gained from his messages to them through pondering the ideas he taught, his demeanor among his disciples and the deeper, less obvious meanings which were essential to his ministry.

Though volumes have been filled with echoes of the prophecies made about the birth and saving mission of Jesus, who among us is really aware of the extent of Jesus' love for the Torah and other Jewish writings or his intense devotion for his Heavenly Father? What can we say of his effort to convince his contemporaries of the truth of his discipleship and his mission? What essential lessons do his parables have for us? We can only wonder at his own anxieties and triumphs as he taught, healed, performed miracles and finally let himself be overcome at the hands of one of his own apostles and then, without using his divine power to save himself, Jesus allowed the Jewish Court of Sanhedrin to condemn him to death, the infinite sacrifice from which he rose in glory.

Only when we understand how perfectly he lived the ideals he taught can we really understand that Jesus Christ was the living embodiment of divine, eternal principles. Then we can more fully appreciate the greatest truths of all; that he lives, that he administrates this earth and its creatures whom he saved forever from physical and spiritual death, and that he will return to live among us in the majesty of perfect grace.

The birth date of Jesus cannot be known but might be very roughly estimated. Luke, in his gospel, says that Jesus was baptized in the fifteenth year of the reign of Tiberius Caesar, about 29 A.D. (See Luke 3) Luke's timing may not have been more than an estimate, for he says that Jesus at that time "began to be about thirty years of age,"(Luke 3:23) thirty being only the then legal age for proselytizing in that region. According to Matthew's account, Jesus was born during the reign of King Herod the Great, who died several years later, rumored to be around 4 A.D.

Errors in calculating the Christian calendar used then (the

Dionysian system, which asserts Jesus was born 753 years after the founding of Rome) make it impossible to know for certain, but various scholars have estimated the birth of Jesus to be between 5-1 B.C. Latter day scripture places the birth at 1 B.C. (Doctrine and Covenants 20:1, 21:3) We know that Jesus' crucifixion occurred prior to the death of Herod Phillip in 33 A.D. and the historian Josephus records it occurring that year on April 3rd,[1] so it is reasonable to assume that Jesus (the mortal) lived fewer than forty years on earth.

Jesus appeared on earth at a time when there was favorable spiritual thinking. In prior centuries the Jews had been subject to Greek culture and language, which had spread over the Occident. The Jewish Diaspora (dispersion after the destruction of Israel and then Judah) saw many thousands of Jews adopt Greek ways or outwardly appear to embrace them under fear of death should their own ceremonies, held mainly in secret, be discovered. In Jerusalem there was at the time internal accord and what seemed like prosperity in the Greco-Roman world, known as the Pax Romana. The Greeks spread culture, language, and philosophy. The Romans built the roads and ruled in the Mediterranean and the Roman Empire spanned the borders of Britain, Mesopotamia and Egypt.[2] Under no threats of war for a time, they kept a somewhat tolerant political rule. A great era of trade was opening up, not to be rivaled until the nineteenth century. Travel for Jews was common then and encouraged throughout the region—the gospels record Jesus' journeys with his apostles as far north as Tyre in Syria.

The Pharisees and members of the Sanhedrin constituted the wealthy class. Other residents of Jerusalem lived in relative squalor. Jesus found himself with almost no middle class to preach to, but there was for a time equanimity between the Roman political and social systems while Jewish moral teachings were spreading throughout Syria, Lebanon and Israel. The Apostle Paul was an example of this, being a Roman citizen (See Acts 16:37) and preaching in Greek the gospel of a Hebrew Messiah. The impression is that this temporary tranquility was but a hiatus between wars, but it gave Jesus the opportunity to establish his Church among them in that dispensation.

The Jews in Jerusalem had become very influential. They were intimately involved with organizing trade in the Mediterranean world, as many routes passed through Palestine toward the seaports to the east. Many prosperous Jews became citizens of an ever-expanding Greco-Roman worldly outlook as well. Their court, the Sanhedrin (formerly Council of Elders), was entrenched there with its chief priests and scribes (See Luke 22:66) and recognized as legitimate by the Romans who tolerated their religious ceremonies.[3] They were recognized in matters of law which did not directly affect Roman interests, and as such it had no power to carry out sentences of death. By Jesus' time, the first century of the new era, the city of Jerusalem had grown in size to about three miles in circumference. The emperor Titus built a wall around the three million inhabitants it housed.

Perhaps the most famous Roman governor of Judea was Augustus Caesar (31 B.C. - A.D. 14), an energetic ruler who demanded order in his government. He worked for financial reform while including careful registration of persons of each conquered town or city, according to their ancestral birthplace. Augustus was essentially concerned with power. He was always suspect of other powers arising in that area that would challenge Rome's further expansion. Palestine was therefore allowed to be only a semi-independent state within a gentile dictatorship full of military sites. Indications of the Roman presence were everywhere, especially near Jewish places of worship. Pontius Pilate, the Roman procurator in Judea who later would give up Jesus to be crucified, is rumored to have built his palace near the Jewish Temple.

Herod the Great ruled Judea for a time (Josephus estimates 34 years until his death in 4 B.C.)[4] as successor to the throne of his father Antipater. Herod was a prodigious builder, but also a murderer. His wife and children suffered death at his possessive and jealous hand. After the death of Herod during Jesus' childhood, Palestine was divided thrice into areas governed by Herod's sons, Philip (areas northeast of Galilee), Antipas (Galilee and Perea) and Pontius Pilate who was made procurator over Judea, Samaria and Idumea. Josephus tells us that Pilate planned to abolish the Jewish laws.[5] Antipas and Pilate shared a love of power in their regions. Both were involved in the trial of Christ.

But it was increasingly difficult for the Romans to rule the Jews because they were mutinous, stiff-necked and insurgent as a captive people in their own country. Pilate even encouraged ongoing conflicts in his attempt to govern them. The more oppressive he became, the more they robbed and protested his edicts, always in the name of socio-political causes. He had a reputation for always denying the Jews what they asked for. His final concession to them in allowing Jesus to be crucified he made reluctantly in an effort to restore order and to protect his reputation with emperor Caesar, for the Jewish zealots exhorted Pilate that "...whosoever maketh himself a king speaketh against Caesar." (John 19:12)

By the time of Jesus' birth the Jews had become but a remnant of their once huge Davidic nation. Ten of the original Twelve Tribes had been led north only to become lost in antiquity following the breakup of Judah and Israel in the latter part of the tenth century. Around 587 B.C.[6] Nebuchadnezzar, king of Chaldea, led thousands of Jews from Jerusalem into captivity in Babylon before burning Solomon's Temple and destroying the city, killing its king. Jerusalem was eventually rebuilt in time for Alexander the Great—son of Macedonian king Philip—and his armies to capture it. There were several more conquests by Egyptian kings who offered sacrifices to pagan gods within the city walls.

By the time Jesus was born, Jerusalem had been conquered nine times, many hundreds of thousands of Jews paying the price of the spoils until the Roman high priest John Hyrcanus begged the Romans for help. They had not long since thrown off some of the yoke of Syria, Greece and Egypt through their great freedom fighter, Judas Maccabeus (who many Jews regarded as their Meshiach), rededicating their precious temple in 165 B.C.[7]

Roman rule in Palestine was habitually neutral but could turn suddenly into open hostility. Pilate, a pagan, was increasingly scornful of Jewish customs. He had a fondness for erecting graven images, even flags with Caesar's likeness. These probably were done rather as a display of power than of open demonstration. This angered and threatened the various Jewish sects. Veiled and then open rebellion followed. Pilate increased his troops at the walls and byroads of the city. Roman watchmen checked incoming visitors and made sure that the Jewish priests never forgot their presence was subject to Roman approval. With time the situation worsened until Pilate's men responded to a Samaritan disturbance by massacre. Pilate's ten-year rule of tyranny ended and he was sent to Rome.

During the life of Jesus the Jews were a suspicious lot because of this outside rule. They were still a conquered people, living in exile through permission of the Roman prelates, hated by many because of their refusal to acknowledge and worship the Roman gods of Olympus. But many Jews were also openly entranced by aspects of Greek life, perhaps in an attempt to disassociate from the political turmoil at home. They felt no real allegiance to Rome. Zealously they maintained their separateness as a "peculiar" people, careful to keep themselves exclusive in acknowledging and respecting the moral laws written in their Torah—the ancient five books of Moses that constitute the major part of the Old Testament. They never forgot that they were "a holy people unto the Lord…chosen…to be a special people unto himself, above all people that are upon the face of the earth." (Deut 7:6)

Every loyal Jew observed the minutiae of the Torah as Moses had written it and presented to them. The Talmud, a collection of rabbinical exegesis upon the Torah, was an ongoing oral tradition, not yet accumulated in book form. They were not tolerant of anyone who would openly decry their long held traditions. Revolving their religion and ceremonies around their temple in Jerusalem, Jews became increasingly self-absorbed, quite willing to mock the Roman religious gods, but unwilling to share their Jehovah (meaning *unchangeable one*, the covenantal Hebrew word for God) with outsiders. They were not interested either, in accepting the gospel Jesus presented to them, for his new doctrines offended their scribes, these especial interpreters and reporters of Judaism whose authority had become almost greater than the written law.

The Jews were slavishly devoted to their laws and traditions and nothing in their Law prevented them from hating all outsiders. Especially hated were the Samaritans (Matt 10:5, Jn 4:9) with whom the Jewish people had shared an enmity from before the Babylonian captivity the result of a war centuries earlier with Shalmaneser, then king of Assyria responsible for besieging Samaria, capital city of the northern kingdom of Israel.[8] His successor, Sargon II (721-705 B.C.) conquered the area and carried off thousands of Jews to the north, replacing them with a polyglot of people descended from other areas of the continent, a policy of "transpopulation." These people eventually became known as the Samaritans.

The Samaritans had worked to prevent the rebuilding of Jerusalem by the newly returned Babylonian Jews. The Samaritans regarded themselves as the true remnants of Israel since the dispersion from Judah. They claimed the city for themselves but were rebuffed when they tried to help build a new Temple.[9] For years afterward they did all they could to frustrate and prevent their rivals from erecting a Temple in Jerusalem. Eventually, through their friendliness to the armies of Alexander the Samaritans were rewarded with their own temple on Mt. Gerazim, which was later destroyed during the Maccabean revolt. The Jews had avoided any contact with the Samaritans for years. Their hatred of each other was historic, therefore, when Jesus wanted to preach in Samaria the apostles had first to confront their own prejudices, but they, of course, followed him and ministered there. (Acts 8:4-25)

The Sadducee caste of the Jews was another thorn to Jesus. They were a reactionary organization from the second century B.C. These men made up the Jewish priestly aristocracy in Palestine and, though few in number, they rejected the mass of rabbinical canon while they upheld the sanctity of the written law as it has been so far preserved. They believed in strict compliance with Mosaic Law, not its interpretations. Where Mosaic Law demanded an eye for an eye, the Sadducees interpreted that to mean punishment equal to the crime must be doled out. There was no flexibility in their position about the soul surviving the body or other weighty spiritual questions. They believed that nothing survived death and they based that belief on the lack of Mosaic scripture to the contrary. This refusal to accept the doctrine of immortality later brought much opposition to the work of the apostles because the Sadducees rejected the concept of resurrection.

Their counterparts, the Pharisees (from the Hebrew parushim, meaning "separated ones"), were far greater in number and better organized. They were an evolved religious sect, demanding scrupulous following of Mosaic Law and at the same time compliance with traditional rules. They differed individually on matters relating to spirit bodies, immortality of the soul, resurrection from the dead and other vital issues. Pharisees believed the Torah and other Jewish texts were to be subject to commentary and explanation and they were tireless in their efforts. They taught the mercy of God and expounded the Golden Rule. Pharisaic tradition asserted that every mind was made to be free because every soul is an independent entity. The synagogue was their answer to the perfect communal institution. But their great weakness was their tendency to reduce religion to a series of many ceremonial rules which they prided themselves on observing. Jesus, tired of the Pharisees asking to see outward signs of his authority later said of them "Ye blind guides, which strain at a gnat, and swallow a camel." (Matt 23:24)

Called the "chief priests, scribes and elders," the Pharisees conducted a house of prayer strict in its observances, keeping themselves separate from the Roman presence which lurked just outside the doors. Many of these Jewish priests were in the Sanhedrin, the Jewish high court. They held influential positions in the city. Jesus, in claiming authority to teach them, endeavored to give them new doctrine. Confused and angered, the Pharisees determined that Jesus was in league with devils, and they eventually conspired to have him killed. They saw him eating with the hated Jewish tax collectors, 'publicans and sinners', and wondered aloud to his disciples. (Mark 2:16) Jesus answered them that he knew the public avoided sitting with these men and that the Pharisees also disapproved, but that he chose to do so because of their low stations in life, in preference to eating with the righteous who did not need his ministrations. (Matt 9:12) Other significant differences arose between Jesus and the pharisaic sect concerning the healing of the sick on the Sabbath. But Jesus' answers only served to confuse and anger them until they reached the point of total rebellion against him.

> When Jesus heard it, he saith unto them, They that are whole have no need of the physician, but they that are sick: I came not to call the righteous, but sinners to repentance.
>
> *Mark 2:17*

Together with other sects, such as the Essenes, the Zealots and the Nazarites, much social, political and spiritual confusion and contention greeted Jesus' entry into the world. The Essenes were a Jewish sect living around the shores of the Dead Sea, which had adopted many Persian beliefs and semimonastic practices. This group wandered into the Judean wilderness near Qumran.[10] Their members were ascetic, refraining from marriage and eschewing the eating of meat. They also refused temple worship. They lived a common law in secluded monasteries, self-appointing their priests, practicing ceremonial washings, administering oaths and covenants.[11]

All these Jewish sects differed greatly from the Zealots, a group of Jewish patriots who advocated any action that would free them from Roman rule. These men were especially harassing to Pilate and his soldiers, threatening to escalate the already dangerous tensions in the region.

The Jewish Nazarite brotherhood believed in the coming of a

Messiah, though Jesus never allied himself with this group or with any other. John the Baptist may have taken Nazarite vows. Manoah, father of Samson (Judges 13:5) may have become a Nazarite, and the prophet Samuel was similarly inclined, though in the Bible this information is not clearly given. (1Sam 1:11) Nazarites were looked upon as holy men. They were among the few allowed to enter the inner court of the Temple. Members were of either sex, bound to abstinence and sacrifice by their vows of service to God. (Num 6:2-21)

Among some sects spoken authority was becoming more influential than the written Mosaic Law itself, making it harder for the Jews to accept a new gospel. Complicating life further, Roman occupation of Jerusalem resulted in the isolation and virtual bondage of the Jews to their traditions and their Law, which eventually evolved into an unwritten law of defense against Roman tyranny or new ideas. When Jesus challenged the dogma of entrenched rituals he met with rejection, fear, confusion and anger from every faction. One recalls the prophet Jeremiah's chastisement against the Jews of Palestine: "...their ear is uncircumcised, and they cannot hearken: behold, the word of the Lord is unto them a reproach; they have no delight in it." (Jer 6:10)

These political, social and religious factors were great impediments to the success of Jesus' ministry. They led to his arrest, trial and murder. Because so much of his Gospel plan fell on prejudiced, confused ears, many of the simple truths he told were often suspect, misconstrued or ignored. Jesus knew much of his work would be misunderstood, yet he never turned back. The Savior knew the end from the beginning. He knew the Jewish nation's soul longed for their Mashiach to save them from the miserable Roman rule, even the rule of all conquerors. Surely Jesus also longed to see Palestine free. Is it any wonder he increasingly spoke in parables to those who would ponder his words? What sadness he must have felt knowing he would soon have to leave his apostles to carry on his work in a hostile world! But again, how great was his joy in his resurrection!

Jesus came to save the human race from the ravages of its sin and the terrible bonds of Satan. He preached the good news of the gospel of brotherly love to all, looking first to teach his own people; to declare his Sonship of their great God, but the political situation in the holy land became so heated among the Jews who rejected him, eventually calling for his blood, that his Gospel of personal religion was lost on many. Fortunately, those who believed in him became the saviors of the uncounted souls who have followed.In retrospect, Jesus of Nazareth was in that time an example of perfection set before the human spirit. Men tend to reject what they do not understand, or what they do not want to change. To lovingly persuade a population to change their ingrained way of life that they might acquire increased spiritual insight to transcend their unhappy lives is a task no mortal can or could accomplish. Through God's infinite charity His Son was sent to us. He alone possessed the necessary items for success: a perfect plan for survival through time and timelessness, a love of mankind so encompassing that the idea of that final darkness at the end of light must be shattered by a perfect redemptive Plan, defeating death forever. Who but Christ can bring the Church of God to the earth?

Jesus Christ came to save forever the very essence of humanity in the hope of its eventual exaltation—the personality, precious with potential, the jewel of every life. It would take a perfect being, one in whom divinity was an accepted fact of form and function, a Creator with immeasurable compassion, leadership, understanding and love for the humanity born of his love. Such a man is Jesus the Christ.

> *And my Father sent me that I might be lifted up upon the cross; and after that I had been lifted up upon the cross, that I might draw all men unto me, that as I have been lifted up by men even so should men be lifted up by the Father, to stand before me, to be judged of their works, whether they be good or they be evil...*

> *3Ne 27:14 Book of Mormon*

Jesus is no alienated god in the misty recesses of our minds. He is ours, he is family. He is the only Begotten Son of God, of spirit and of flesh, the vital spiritual link in the ever-reaching chain of brotherhood that encompasses us all. He knows who we are, but we, knowing very little, have come here to learn again that we are his.

Notes to Chapter One

1. Flavius Josephus: *The Complete Works of Josephus*, p. 379

2. Galbraith, Ogden, Skinner: *Jerusalem The Eternal City*, p. 153

3. LDS Bible Dictionary, p. 769

4. Flavius Josephus: *The Complete Works of Josephus*, p. 379

5. Op cit, p. 379

6. LDS Bible Dictionary, p. 639

7. Op cit. p. 642

8. Galbraith, Ogden, Skinner: *Jerusalem The Eternal City*, p. 85

9. Op cit. p. 121

10. Op cit. p. 148

11. Vermes, Geza: *The Dead Sea Scrolls: Qumran in Perspective*, p.87-115, 142-146.

All things must be fulfilled, which were written in the Law of Moses,
and in the prophets, and in the psalms concerning me
Luke 24:44

For had ye believed Moses, ye would have believed me: for he wrote of
me. But if ye believe not his writings, how shall ye believe my words?
John 5:46-47

CHAPTER TWO

THE JEWISH MASHIACH

JESHUA. THE NAME, A FORM OF Jehoshua, means *the Lord saveth.*[1] Jeshua
was born of a Hebrew mother who raised him with her husband
Joseph as their first born son. We have only to read of his special
lineage in two of the Gospels, as Matthew gives in Matt 1:17 and
Luke recounts a little differently in 3:23-38. His line of descent comes
more properly from his mother, Mary, who was Joseph's cousin,
because the Lord cursed Jeconiah, a sinful king of Judah who ruled
in 598 B.C., casting out he and his seed (See Jeremiah 22:24-30).
Mary's lineage was traceable to David, and before that to Abraham
and so to Adam, the earthly patriarch of us all, and finally to our
Father in Heaven, whose spirit children we all are.

We can assume that as Jeshua, called Jesus of Nazareth, grew to
manhood he observed the many rituals and traditions of his faith. As
a boy and as a man Jeshua would have daily worn a yarmulke, or
skullcap, to show his great respect for God. He would have been
educated in all the formal rites and rituals of a Jewish household and
coached to study and to master the first Semitic languages; Hebrew
and its precursor Aramaic, the common language of the Jews after
their return from Babylon and the everyday speech for much of
southwest Asia at that time.[2] How often did he listen to his father in
synagogue reciting scriptural passages? How many intense hours
did Jeshua spend in deep contemplation and study of Hebrew,
intoning the guttural consonants over and over, adding as he taught
them the necessary vowel sounds to soften and round out the harsh-
ness until his grammar was perfect? He would be called to read
Torah with the elders of the synagogue, to sing with the cantor

(conductor of liturgical portions of synagogue service, also has officiating duties) during Sabbath services.

Reverently draping the special, *tallith* prayer shawl with its
fringed corners (called *zizith*) upon his shoulders for the reading of
the Jewish book of divine laws, the Torah (five books of Moses and
Prophets),[3] Jeshua the boy was ready for his father to teach him the
ritualistic daily prayers, the *tefillah*. It was like reliving the time of the
ancient rabbis in Israel before its fall. If Jeshua was expecting to offer
prayers of thanksgiving as they came to his mind, he was instructed
early in his training that Jewish communal prayers are not sponta-
neous but unchanging in detail and recitation. Nevertheless, Jewish
prayer seeks a solemn and passionate communication: It is intense
concentration upon asking for God's daily assistance. The pious pray
throughout the day and evening, hoping their personal petitions will
find their way to God. As Jews contemplate the meaning of life and
death, they plead with God and petition for their spiritual and physical needs, for the needs of Israel, for the rebuilding of Jerusalem and
for the swift coming of the Jewish *Mashiach*, (Messiah).

> *God longs for the prayers of the pious, for their ever renewed affir-
> mation of the covenant. Therefore, even an iron wall cannot
> separate God and a Jew in prayer.*
>
> Quoted in The Complete Book of Jewish Observance, p. 41.

Talmudic writings remind us that the Shekinah, the presence of
God, stands before us as we pray. Jesus was born too early to read
from the Talmud (research), a compiled volume of rabbinical commentaries on Torah for the Jews in world exile (diaspora). Written
compilation began in the years following Jesus' death and took several
hundred more years to finish.[4] But the uncodified oral Talmud was
very much alive in those days and had been since the fourth century
b.c.e. Thousands of rabbis contributed to it for generations before and
after the birth of Jesus. Through constant association with the ideas of
ancient patriarchs he discovered, absorbed and taught the themes of
brotherhood and charity, grasping perfectly the central theme: the Jew
is being called upon to love his fellows:

> *Who is the strong man? He who changes his enemy into a friend.*
>
> Talmud

Take the yoke of the Kingdom of heaven upon you, outdo one another in the fear of God and practice acts of love toward one another. Talmud

Jeshua the boy learned those fine points of Talmud commentary upon the words of God and it became a part of his spiritual heritage. Many of his Gospel teachings reflect that early Talmudic teaching, especially as reflected in the style of the parables and in Christ's rigorous insistence upon being charitable to others, even to the extent of giving away of one's own possessions to those in need.

Jesus would have been very familiar with the three "offices" of prayer in synagogue, or *shul*. The morning prayer, called the *Shaharit*, was instituted by Abraham who hurried to stand before the Lord as each day began (Gen 19:27). In this prayer the Jew is called upon to render his utmost obedience to God and to endure whatever sacrifice is required of him. The *Shema*, creedal Jewish affirmation of faith is then recited. On special days the Torah is read and on holy days the *Alenu*, a prayer which speaks of God's greatness and His covenant with the Jews, is added. It is a prayer of great beauty, beloved by those who sing it, for they often feel the presence of the great and mysterious *Shekinah*.[5]

In the afternoon the *Minhah* prayer is recited, opening with Psalm 145. Each Sabbath a portion of Torah is also read. Torah readings are pre-assigned for each day of each year, so that in every synagogue readings will cover the same portions. The *Amidah* gives praise to God. It is a time to lift the weight of worldly concerns and to seek forgiveness.

At evening prayer, the *Ma-ariv* service includes *berakhahs*, calls to worship. In these structured prayers Jews offer thanks for the Torah and the lifetime we have to study the Law. Jews again pledge their affirmation of faith. More ritual prayers follow which speak of God's love for his covenanted and their love for Him, including thanks to Him for redemption of the Jewish people.

In its essence the prayers of the orthodox Jews follow ancient rabbinical attitudes, centering on four major themes: the Temple and its gathering of the devout, man's humility and helplessness, the wrath of God, and the body of ideas and symbols which are part of Israel's sacred history. Jesus very likely had to adhere to this strict program of prayer, but it is significant that he later introduced new aspects of worship. In his ministry he cautioned against eloquent phraseology and thoughtless repetition, reasoning that personal petition has more value as a heartful expression of love for God.

> *But when ye pray, use not vain repetitions...for your Father knoweth what things ye have need of, before ye ask him.*

Matt 6:7-8

This attitude did not endear him to any of the Jewish sects. But Jesus knew that when the human spirit is in full accordance with divine will, answers to prayer will always be forthcoming. During his ministry he opened the way for prayers that concerned the personal and spiritual welfare of individuals and families. He taught through the Beatitudes that the welfare of others was worthy of prayer, though it didn't take the place of personal ministering.

To a significant extent Jesus was a contrarian. In the face of Jewish rituals and rites Jesus came forth teaching the higher law. Mosaic Law required animal sacrifice to symbolize human repentance. Jesus told his followers in the Sermon on the Mount (see Matt 5:17) that he had come to fulfill the Law of Moses. Whereas the complex ordinances concerning animal sacrifice was given of God through Moses that the Jews should observe those laws of performance and ordinances, the rituals were only a type and shadow of Christ who, through the shedding of his blood and the giving of his life, showed mankind that even the spiritually dead can be reborn, not through sin offerings of sacrificial animals, but through the redemption of God.

> *Wherefore the law was our schoolmaster to bring us unto Christ, that we may be justified by faith.*

Galatians 3:24

The apostle Paul, in his letter to the Galatians admonished them:

> *Knowing that a man is not justified by the works of the law, but by the faith of Jesus Christ, even we have believed in Jesus Christ, that we might be justified by the faith of Christ, and not by the works of the law: for by the works of the law shall no flesh be justified.*

Galatians 2:16

Jesus encouraged prayer for the salvation of the individual soul because it enlarges the human spirit and puts the petitioner in contact with God. He went about praying for mankind in general, also for his disciples and for those he healed and encouraged to greater strength of character and nobleness of spirit, always subject to the will of Heavenly Father. "Lead us not into temptation..." he implored humbly of his Father (See Matt 6:13). Always he taught that praying for divine guidance on a personal level was necessary because of its power to enlarge our capacity for communication with the Holy Ghost.

As he studied with his father, Joseph, and the rabbis in the synagogue, Jesus would have received the full education of one who was expected to take his place in the temple as a teacher and priesthood holder. His daily learning would include an understanding of the Jewish law of performances and ordinances according to the Book of Leviticus (Law). These laws cover the practical day to day rules of cleanliness and uncleanness of animals and men. Jesus knew the laws of sacrifice and the various types of sin offerings to be made to the priests who administered the rites. His Gospel teachings required that Jesus have a thorough understanding of *zaddik*, the qualities of the Jewish moral code: justice and charity. Recall one of his comments on charity as recorded in Mark 9:50:

> *Salt is good: but if the salt have lost his saltness, wherewith will ye season it? Have salt in yourselves and have peace one with another.*

Jesus knew that in the kingdom of God all are equally beloved of God. During his youth Jesus was undoubtedly gaining increasingly mature impressions of the Semitic world about him. He must have become deeply aware of the selfishness and spiritual blindness inherent in human nature (for example, Mark 6:1-6), and in his teachings Jesus counseled that each person is endowed with a spiritual spark from their Creator. (See Matt 6:22) He saw charity to one's fellows as a measure of maturity but he realized that people lack the understanding of the father/child relationship of God to his children on earth. When he reproved the Pharisees for their false traditions he chastised them for such strict adherence to ritual that they neglected to learn brotherly love. (Mark 7) Love, he tried to teach them, is a divine inner urge we all possess. It must be founded in service, honed by understanding. It must be practiced on a constant basis, for that is the will of God and the only true way to know Him.

> *Thou shalt not avenge, nor bear any grudge against the children of thy people, but thou shalt love thy neighbour as thyself: I am the Lord.*

> *Lev 19:18*

From the Torah Jesus learned of the sanctity of the marriage vows and the role of women in Jewish life. Though he was celibate, Jesus evidenced a great understanding and respect for women and their right to self-determination, no doubt gleaned from his childhood experiences with his mother and sisters. He spoke with women as equals. The Samaritan woman at Jacob's well found him pleasant and helpful, as she divined he was a holy man. Mary Magdalene was given new life through his forgiveness of her sins.

We do not know Jesus' thoughts as he studied and reflected upon the hundreds of rules and social taboos for every part of a Jew's life: dietary, marriage, usury, credit, private property, murder, government, cleanliness, worship, repentance, sin offerings and the like. But from his magnificent sermons and parables it is evident that Jesus knew well the Jewish spirit, and knew far better than his teachers that all people are the spirit children of their Heavenly Father who loves them unconditionally. Surely, as the Son of God, Jesus was also being taught by heavenly beings who prompted and inspired him to ponder profoundly the many Gospel principles taught by the Hebrew elders and priests of his time.

Jesus' reading of the Torah included the books of the Prophets. There he read in Hebrew the chastisements of Isaiah to the Jews for their sinfulness, exhorting them to never forget the fall of their nation to Assyria and later to Babylon. Jesus knew he was soon to play the central role in the unfolding of Jewish history. Surely he pondered Isaiah's prophecies of the fallen kingdom of Israel. He may have been moved to tears as he read the many passages telling of desolation and imprisonment to come upon his people through their stiffneckedness and insularity: Isaiah's warnings were echoed throughout the centuries preceding the Savior. All the major and most minor Old Testament prophets prophesied in strong, colorful language of the fall of Israel as a nation and of their eventual captivity and dispersion throughout the world.

> And I will punish the world for their evil, and the wicked for their iniquity; and I will cause the arrogancy of the proud to cease…
>
> *Isa 13:11*

Yet God is merciful to His wayward children: "For the Lord will have mercy on Jacob, and will yet choose Israel, and set them in their own land:" (Isa 14:1) He promises eternal life to those who believe in

Him. "Thy dead men shall live, together with my dead body shall they arise. Awake and sing, ye that dwell in dust: for thy dew is as the dew of herbs, and the earth shall cast out the dead." (Isa 26:19) He promises new spiritual leaders to come in a future that can be seen only by his chosen prophets: "All ye inhabitants of the world, and dwellers on the earth, see ye, when he lifteth up an ensign on the mountains..." (Isa 18:3)

How the heart of our Savior must have gone out to his people as he read the long history of their spiritual blindness, reflecting as he read upon their ever-present shortsightedness. Isaiah's words surely quickened the dedication of this maturing man of divinity toward his impending mission among them. Did he in the privacy of his thoughts wince at the prophecies of the scattering of Israel who forgot their God as he read of the fall of the Jewish nation, especially the sieges against Jerusalem and the overtaking of Israel by Assyria?

> For it is a day of trouble, and of treading down, and of perplexity by the Lord God of hosts in the valley of vision, breaking down the walls, and of crying to the mountains...And it shall come to pass, that thy choicest valleys shall be full of chariots...
>
> *Isa 22:5,7*

But faithful Isaiah also assured the multitudes that redemption is sure. Israel is to inherit their land in the Resurrection, gathered and cleansed. The Messiah will be their Shepherd and they shall receive their everlasting Gospel covenants through the Restoration of the Gospel in the latter days when the Bible would be joined by another work which would contain the writings of the fruit of Jacob's son, Joseph. How the Son of God must have loved that great prophet as even now he is looking forward to the prophecies he will bring to pass upon his return.

> And it shall come to pass in that day, that the Lord shall beat off from the channel of the river unto the stream of Egypt, and ye shall be gathered one by one, O ye children is Israel.
>
> *Isa 27:12*

> So I prophesied as he commanded me, and the breath came into them, and they lived, and stood up upon their feet, an exceeding great army...Behold, O my people, I will open your graves, and

bring you into the land of Israel. And ye shall know that I am the Lord...and shall put my spirit in you...

Ezek 37:10, 12, 14

Moreover, thou son of man, take thee one stick, and write upon it, For Judah, and for the children of Israel his companions: then take another stick, and write upon it, For Joseph, the stick of Ephraim, and for all the house of Israel his companions: And join them one to another into one stick; and they shall become one in thine hand.

Ezek 37:16-17

But for all the drama of these prophecies of doom, resurrection and latter day restoration, there was cause for even greater happiness. None but Jesus discerned the timeliness of the many great predictions of his own life and mission. Was his beautiful spirit moved to share the joy that pervades these writings? We can only wonder at Jesus' thoughts as he heard those Torah portions read which foretold the advent of his earthly mission, the long awaited Word of God come to fulfill the Law:

And there shall come forth a rod out of the stem of Jesse...with righteousness shall he judge the poor, and reprove with equity from the meek of the earth; and he shall smite the earth with the rod of his mouth...

Isa 11:1,4

And in mercy shall the throne be established; and he shall sit upon it in truth in the tabernacle of David, judging, and seeking judgment, and hasting righteousness.

Isa 16:5

All the ends of the world shall remember and turn unto the LORD: and all the kindreds of the nations shall worship before thee. For the kingdom is the LORD's: and he is the governor among the nations.

Psalm 22:27-28

When a Jewish male reaches thirteen years, his religious initiation begins with graduation, the traditional *bar-mitzvah* ceremony in which the boy becomes a "son of the commandments." It marks formal separation from synagogue training. In his Gospel, Luke tells us that Jesus "…increased in wisdom and stature, and in favour with God and man." (Luke 2:52) Though we know little of Jesus' early years, his great spirituality and serious nature can be sensed through this passage of scripture which likely refers to his growth in synagogue affairs.

This rite of passage from boyhood initiate to responsible manhood must have brought great joy to Jeshua. *Bar-mitzvah* confirms allegiance to Torah as orthodox Jews believe it was received by Moses on Mt. Sinai. The ceremony is attended by great happiness, lots of food and gift giving. The graduate now becomes part of the *minyan*, a group of ten men required for synagogue services. He is expected to read aloud from the Sepher Torah scrolls on occasion. These are parchment rolls inscribed with the words of the Old Testament books, rolled around two wooden sticks, each with a sort of disk at each end. A cloth envelops the scrolls that often bear a Seal of Solomon. During solemn moments in the services of today it is taken from its cabinet and carried throughout the congregation. Graduation from synagogue as a responsible Jewish adult is of solemn consequence in Jewish life. He must now be determined worthy of receiving the Levitical lay priesthood. The Levitical, or lesser priesthood, is a sacred honor bestowed by God through Moses upon the heads of Aaron and his sons (Ex 28:1-4,29, Heb 2:17-18, 3:1, 5:6, 10; Doctrine and Covenants 84, 107) at Mt. Sinai and conferred upon following generations through the laying on of hands until the death of the apostles. This Aaronic[6] priesthood prepares its members for the oaths and covenants of the greater order of Melchizedek(c). It was conferred upon worthy male Jews of the Levite tribe between the ages of 30 and 50, essentially to school Israel for the time when they would be presented with the whole Gospel. It has been restored, along with the Melchizedek priesthood, in these latter days through The Church of Jesus Christ of Latter-day Saints.The right to the Levitical or Aaronic priesthood originally had lineal restrictions. From the time of Abraham it belonged only to the Levite tribe, but was apparently lifted when the Law of Moses was partially fulfilled. (Heb 7:13-14) According to scripture, Levite priests were empowered by God to offer sacrifices for the people, to burn incense upon the altars, teach the Law, cleanse and maintain the synagogue (and the Temple). They held the "keys" (responsibilities) of the ministry of angels, performed baptisms and ritual washings for spiritual cleanliness, and otherwise assisted other priests. (1Kgs 8:4, Ezra 2:70, John

1:19) Zacharias, the Baptist's father, was a Levite priest. John also held the Aaronic priesthood, but it was bestowed upon him when only eight days old (also the ritual time of male circumcision) by the Lord, "to overthrow the kingdom of the Jews, and to make straight the way of the Lord before the face of his people, to prepare them for the coming of the Lord..." (See Doctrine and Covenants 84:26-28)

The Melchizedek(c), or greater priesthood, is non-lineal.[7] Named after a beloved teacher of the Gospel and high priest in ancient Salem to whom Abraham paid tithes, this sacred office enables the holder to perform holier duties: bestowing the gift of the Holy Ghost after baptism, overseeing the Levite priests, officiating in the synagogue. (See D&C 107:18-19) Prophets of God throughout history have held this "higher" priesthood, but Jews in general did not. Holders of both priesthoods must be called of God through the laying on of hands by one having similar authority. They may be called to prophesy, to heal the sick, and generally to perform whatever ordinances God dictates that have eternal or miraculous consequences. (Heb 7:25-28)

Though we have no dates when Jesus' received his priesthoods, we know that through them he was empowered to give benedictions, to carry the sacred scroll of the Law throughout the synagogue, to minister to the congregation and to the world. Believers understood that the miracles he performed during his ministry were not solely of Jesus' making, but occurred through union with his Father in purpose and testimony. Without the authority given him through the holy priesthoods he held, Jesus would not have been able to accomplish what he did. (Hebrews 5) He was now a "son of the commandments," an ordained servant of God on earth qualified (at the very least) to speak with the scribes and teachers in the synagogues.

Jesus surely participated with his parents in yearly Passover celebrations as he grew, traveling with Joseph to the synagogue. Occasionally he might have been the speaker of the beautiful liturgies, which proclaim the exodus of the Jews from Egypt and the flight through the Red Sea. In this service God, who receives all praise and glory, is the lover while Israel is the beloved who feels the intimate presence of God's saving grace. Jeshua on many occasions in his young life must have helped to commemorate those wondrous events which Jews have always maintained is a main theme in their secular history.

Central to this theme of redemption is the creedal affirmation of faith in one God, the *Shema*: "Hear O Israel, the Lord our God is one God." (Deut 6:4) During his Jerusalem ministry Jesus emphasized this as the seed of the first great commandment (Mark 12:29) with the admonition to "...love the Lord thy God with all thy heart, and with all thy soul, and with all thy mind, and with all thy strength..." The accompanying command was to love all people as the spirit brothers and sisters we are. Two thousand years later we again await the author of these messages, and the inhabitants of this age, in their worldly milieu, are as little inclined to hear the cautioning words as were inhabitants of ancient Judea.Learning in this way the history, worship and mindset of the Jewish spiritual and communal life helped greatly to prepare Jesus for the mission that lay ahead. As a young man of divine, inspired parentage we know that he often received inspiration from unseen, holy advisors as to his true nature and purpose as the Begotten Son of God who would soon walk into the waters of baptism through the priesthood authority of John the Baptist, his cousin. As a young citizen of the Jewish world of his day Jesus continued to watch and understand the thoughts and feelings of mortals. He learned that to do the will of his Heavenly Father he would have to consecrate his life through service to others. Every day he added to the knowledge and experience he would need when he came forth to begin his personal ministry as a merciful Savior, the chosen leader of mankind to God and of a loving Heavenly Father to His children.

Notes to Chapter Two

1. Bible Dictionary, p. 713. Jeshua also a form of Joshua.

2. Op cit. p. 613. Also see Jesus and His Times, p. 142. Jesus and his disciples may have spoken a Galilean Aramaic, a dialect considered rustic and uncultured for the times. Aramaic words are found in portions of the Old Testament and Psalms. It was one of the primary languages of the historian Josephus. Because Hebrew was increasingly used as a language of the Temple, passages of Torah were often translated into Aramaic for the general congregation.

3. Random House Dictionary, p. 77. In the first five books of Moses; Genesis, Exodus, Leviticus, Numbers and Deuteronomy are contained the essential Mosaic Law, generally considered to have been written by Moses. The second portion of Torah contains the historical and prophetic books, while the third portion encompasses the Psalms, Proverbs, Job, Song of Songs, Ruth, Lamentations, Ecclesiastes, Esther, Daniel, Ezra, Nehemiah and Chronicles I, II. In Jesus' time the Torah was copied on parchment which was stitched together and wrapped around wooden poles. Family Torahs were commonplace in Jewish homes, in synagogues and the Temples. For Jews the Torah carries the sum of all wisdom, all guidance necessary for life. The daily and serious study of Torah is a lifelong obligation, which God has assigned, the neglect of which is said to bring eternal punishment.

4. LDS Bible Dictionary, p. 780. Also see Jesus and His Times, p. 152 and Holy Mountain, pp. 79-83. Children of Jesus' time learned Talmud by chanting the rabbinical writings, to speed memorization of commentary upon the Law. Stories, tales, legends made up a Midrash portion of Talmud which consists of two sections, the Mishnah, or text, and the Gemara, the commentaries dealing with many aspects of Jewish life. Talmudic rabbis have always had great influence upon Jewry, developing elaborate systems of dietary laws and rituals to insure cleanliness, regulate marriage and divorce, adjudicate civil and social laws and contracts. This was in partial effort to restrain Jews from keeping any significant company with non-Jews, thus preventing intermarriage

and disagreement. The written Talmud dates from about a.d. 200 and was added to for centuries afterward.

5. Sheckinah, meaning presence. The idea of the Sheckinah can be expressed in Exodus 3:1-6; 1Kings 8:10-11, among other scriptures. These citations refer to a physical manifestation representing the glory of the Lord. In the early Temples the Holy of Holies area was the place where the presence of God was expected and received. Latter day experience of the equivalent of the Sheckinah occurred when the Prophet Joseph Smith was given the bright light and vision of God the Father and Jesus Christ while praying in the Sacred Grove to know which church to join. See Joseph Smith History 1:16-17. This divine presence is believed to be a prophetic occurrence, mystical and mysterious, given to mankind in rare circumstances accompanying a message of great import. The Sheckinah should not be confused with the influence of the Holy Ghost, however, the author believes that portion of the Godhead is always involved in heavenly manifestations.

6. LDS Bible Dictionary, p. 600. "The Aaronic (or Levitical) Priesthood thus functioned only within the tribe of Levi, and the right to have it conferred upon one was determined by lineage and worthiness...The lineal restrictions...were lifted when the law of Moses was fulfilled, and thereafter the offices of the priesthood were conferred upon worthy men without limitation to the tribe of Levi."

7. McConkie, Bruce R.: Mormon Doctrine, p. 475-483. This section gives a wealth of information on the Melchizedek Priesthood. Everything on earth is subject to its power and authority because it is the repository of God's eternal laws, being a perfect law of theocracy (See The Teachings of Joseph Smith, p. 322) which gives eternal laws to the people as servants and representatives of the Almighty, thereby to administer in righteousness, humility and with exactness of attention to the keys and powers of the Gospel, ancient and restored.

Verily I say unto you, Among them that are born of women
there hath not risen a greater than John the Baptist:
notwithstanding he that is least in the kingdom of heaven
is greater than he.

And if ye will receive it, this is Elias,
which was for to come.

He that hath ears to hear, let him hear.

Matt 11:11,14-15

CHAPTER THREE

TOWARD ENLIGHTENMENT

THE ONLY CHILD OF ZACHARIAH AND his wife, Elizabeth, cousin to the
Savior's mother, John the Baptist was a child of heavenly promise and
prophecy and his parents doted on him, teaching him to be serious and
spiritual. Zachariah was a Levite (See Num 1:50-53) in charge of
lighting incense in the Temple, but John chose to exercise his priesthood in a different way. Luke's record tells us of John's divine purpose
as a chosen prophet who was sent to earth to "...go before the face of
the Lord to prepare his ways." (Luke 1:76) He may have taken Nazarite
vows, practicing self-denial, abstaining from wine, not cutting his hair,
living an impoverished life and consuming little. He began to be
clothed as the prophets of old (2Kings 1:8), wearing hairy garments
with a leather girdle and eating "...locusts and wild honey"(Matt 3:4),
adopting the monastic ways of that sect as a desert wanderer,
preaching of the time the Messiah should appear unto all men.

The Baptist became a total believer that a new age was coming.
He knew by prophecy and revelation of the power of the Son of the
Almighty God, though scripture does not record that they met. He
surely trusted entirely in the prophecies of Isaiah and Malachi
heralding the coming of the Messiah. We are told in Luke 1:44 that
the unborn John "leaped in (his mother's) womb..." when
Elizabeth's cousin Mary spoke of the Lord. That John was chosen by
God to prepare the way before the Savior is evident when his father,

Zachariah said of him "And thou, child, shalt be called the prophet of the Highest: for thou shalt go before the face of the Lord to prepare his ways…to give light to them that sit in darkness…" (Luke 1:76, 79)

The biblical record describes John as a man deeply committed to preparing many souls for Christ through baptism in the Jordan River for remission of sins. To those travelers who came out of the Judean wilderness it must have seemed that this tall and oddly dressed man who made his station the banks of the Jordan was the very prophet he spoke of. Such exhortation was unheard of in that vicinity and we can have small doubt that news of his preaching and baptisms must soon have carried throughout Palestine, for John had chosen a traveled public place for his ministry. He attracted large and curious crowds that included many Jews who were whetted for the restoration of their kingdom and the overthrow of their Roman oppressor's yoke.

Such is the value of knowledge that while given freely it imposes a new order upon the learner. The religious truths the Baptist spoke of were meant to heighten and refine in men and women their spiritual awareness, strengthen and deepen character, affect their daily pursuits for good and increase their faith in the reality of eternal lives. John preached that the time of change and new opportunities to make great strides toward the kingdom of God had arrived. The fulcrum of John's mission on earth was to baptize his cousin, Jesus of Nazareth 'to fulfil all righteousness' (Matt 3:16) and to bear witness of John as the greatest prophet. (Matt 11:7-11)

Members of Jewish sects were in the gatherings where John preached, full of wonder and perhaps hopeful that their Mashiach was truly arriving. When the Pharisees demanded to know of John's authority to baptize, he humbly told them "He it is, who coming after me is preferred before me…" (John 1:27) Many knew the story of the angel Gabriel prophesying to Zachariah of his son's coming ministry among men. (See Luke 1:5-25) As mentioned in a preceding chapter, John was of priestly descent through his parents' lineage. His mother was the daughter of Aaron. (See Luke 1:5, 8-17) He had the distinction, too, of being the last prophet under the Law of Moses as well as the first of the New Testament. He was ordained when still a newborn. Though he was a Levite priest who performed holy duties which included baptizing (immersion for remission of sin), he could not bestow the gift of the Holy Ghost upon those he baptized. That ordinance was withheld until Jesus instituted it through the

Melchizedek priesthood. (Heb 2:17-18; 3:1; 5:6, 10; 6:20; Mark 1:8) Recall also that the prophets Isaiah and Malachi had foretold John's great mission. (See Isa 40:3, Mal 3:1) Jesus said of the Baptist:

> *I say unto you, Among those that are born of women there is not a greater prophet than John the Baptist...*

Luke 7:28

John the Baptist's greatness lay in his perfect obedience to God's command to prepare the way for the Christ. He performed no miracles but was elected to baptize the Son of God so he could "fulfil all righteousness." (Matt 3:15) What a privilege! John was great among the prophets because of his complete trust of his Father in Heaven's Plan. He alone at that time "was the only legal administrator holding the keys of power on the earth,"[1] as that privilege was no longer in Jewish hands.

The Jewish reaction to John's baptizing was to deny it as a new social and religious way of life: A Jew's Hebrew heritage is a birthright through the matriarchal line. One born of a Jewish mother is automatically a Jew, usually raised in compliance with Mosaic Law. (Male Jews are still circumcised in accordance with ancient commandments. See Gen 17:10, 23; 21:4.) Most Jews who did allow themselves to go down into the water with John to be cleansed of sin continued upon re-emergence to live and practice the Law of Moses as a matter of course, before and during Jesus' ministry, except those relative few who accepted the full Gospel after Jesus' death and resurrection, recognizing the Christ as their Messiah. These people were baptized as converts to the new Christianity.

A word of explanation may help to clarify this issue. Baptism after the resurrection of Jesus Christ referred specifically to acceptance of Christ as a personal Savior and Redeemer. Baptism follows faith, repentance and obedience to the commandments of God. Christian baptism signifies acceptance of the whole Gospel, but is not complete without the laying on of hands by one having authority for the reception of the gift of the Holy Ghost. (John 3:3-5, 3Ne 27:20, others) This sacred rite symbolizes death, burial and resurrection in similitude of Christ's infinite sacrifice. The newly "golden" convert makes sacred covenants with God and thereby gains membership in the Church and kingdom of God on earth. He covenants to take upon him the name of Christ and to be his witness (Doctrine and Covenants 18:17-

25), to submit in humility to the will of the Father in all things, to obey the commandments, to bear each other's burdens. (See Mark 1:4; Mosiah 4:3; 18:10; Acts 16:31; Moroni 6:2) The Lord covenants with man that he may gain him entrance into the Celestial kingdom (1Cor 15:40; Doctrine and Covenants 76) where he will be numbered in the First Resurrection of the Just and have eternal life with God. The Lord also promises to bestow his spirit more abundantly upon man through the baptism of fire and the reception of the Holy Ghost as his constant companion. All promises are conditional, based upon the convert's worthiness. (See Matt 10:38-39; 2Thess 1; Doctrine and Covenants 51:2,4,5, others)Because most Jews never accepted Christ as their Savior they looked upon John the Baptist's invitation to immersion with a different mindset. That was partly due to strict Torah rules for ritualistic cleansing of all or part of one's body to restore worthiness before God. Jews did baptize (and also circumcise) their gentile proselytes. They baptized converts to Mosaic Law through washings and anointings for spiritual cleanliness as an essential part of Mosaic Law. (See Lev 7:6; 12: 7-8,15; 22:6-7) It was a traditional Jewish belief and practice that as the body was washed and cleansed the soul was also purified. (See Isa 1:16) This included washing of the feet, an act of service and love with which Jesus amazed his disciples at the Last Supper. These washing and cleansing practices were assimilated anciently into Judaism from other religious orders to the East through Asia Minor. (History of Judaism, p. 230) Once cleansed from all unrighteousness in compliance with Mosaic Law, converts were allowed to gather in the outer court of the Temple. We know now that these rites were really preparatory to the fullness of baptism as members of Christ's Church on earth.

Jewish washings and cleansing by immersion were a common ritualistic practice of ancient Judaism long before Jesus' birth. The Old Testament is almost mute on that point, unfortunately, though Paul in 1Cor 10:1-4 speaks of the children of Israel being baptized "unto Moses in the cloud and in the sea," probably referring to their crossing of the Red Sea while fleeing Egyptian tyranny. Again, the Temple of Solomon was built to include a "brazen sea" (fonts) which rested upon the backs of twelve oxen. (See 2Chr 4) Recently, excavations in what was Judea, at the site of Qumran, a ruin just 13 miles east of Jerusalem near the Dead Sea, have presented strong evidence that this ancient area was a religious settlement containing fonts used for ritual baths during the Second Temple period. (37 b.c.e.-70 .c.e.)[2]

So the ordinance of baptism in early Judaic practice had Messianic undertones because Jews sought to sanctify their covenantal relationship with Jehovah, who they believed was God. Jewish rites of repentance and petitions to God for forgiveness were also regularly expressed through frequent animal sacrifices, prayer and fasting, and during annual High Holy Day observances. Surely the Lord, in bringing God's priesthoods to earth through His prophets, hoped to teach his Jewish brethren that salvation would ultimately come only through Christ, but the majority of Jews have never sought that blessing or recognized the Lord's magnificent promise. He waits for them still and invites them to knock, that he may enter their hearts with his message of love and resurrection.

In light of the many prophecies of Jesus Christ, as well as the ordinances and covenants which God bestowed upon the Hebrews through prophets, and the trials they endured in Old Testament times to carry out those commandments, it is fair to state that these especial, chosen prophets of the Lord were taught the full Gospel through the ministration of the Holy Ghost. They knew that the Christ would come to lay down his life for all mankind. Since the time of Adam men have been practicing baptism. A passage in latter day scripture describes his baptism:

> ...he was caught away by the Spirit of the Lord, and was carried down into the water, and was laid under the water, and was brought forth out of the water. And thus he was baptized, and the Spirit of God descended upon him, and thus he was born of the Spirit, and became quickened in the inner man.

Pearl of Great Price, Moses 6:59-65

The murder of John by King Herod Antipas, himself a Jewish convert, was precipitated in part by a great misunderstanding of the Baptist's role as a teacher. Herod likely could not reconcile the institution of baptism replacing the ancient Jewish practice of circumcision, and certainly was very concerned that John claimed authority to change the doctrines of God, their application, and places of worship. He also suspected the Baptist of aspiring to greatness by making impressions "upon the ignorant."[3] Herod no doubt viewed the crowds which gathered around John who preached of a Savior to come, and feared rebellion of the people against his rule. Mark 6:16-29 records that John criticized Herod's unlawful marriage to Herodias. This incurred the king's anger further, and fearing John's growing popularity and influence over the people could lead to a political power play, Herod quickly imprisoned him and later put him to death. (Matt 14:3-12)

Despite these differences, the Jewish people heard John's message with interest because they, too, were waiting for the new era of the kingdom of God on earth. It is probable that numerous Jews allowed themselves to be baptized (cleansed of sin) by immersion for the good of their homeland, afraid that one sin might delay their Mashiach's arrival.

The Jewish vision of the Mashiach was based upon the grandeur and greatness of the prophets Abraham and Moses. Like these earlier heroes the Jews expected their Deliverer to be a prophet, priest and king who would soon come to deliver them as a people from Roman domination through miraculous powers and deeds. They wanted a restoration of their former national glory. Their Deliverer would ride as a general at the head of his army, human or divine, invincible and Jewish. He would not come to "save" mankind, in the sense that salvation depended upon believing Jesus to be the Christ. This longed for Mashiach would lead only his "chosen" people into freedom and out from under the Roman yoke, where he would reign as their leader, end the miserable Diaspora and restore to them forever their Israel.[4]

They knew, when Jesus came among them that he was a high priest in the Melchizedek priesthood (Gen 14:18; Heb 5:6) through his lineage, but few recognized him as a prophet or of human and divine parentage, and fewer came to know he was the Mashiach. The Jews of that time missed the mark: Impatiently, they awaited a dauntless leader with the trappings of a conqueror, a man such as the intrepid Alexander the Great, come to rescue the children of Abraham from their hated Roman conquerors.

Instead, they beheld a gentle, simply clad wanderer who preached that the kingdom of Heaven was for all to seek, Jew and Pharisee alike. He preformed miracles and he sent the Jewish moneychangers from the temple. He raised the dead, then said he had come as the Son of God to fulfill God's law. When he spoke of baptism to Nicodemus (See John 3), the Torah scholar and member of the Sanhedrin was confused by the depth of spiritual vision Jesus presented to him. When Jesus reproached Nicodemus for his lack of spiritual insight this influential man and his fellows refused to accept the testimony they were given or the witness they must have been offered.

Nicodemus' reactions to Jesus' teachings were typical of the Sanhedrists and the majority of the wealthy, popular citizens of Jerusalem. Deeply immersed in their rituals and their Torah scrolls, the Jewish priestly class was first to disdain Jesus and his saving message. His teachings were simple: All were called to repentance, even the children of Abraham. None was spared. To gain eternal life, one must unreservedly comply with the eternal laws and ordinances of the Gospel as Jesus presented them from the Father: Faith in Christ, heartfelt and complete repentance, baptism by immersion for the remission of sins by one having authority and new birth through the laying on of hands for the gift of the Holy Ghost.

Ironically, Jesus found it easier to perform miracles and to raise the dead than to raise the general consciousness of Jerusalem. While the Jews waited and watched for their promised Mashiach, the gentle, simply clad Son of God quietly and purposefully walked out of obscurity into the Jordan to be baptized of John the Baptist—not for remission of sin or for repentance, but to consecrate himself to Heavenly Father's will. The holy event, celebrated today among Christianity, was regarded throughout the Jewish community with suspicion and incredulity. Few guessed he came to fulfill the prophets. Their reactions, though predictable, were understandable, but most Jews, then as today, rejected him. They would not open their hearts or prepare their spirits to accept the saving truths that the Savior taught during his brief ministry among them. Faced with this great handicap, the new teacher, when he came, marked the meridian of history and with his message of infinite love moved the world from its long season of doubt and sorrow toward the light of truth that brings supernal joy.

Notes to Chapter Three

1. Jesus the Christ, p. 275

2. Biblical Archaeology Review, pp. 26-34.

3. The Complete Works of Josephus, p. 382

4. In modern times an accepted thought among Jewish congregations is that the return to Israel which has been occurring in great numbers, is a symbol of a Jewish Mashiach. This Zionist movement was begun in 1896 by Theodore Herzl to restore Palestine as the national home of the Jewish people. Also, from time to time a revered rabbi has been spoken of by certain Jewish sects as a Jewish Savior. Jews today recognize no single spiritual head or religious hierarchy.

Behold, I am Jesus Christ,
Whom the prophets testified
shall come into the world.

And behold, I am the light and the life of the world;

and I have drunk out of that bitter cup
which the Father hath given me,

and have glorified the Father in taking upon me
the sins of the world,
in the which I have suffered
the will of the Father
in all things
from the beginning.

3 Nephi 11:10, 11
See John 1:17, 7-9

CHAPTER FOUR

LESSONS FROM THE MASTER

JESUS HELPED MANKIND SEARCH FOR and find God. He saw that people searched for many things but understood that what they really longed for was to know their Heavenly Father, the true father of their spirits, for then they would know everything. They would have discovered the miracle of divine love which fills every soul with faith and fulfills the immortal spirit. Love is vital to life. It cannot be captured or stilled because it is forever alive and increasing, adding upon us as we seek to know our Heavenly Father and to emulate Him. As Jesus taught of his Father's love he in essence presented the great Plan of Salvation, which "comprises all the laws, ordinances, principles and doctrines by conformity to which the spirit offspring of God have power to progress to the highest state of exaltation enjoyed by the Father."[1]

The Fall of Adam changed the state of earth, mankind and all forms of life from a paradisiacal and primeval one to a mortal and corrupt one. But, as Adam brought mortality upon the earth, so

Christ brought immortality.[2] Through the grace of God and the infinite Atonement of our Lord Jesus Christ (Eph 2:8), mankind and all
forms of life are forever ransomed from mortal death. Salvation in
general is synonymous with mortality, for all but the sons of perdition (See Doctrine and Covenants 88:32) will experience "the
inseparable connection of body and spirit so that the resurrected
personage lives forever."[3] After they are judged these rebellious souls
must endure a lasting torment, as they are filthy still. (2Ne 9:13-16)

According to the Plan of Salvation there is further opportunity
for all who are resurrected to live with God and Jesus Christ
(Doctrine and Covenants 20:29). This conditional salvation is
obtained by obedience to Gospel principles while still in mortality
and the individual soul then receives its inheritance in God's celestial kingdom, whence it originated, inheriting all that the Father has.
(See Prov 28:18; Matt 25:34; Acts 2:33; 2Phil 2:10-12; Rev 21:7;
Doctrine and Covenants 76, others)

This is full salvation, obtained "by virtue of knowledge, truth,
righteousness and all true principles... Without the atonement, the
gospel, the priesthood, and the sealing power, there would be no
salvation. Without continuous revelation, the ministering of
angels, the working of miracles, the prevalence of gifts of the
spirit, there would be no salvation."[4] (See Rev 1:5-6;3:21; Alma
34:16 Book of Mormon; Doctrine and Covenants 128; Moses 1:39;
Abra 3:24 Pearl of Great Price).

When Jesus gave his Sermon on the Mount (Matthew 5-7) he
emphasized that when men wanted to experience fully the love of
God in their hearts they would happily bestow that same love upon
their fellows. As they discovered greater and deeper love for others
and for God through living these great principles, they would come to
understand the transcendent possibilities inherent within themselves
which can be realized through, first, a living faith, then a life of godly
obedience to the saving principles of the Gospel including repentance
of sin, baptism by one having authority and heartfelt charity toward
all and long-suffering adherence to saving truths under any and all
conditions of mortality. Jesus himself was our perfect example of great
self discipline and nobility of thought. As he began his ministry, the
Adversary came to tempt and test his divine obedience. "But he
answered and said 'It is written, Man shall not live by bread alone, but
by every word that proceedeth out of the mouth of God.'" (Matt 4:4)

This eternal cycle is extended from our Father through His Son to all mortal creatures: "As the Father hath loved me, so have I loved you: continue ye in my love... This is my commandment, that ye love one another, as I have loved you." (John 15:9,12) Mankind must learn that to know God is the greatest experience in existence and that each of us possesses at birth the potential to be Christlike. And we have the true Gospel of the risen Christ that we might learn the truths of the kingdom of God.

Without knowing and living the Plan our Almighty Father has prepared for us we reject the best that is within us, becoming blind to our own precious birthright. How can we resist sin and temptation without the teachings of Jesus Christ made known to us through the Holy Ghost? Recall the advice of Paul in 1Tim 5:22: "Keep thyself pure." Whenever we turn away from God we invite deception and the potential for evil into our lives. Recall the point Jesus made in his conversation with the scribes in Mark 3:24-25: "And if a kingdom be divided against itself, that kingdom cannot stand. And if a house be divided against itself, that house cannot stand." In another conversation he reminded his followers: "No servant can serve two masters... Ye cannot serve God and mammon." (Luke 16:13)

The operative idea is that we as God's children—pure of heart and mind on arrival—should strive to remain totally focused upon what is good. The Savior taught that righteousness and unity of purpose were of utmost importance. Though we are different in our thoughts, opinions, physical makeup, etc., we will fare best if we are united in Christ's teachings so we can achieve our goals and purposes. In this way we will continue to grow in the clarifying light of Christ through the Holy Spirit which testifies to us of truth and error. To this end Jesus often would cast out "unclean spirits" from those who were afflicted with them and gave his apostles the power to do the same. (See Mark 5:7-9, Matt 10:1) "For everyone that doeth evil hateth the light, neither cometh to the light, that his deeds may be made manifest, lest his deeds should be reproved." (John 3:20) He taught that error and evil are the results of not understanding that we are all sons and daughters of God: We are, then, children of a King, each given the Spirit of Christ, and the salvation we all seek God wants us to attain.

For behold, the Spirit of Christ is given to every man, that he may know good from evil; wherefore, I show unto you the way to judge; for every thing which inviteth to do good, and to persuade to believe in Christ, is sent forth by the power and gift of Christ; wherefore ye may know with a perfect knowledge it is of God.

Moroni 7:16, Book of Mormon

Jesus' teachings spoke to the souls of men and women. He sought to inspire a living trust among them and to present eternal and saving spiritual truths for their edification and instruction. He always saw the end from the beginning, the rewards of charity and the penalties of sin. The reward in this life for learning the truths he taught is joyous love for our Creator and His creations. In the world to come that joy can continue as each soul progresses toward its eternal and desired glory.

Blessed are the pure in heart, for they shall see God.

Matt 5:8

Some of those whom Jesus taught were no doubt at odds with their lives, living as they did in politically dangerous times. He knew of their difficulties and despair, their sinfulness and their spiritual blindness. He gently but firmly spoke peace to their souls. He taught that our aim should be true humility before God. The Savior's own faith was based unquestioningly upon his Father. In the face of worldly sorrow Jesus was supremely tranquil because his trust in God was complete. God was a living reality within him and he sought to teach the necessity of attaining that personal experience to each yearning soul. Recall Matthew's description of the Christ as he went about his ministry:

And Jesus went about all Galilee, teaching in their synagogues, and preaching the gospel of the kingdom, and healing all manner of sickness and all manner of disease among the people.

Matthew 4:23

The faith Jesus experienced was total, it was free of doubt and without conflict. He always trusted God with the purity of a child (though not childishly) in that he depended totally upon that divine authority. Jesus' mortal life was based upon a living experience of an ever-present God. He was so in tune spiritually that he lived an inspired life. There is no evidence in scripture that he ever relied upon voices or claimed to have visions, but he attained spiritual perfection through his great faith in and consecration to the will of his Father in Heaven toward whom he exercised the most reverent and humble worship. Faith in that sacred trust enabled him, as it does all of us, to accomplish mighty miracles in service to others.

Jesus always urged people to experience with him the joy of the complete security he felt through knowing God's love. Every principle of life that he taught he attributed to his Father, a fact that becomes obvious from a cursory scan of the gospels. When he urged people to "follow me," he was asking them to share his own faith and to give their lives in unselfish service, as he did, that all might be instructed in the ways of God and live by those saving principles. In the directness of his teachings, Jesus seemed to take for granted that his followers had already developed a love for their Heavenly Father. He urged them further, to have the will and confidence to live a life inspired of God; to continue on that very narrow path which leads us gloriously and gratefully back into His presence.

> *And when he had called the people unto him with his disciples also, he said unto them, Whosoever will come after me, let him deny himself, and take up his cross, and follow me. For whosoever will save his life shall lose it; but whosoever shall lose his life for my sake and the gospel's, the same shall save it.*
>
> *Mark 8:3*

When we read of Jesus' life and travails we do not usually consider that he, too, had a lot at stake personally. That he struggled with his cosmic responsibilities becomes apparent when we read his beautiful Intercessory prayer in the Garden of Gethsemane:

> *Father, if thou be willing, remove this cup from me; nevertheless not my will, but thine, be done.*
>
> *Luke 22:42*

Of great urgency to him was his mission to do the Father's will in all things; to reveal God's great love for His children and the security to be found in that divine love. In his final mortal hours Jesus took upon him the sins of all mankind, from Adam to the last who will be born. He told his Father "I have glorified thee on the earth: I have finished the work which thou gavest me to do." (John 17:4) But for his work, his caring and his longsuffering he was brutally tortured and crucified, a fate he predicted and yet bore like the innocent and holy man he was.

It was urgently important to Jesus to win the hearts of everyone who would hearken to his message to accept him and the spiritual kingdom he offered, to find brotherhood and joy in sharing and service. To that end he went without belongings or money, often without food or lodging and without acceptance or safety into the world, meek, gentle, submissive and humble, loving each whom he met. He saved many souls at the expense of his own life, which he so magnificently gave up as the supreme example of love and sacrifice.

To that end Jesus never sought to reform oppressive governments. He was very much aware of the very strained relations that existed between the Jews and the Roman government, yet neither he nor his disciples became involved in their political problems. Though he condemned the exploitation of the weak and the less fortunate, he was careful to observe all laws and ordinances. It behooved him to ignore the economic and social problems within the towns and cities where he preached, for he had committed himself to finding and saving every possible soul for the Kingdom and Jesus knew his time among them was short.

He did not wish an open clash with the established Jewish sects and Roman religion. While he was non-committal with regard to civic affairs, Jesus did not seem fearful for his own safety. We recall the numerous times when his capture or arrest was imminent, and yet he slipped quietly away to preach again elsewhere. When finally apprehended, the Savior even refused to use his divine powers to free himself or to damn his persecutors, choosing instead to endure their blasphemies and their cruelties. He surely did not approve of their behavior, but in respecting their free will he allowed their malicious acts to condemn them. He knew that men were afraid to understand his gospel and to be like him.

Those who heard Jesus deliver the Sermon on the Mount must have been overwhelmed at his brilliance and strength of character. How he astonished them with his declaration "Think not that I am come to destroy the law, or the prophets: I am not come to destroy, but to fulfil." (Matt 5:17) He proceeded to tell them that men were all brothers, that their anger and revenge toward each other would earn them only the severe judgement of God, that they should love one another and become more righteous than the Pharisees and scribes. He admonished them that habitual oaths upon the name of God were forbidden. He reaffirmed that adultery a crime and denounced men for divorcing for the purpose of fornication. He spoke for a long time to them about the proper way to live. And then Jesus commanded them all to be perfect. (See Matt 5, Luke 6)

> *And they were astonished at his doctrine: for he taught them as one that had authority, and not as the scribes.*
>
> *Mark 1:22.*

Jesus was a revolutionist, but his method was to be persuasive. He sought through appealing to men's hearts to influence the enlightenment of souls, hoping that men and women would choose to lead righteous lives. We can learn much about perfection from the life that Christ led among us. Jesus paid no attention to public opinion. He was in the world but not of it. He was invariably tender and compassionate, always self controlled and dignified. Praise never seemed to influence his words or actions. He prayed constantly, and so was always in communication with his Father. He was totally free of religious intolerance, possessing extraordinary wisdom. He regarded women as equals, coming often to their defense. He appeared first to Mary Magdalene upon his resurrection (John 20:15-18). It was she who then delivered the message to his disciples of the risen Christ. Jesus always communicated with men on their own terms, because he had been raised among them and knew their thoughts. He prayed for them, he blessed and healed them and raised their dead. He forgave their sins. He taught them to pray, he exhorted them to have total faith in God and to love one another. He asked them to lead lives of service and hard work. He loved all people unconditionally.

Having perfect self control he was meek but fearless. He exhibited great patience in suffering. He loved us more than his own life and in his last agony he cried out "Father, forgive them; for they know not what they do." (Luke 23:34) He perfectly carried out his Father's will, never wavering, until the end when he said "Father, into thy hands I commend my spirit..." (Luke 23:46)

His ministry lasted only about three years; certainly most of his words are not recorded. There are numerous times in the Bible when

Jesus admitted his divinity (See John 14:2,25,26; Luke 4:21;7:26-27,34;9:20-22;22:70-71) It is testimony to his divinity that even the unclean spirits he cast out of men knew he was the Son of God. (See especially Luke 4:41,8:28) Jesus was always aware that there is opposition in all things and that those who hated him were unteachable. He knew they were blinded, being guided by the wrong spirit. But he knew also that he was their martyr, that he must become the final and infinite sacrifice. Peter said of him "For Christ also hath once suffered for sins, the just for the unjust, that he might bring us to God, being put to death in the flesh, but quickened by the Spirit." (1Peter 3:18) Such was the great love for mankind which Jesus lived and exhibited to the end of his mighty life.

The ministry of Jesus Christ was necessary to mankind. The only Begotten Son of God, he came not only to die for us but to bestow upon our world those saving and sacred truths, covenants and ordinances which are necessary for the perfection of our spirits. He instituted for us the ancient Aaronic and Melchizedek priesthoods to carry out the holy will of God, enabling baptisms, blessings and other ordinances to be sanctified by those having that authority. He added to baptisms the great bestowal of the gift of the Holy Ghost and commanded that the Comforter, the "...Spirit of truth..." (John 14:17) remain among us. He endowed all who are born with his Spirit. He brought to mankind the sacrament and covenanted with us that those worthy may take upon them his name and always have his spirit to be with them. If we always remember him and keep the commandments, we have the promise of eternal life with him. (John 6:54)

Jesus instituted the ordinance of baptism for the dead by proxy for all who have ever lived and died, as a means whereby all worthy can come to him as heirs of salvation. This ordinance is the gate to God's celestial kingdom, and a just God has provided that all His children will be given every opportunity to hear and accept his full Gospel, in life or death, through this vicarious labor. (See 1Cor15:29, Doctrine and Covenants 124:28-36;127; 128) He told of the mansions of the Father that had been prepared for us, exhorting us to live lives of righteousness and purity on earth, our proving ground. He extolled the value of eternal relationships (e.g. John 3:15-16; Matt 19:26,29, The Doctrine and Covenants Section 14:7; 76) and his mission showed mankind that the way toward the promise of eternal lives can only be fully understood in the latter-day temples of God.

Jesus conquered sin and death through his own death and resurrection. He became the infinite sacrifice, doing away once and for all with animal sacrifice and its bloodletting: No more would blood be spilled in similitude of the Savior. His single sacrifice is sufficient for all mankind, forever, in that all who have lived will have their spirits and bodies reunited in resurrected immortality. All will not be resurrected at the same time, however, for there are differing degrees of glory a spirit can obtain: everyone will be raised to his or her own order. (1Cor 15:23; John 5:28,29; Rev 20; Doctrine and Covenants 76)

Jesus came to tell us that we are the children of God and to show us what we can become. His own life was the perfect example of how one's life will be when God is the basis of all that person does. If mankind would recognize that divinity is within, his potential for Godliness could be expressed in daily life. After mortality, for those who strive to be like God, that is the state they will obtain.

Jesus told us that faith in God through him is the threshhold step into the Kingdom: "...I am the way, the truth, and the life: no man cometh unto the Father, but by me." (John 14:6) He asked us to love him enough to make that saving choice and gave us his promise of his constant companionship.

If a man love me, he will keep my words: and my Father will love him, and we will come unto him, and make our abode with him.

John 14:23

Jesus' mission brings all mankind hope and offers us the peace that comes with righteousness, which "...passeth all understanding..." (Phil 4:7) and speaks joy to our spirits. "These things have I spoken unto you, that my joy might remain in you, and that your joy might be full." (John 15:11) Latter day scripture reaffirms that we are on earth to be happy: "Adam fell that men might be; and men are that they might have joy." (2Ne 2:25, Book of Mormon)

Most marvelous of all is that he lives. Uncounted number of people have testified that Christ's spirit is ever among us, and that he has promised he will soon return as the perfected and glorified being he is to rule and reign among us, and that the Adversary will be banished during his reign. "And, behold, I come quickly; and my reward is with me, to give every man according as his work shall be." (Rev 22:12) Indeed, Jesus Christ lives. He is our friend, our brother, our personal Savior and Redeemer. He will be our Advocate with the Father when our journey here is finished, and he is our only true hope for eternal life.

We owe him everything. Praised be his name!

Philip findeth Nathanael, and saith unto him, We have found him, of whom Moses in the law, and the prophets, did write, Jesus of Nazareth, the son of Joseph.

And Nathanael said unto him, Can there any good thing come out of Nazareth? Philip saith unto him, Come and see.

John 1:45-46.

NOTES TO CHAPTER FOUR

1. McConkie, Bruce R.: *Mormon Doctrine*, p. 575-6

2. McConkie, Bruce R.: *A New Witnessfor the Articles of Faith*, p. 81

3. McConkie, Bruce R.: *Mormon Doctrine*, p. 669-73

Testimonies
of
Jesus Christ

But as it is written, Eye hath not seen, nor ear heard,
neither have entered into the heart of man,
the things which God hath prepared for them that love Him.

But God hath revealed them unto us by his Spirit:
For the Spirit searcheth all things, yea,
the deep things of God.

1Corinthians 2:9-10

SUSAN'S STORY

Born: Texarkana, Tx   Divorced, no children
Youngest of three. Two older brothers   Lifelong Christian
Professional Designer   Age: 50

IN DIFFERENT PERIODS OF MY LIFE I went through varying degrees of faith. I can tell you of something that happened to me many years ago when I was in college. This was a time when I began to drift away from my Heavenly Father in many ways. I began to be confused. I still wanted a contact with Him. I wanted it so badly that very often I would go to a church across from my dorm and pray. I would pray for long periods of time to know His will in my life. But I still was not getting the answers, the direction that I was seeking. I was still confused. I remember I was particularly distraught one time. I found the church doors closed. Before then all the churches remained open so that people could go in and pray. Then we started experiencing times of vandalism. Eventually people began to close and lock the doors of churches at a certain time.

I don't remember what time of night it was when I went out but I was desperate, desperate. I felt I had to go into a place like that church to pray, to receive answers. I was distraught when I found the church locked. I went to the home of the priest and knocked on his door. I told him "Please, I need to go inside the church. I need to pray." He saw how desperate I was and unlocked the church door for me.

At this period of time I was actively seeking Heavenly Father's will and yet rebelling against His will. I knew that I was doing wrong

49

things. But He also knew I was searching. I remember one early evening I went to my room. I was so exhausted, more emotionally and spiritually than anything else. I fell into a deep sleep. As I slept I had an experience.

First, the most incredible light filled my eyes. They were not open and yet I could see with my mind and think with my eyes. The intense light totally filled my whole being. It just radiated within me and out of me and beyond me. I had the most overwhelming feeling of love I have ever known. I knew when I awoke what it was. There wasn't a doubt in my mind. It was the love of God. He wanted me to know His love for me. He filled me with that love. He filled me with light. I felt wonderful.

But there were so many things going on in my life at that time pulling me in the opposite direction. So many that I still faltered, still continued to be confused. If I only had the strength to resist all those other influences in my life that would have been the complete turning point. Unfortunately I had to go further and into more despair before I reached that true turning point. One of the most important lessons I received from that experience is that He loves me, no matter what. He reached out to me and I almost took His hand but then I turned away. I had the free agency to turn away even after that incredible experience, but when I turned away there were consequences and the consequences were far reaching. I endured a lot of suffering for the next few years as a result of turning away.

That was before I learned something very important; how to create, how to find spiritual peace wherever I am when I need to pray.

There was a period when I did not know how Jesus' life fit into my life but that was only briefly in my college days. I began to wonder what was his real role. Prior to that time of confusion I cannot remember a time in my childhood that I did not love Christ and have a testimony of him.

My parents raised us in church. They were very faithful about that. They knew it was important, so we always went to church. And I suppose I was taught not only through the example of my parents, but by ministers, teachers and others. I was taught from a very young age that scriptures are important and I remember as a child pondering the scriptures to find the truth in them, trying to find answers.

I have read scriptures throughout my life and they have always been very important to me. I always had in my mind the question 'Why is it that God talked to people in the past and revealed things that were written anciently? Why don't we continue to have prophets? Why don't we continue to have scripture in our day? I even went to two of my ministers. I was probably fourteen or fifteen years old then.

The first minister, I remember, was very confused at my questions because he really didn't have any answers for me. Then a new minister came to our church and he used to spend a lot of time with me talking about those kinds of things. I always wanted to know why God was not revealing things now, today because we need it so much. That was something I believed should be. There will always be many questions yet to be answered but I know of a surety now that God has continued to reveal truths to us throughout the ages and that He will continue to do so. Very often people see God in the scriptures as the utmost authority figure who is strict and in command and demanding of our lives. But the scriptures teach us that He is our Father. He is our comforter, He is our friend, our guide. He's really everything to us.

Our Savior, Jesus Christ is also everything to us. I often think of his life here. He was born as a regular person, just like any of us. We know through the scriptures that his father was Heavenly Father. He had a normal birth. We know through the scriptures that he grew and learned as normal children do but apparently in an accelerated manner because he was already brilliant enough to argue with the rabbis of the Temple at a young age.

We don't learn a lot about his life until he serves his mission at about thirty years of age. Then we learn about the attributes he had. Jesus was incomparable, full of compassion. He could not stand to see people suffer. He was moved always to healing when he saw suffering. His life, death and resurrection have great meaning for me. I think that we all need to reflect upon his life, which he lived for us and the example he set for us, the things he tried to teach us about our Heavenly Father. Jesus told us that he didn't do anything but that which the Father told him to do. So if we follow his life we know we're doing what our Heavenly Father wants us to do.

Whenever we partake of the sacrament we're always thinking on his death and his suffering just prior to death. It's incomprehensible to me that he went through it all. I probably will live all my life and never fully understand the extent that he suffered. I can't imagine being able to endure that as he did, for anyone or anything. I know that he did endure it all.

His example gives me faith because when I think of all the things people may go through and what we're going through right now in the world, it's so overpowering. But then, when I think of what he went through, the suffering, the humiliation, every degrading thing, then there are no problems in life, not really, not compared to what Christ suffered for us. Oh, there's so much more that I need to learn of Christ!

There were times that I questioned the truths I had learned. There was a time I was unsure, truly like a boat without a rudder, easily pulled in one direction or the other. I was easily tempted by things that are bad for me. But the Gospel gives such peace. In the Bible we read about the "peace of God which passeth all understanding." (Phillipians 4:7). There's only one way that we can have that; through our relationship with our Heavenly Father, else we have confusion and doubt.

We do need direction. And really, even in the age we live in where there is so much information available to us through sophisticated technology and the Internet, especially in this day and age when we have such a vast amount of knowledge and information available we need a way of sifting through it to know whether it is valid and what's important, and we need to rely on Heavenly Father more than ever. Our lives are not simple in this day and age. It's easy to become confused. That is why we need to depend upon the Holy Ghost to lead us to truth.

Jesus Christ, when he went back to the Father after his resurrection, left us the Holy Ghost "to teach…all things." (John 14:26) So the Holy Ghost continues to teach us, continues to testify of the Father and of the Son and of all truth. On a day to day basis other than my prayers I have most interaction with the Holy Ghost. He's the one that is constantly teaching, constantly testifying to me, constantly bringing me peace from the Father.

When I was young I just frankly wanted to know about Christ. When I got older and needed to understand in a deeper way who he really was and why he is important to us I tried to understand his Atonement.

Everything is based upon the Atonement. When I began to understand what the Atonement really is about and the fact that none of us mortals could ever have accomplished the Atonement, then I began to see his role; a role that nobody else could fill no matter how great a prophet they may have been.

There are different levels of the Atonement and I suppose it is something that I will learn and it will deepen my understanding. On one level the Savior made it possible that all of us will live again. Death will always be temporary. We will be resurrected as he was resurrected. The New Testament is very clear on that. It is a free gift from God.

The next level is Christ's atoning for our sins. I have only begun to understand that he led a perfect life, one without blemish. None of us can qualify for that, even if we offered ourselves we could not atone for another person's death. But without that At-one-ment we can never be truly forgiven and at one with Christ. We can never really be cleansed. And if we are not cleansed, we know that the scriptures are exacting about the consequences of unforgiven sinfulness.

Sinful or not, however, we are always subject to the Adversary. Just because we are obedient doesn't mean the Adversary will stop working on us. He continues to work on us, usually in subtle ways. It may, in my particular case, concern the use of my time. Oh, he doesn't tempt me with gross sins anymore. Now the problem is with my resources; my time, the use of my mind and talents. I'm easily distracted. Not that I do bad things but maybe I could make other choices that are better, so he tempts me to pick out the faults I have to see how miserable I can become.

I can resist him but he will focus on our weaknesses. He tempts people in different ways. Some he can tempt with immorality, some with money. He just helps some of us waste our time so we don't do as much as we should do. We don't always do the best things. We choose second or third choices that are not as good for us as they should be.

But that's natural. When you're starting to learn as a child—and then when you challenge the things you were taught—you begin to question all of your beliefs and dig deeper and you have to know more at that level. I realized that as a child there were certain concepts that I didn't fully understand. I didn't understand Christ's role. I knew that he was the Son of God. I knew that he came to save the world. I knew that he came to give an example. But how he is different than other great prophets, the philosophers or the good men of the earth? That is what I had to separate out. I had to find out why Christianity is important.

When I was a child I wanted to be a missionary. I remember even in my seventh grade math class telling my math teacher who asked me 'What do you want to be when you grow up?' But you know, if I saw him today I could tell him 'I have realized a dream. I was able to go serve the Lord for a year and one half as a full time missionary.' But what a turnaround from rebellion against Him. He completely forgave me. He allowed me to go and to use His name in that way. That is proof to me that my Heavenly Father is totally loving, totally compassionate, willing to forgive. After the mission I came back to my normal life working as a designer, but I still seek ways to serve Him through an everyday life.

I know my shortcomings, but I also know what is expected of me. I know what my Heavenly Father expects of me and I know how far I can go. I can't help but know that He has a time for me to come home to Him. But first I have work to achieve. We all have work to achieve. Of course, I fall far short of the glory of God. I am like the stock market: I rise and I fall. Sometimes I am in a bear market and sometimes I am in a bull market! I wish I could say to anyone that I was completely consistent, but my love for my Heavenly Father and Jesus Christ is consistent.

I have lived my life in stages, as everyone does. First as a child in a Christian home with parents who taught us Christian principles. And that laid an excellent foundation in my life. I later went to college. I was somewhat rebellious, mainly through a flaw of my faith and I did things that I had to repent of. But Heavenly Father did not forget me. He gave me a chance to find the truth, though I was too arrogant to recognize it. And then He gave me another chance to partake of His love, but I was too confused to take full advantage of it. He reached toward me again in a crisis point when my marriage fell apart. I felt my life had fallen apart.

I was calling on customers in Houston one day after that. I walked into a customer's office and there was immediately a most unusual and strange feeling between me and the young woman that I met, one of love and understanding. We began to talk and she said "You know what your problem is? You have got to deal with your relationship to God." I absolutely broke down and started crying.

She was the first person to make me confront the fact that I had to deal with God and set my life straight. I knew that was the problem with my entire life, why my marriage was wrong. When I left that office I resolved to rectify my relationship with my Heavenly Father. I began my search again for truth.

In another two weeks I met another person who was crucial to my life. We spoke of spiritual things and I could see how the Lord put people in my pathway as I began to search again. And each step of the way the Lord was back. He was leading me. And really, from that time forward it has been an upward path. I eventually reached the point where one of my childhood dreams was finally realized and I became a missionary.

I was able to teach that if a person does not know for himself that God lives he must come to know it. He must come to resolve that in his own mind. And he can know. He will not be denied that knowledge. He can know for himself because the Source of that knowledge is waiting to give it to him.

Jesus came to teach us how we can become more like our Heavenly Father because he is like Heavenly Father. And as we look to him and imitate him we can become more like our Heavenly Father. There are many themes that he taught us. The greatest theme was love—pure love to each other. When we learn that lesson we can gain the greatest gift of all—eternal life, if we live as he lived, a life full of love. If we love him we will help others. It's based on love. Gaining eternal life means returning to the presence of our Heavenly Father and living with him for all eternity.

The scriptures teach us that we will have to await the resurrection and in the Old and New Testaments it does tell us that there is a spirit world (Neh 9:20, Eccl 12:7, Luke 24:39, Matt 10:1, others). When we die we will go there. The New Testament has some very sure passages on that. Because Adam brought death into the world Christ brought the resurrection to everyone. That is very clear in 1Cor 15:21-22.

So we will go to the spirit world and there we will await our resurrection. But we will not all achieve the same glory at that time. Not according to Paul. The writings of Paul indicate that there are levels. There are different degrees of glory. Some are like the sun, some like the moon, some as the stars. That would indicate that we aren't all resurrected the same way or to the same gloriousness: 1Cor 15:35 through 42 speaks of that.

For example, Paul compares the resurrection to these things: *There are also celestial bodies* (resurrected) *and bodies terrestrial:* (earthly) *but the glory of the celestial is one, and the glory of the terrestrial is another.*

1Cor 15:41 is also enlightening. Paul was teaching the Corinthians something about the resurrection, probably more than they knew at that time. It is obvious that we will receive different rewards, so you would have to ask 'How are the rewards given out?' It apparently has to do with our faith and our actions and how we have lived our lives. If we love the Savior we will want to do his works and that is why there are different rewards given to different people. Their resurrection is compared to different celestial bodies in the heavens; compared to the sun, compared to the moon, compared to the stars. Even among the stars, some twinkle more than others.

Works are very important to being saved spiritually. We know that we're saved from death by the grace of God. Jesus Christ brought the promise of resurrection to everyone, the just and the unjust. But we're not talking about resurrection only. We're talking about where we will be and what we will be doing after we're resurrected. I know these things are true and that they are a part of our Heavenly Father's great plan for us. It was obviously planned out because all the prophets spoke of it. It was revealed to them throughout millennia. The prophets received their knowledge through revelation, the revealed mind and will of God.

We know this because Jesus, before he left, taught us as well as his disciples and apostles that all can receive revelation. I believe that. I could not know only through reading that this is true. Yes, I believe in continuing personal revelation as I am worthy to receive it and as I seek it. Our Heavenly Father grants that to me. I believe that He continues to reveal in many ways His will among the family of man. Many do recognize it, but many people turn away from it.

Do we need continuing truth revealed? Just look at the world. We need it more than ever. More than any people in the history of the earth. Our lives are complex, our lives are in turmoil. We need and receive revelation individually and as a species. God gives us truth because of His perfect love for us all.

I continue to read my scriptures. I read the Bible and other scripture. I read the writings of the prophets. They're very clear that there is life after this life. I know that God at different times has used different prophets to communicate with His children. I know that in the 1800's He used a prophet by the name of Joseph Smith to communicate with these last generations. I believe that Joseph Smith was a prophet of God and that he served Him with faithfulness. As most prophets have, he sealed his testimony with his own life. I know that he was persecuted unjustly; he was persecuted for telling the truth.

I also believe there is a prophet on the earth today. I believe absolutely that there are disciples of Christ here in these times. I believe it because I have heard our Church leaders speak and what they speak is from the Lord. I know they have the power of God with them. That power is based upon love. There is a scripture which sums up the type of men all prophets are:

> *...and they had waxed strong in the knowledge of sound under-standing and they had searched the scriptures diligently, that they might know the word of God. But this is not all; they had given themselves to much prayer, and fasting; therefore they had the spirit of prophecy, and the spirit of revelation, and when they taught they taught with the power and authority of God.*

Alma 17:2-3, Book of Mormon

I hope to attain that type of love because Heavenly Father and Jesus Christ taught me that no matter what I do they'll love me. It was very clear years ago that they did not approve of my actions but I was allowed to make my choices and to experience the consequences. But their love did not cease for me. Even after that they reached out again. They continued to try to retrieve me. Their love is unrelenting.

I know unequivocally that they love us. They want us to be able to return to them They will help us if we ask. But we have to ask. Once we are given the answers it is up to us to take action. They will guide us but we have to take the action. And if we do the blessings are immeasurable. The peace is immeasurable. And our potential is immeasurable. Our reward is given according to what we choose.

I would like to say that I have given my life to Christ. But I know from my actions that if I had given 100% to him every day I would be home free. I honestly do. To truly give one's life to Christ means simply that now our time is his time. Our thoughts are his thoughts in the sense that we would walk as he has walked to try and live as closely as possible to the way that he lived. I think that is a struggle on a daily basis. Almost everyone I know—they cannot keep that focus. We're completely trapped in our day to day responsibilities.

When I think of what Christ did for us it is incomprehensible. And yet I truly believe it because as I live each day I have absolute confidence and hope in the Resurrection. And if it had not been for Christ providing that I would not live my life with hope every day because I would see an end to it. I can't imagine there not being something beyond this life. I know that there is; that is my greatest hope. I know I will go on beyond here and continue to improve, continue to live, to grow, to have happiness and joy. I can't imagine death or ending up in a place where there was constant torment.

But there are days I just cope. And there are days I only focus on my own life. I think the big thing is, we have to truly love others and we have to show them that we love them. Because the only way that anyone is going to listen to us is if they believe that we truly care about them. So the challenge in our lives is that no matter how busy we are we need a way of showing our love to someone each day and reaching out to them and maybe through us they can feel the love of the Father.

Of course, it does help to be forever faithful in our prayers and to pray constantly. It does help to read the scriptures every day to keep in focus. Going to church is very important. We have to do things to keep ourselves focused: Prayer, scripture study, serving others and keeping our thoughts true to that which is good. In these ways, I believe everyone should take the opportunity to get to know the Savior. One reason is that they have to resolve questions. We're all trying to find the truth. Any important question in the mind that looms over all of us we must seek out the answers to. We must come to know for ourselves. Certainly many have questions and unresolved feelings about Jesus. They need those questions resolved.

When Jesus came here he saw how people relate to each other. He saw how unlike our Father in Heaven we are. He knows that we fight, how we're avaricious, jealous, angry. He knows we do things to others to hurt them. And there were certain things he came definitely to make possible in the Resurrection. But what good is the Resurrection if we can't all live in love afterward?

Our Heavenly Father does not give up on us unless we give up on Him. And we do give up on him. His desire is that we turn to Him. His desire is that we love Him and allow Him to love us back. His desire is that we love one another and He will show us how. He will guide us. When we make mistakes He will forgive them if we will turn to Him. He is always there for us. We have only to acknowledge Him, to seek Him.

Baptism is one way of turning to God. I would think that if the only perfect person who walked upon the earth needed baptism, we do, too. So it is a sign of our faith. Faith means our obedience. We are following the Savior when we do that. We are walking in his path. The Savior was baptized to fulfill all righteousness. If he had not done it, then we would say it is not important. He did not have time to do anything that was not important. His life was very short. Once he was a mature man his mission was very short. Everything that he did was to show us the way to go.

If you study the scriptures carefully you will read that he went to John the Baptist. He sought a person who was ordained to baptize him, he went to one with the authority to do it. He didn't go to anyone randomly. So that teaches us that we have to go to those who are ordained.

I know that God loves us, that we are really His children and He is the father of our spirits. I know that He wants us to return to Him. I love Him for forgiving me, for giving me any chance to return to Him, for giving me hope that there is a way of returning to His presence one day. I love Him for giving me daily help and guidance and strength and encouragement to keep on the path that will eventually lead back to Him.

I know that God lives and that Jesus Christ is His Son and that he came here to make it possible for us to return to our Heavenly Father, to make it possible for us to become like them. It is possible. He has shown mankind the way. It is possible through God to try to become like Christ. I know that Heavenly Father has given us ways to know the truth about him. He has given us scriptures to come to know him. He has given us prayer to be able to communicate with Him and to learn more of His ways. He has given us the Holy Ghost to guide us each day and to teach us all truth if we are willing to receive it. He has given us a prophet on the earth today to help us know His will and His direction for us in this time that we have. He has given us apostles to further teach us as the apostles of old did. He has given us The Church of Jesus Christ of Latter-day Saints that is organized according to the way Christ set up his Church when he lived upon the earth, because it has all of the ordinances, offices and direction that we need in order to return to Him.

I know that without the Savior I could not repent and my debt of gratitude to him could not be expressed. I know that he suffered in the Garden of Gethsemane for us and that he took all of our sins upon him. I know that he died for me and that I will be resurrected and I hopefully will live forever in his presence if I can just endure and obey. I love him for all that he has done. These things I say in the name of Jesus Christ, amen.

For God hath not given us the spirit of fear;
but of power, and of love, and of a sound mind.

Be not thou therefore ashamed of the testimony of
our Lord, nor of me his prisoner:

but be thou partaker of the afflictions of the
gospel according to the power of God;

2 Timothy 1:7-8

Adam fell that men might be; and men are, that they might have joy.

2Ne 2:25 The Book of Mormon

CHRIS' STORY

Born: Fontana, California	High School grad, single
Family: Middle child of five	Devout Christian at 16
No chosen profession	Age: 19

I'M NOT QUITE SURE WHAT PROFESSION I will choose, but I want to help people. That is one thing I do know—something that will be of use to people, but not necessarily something that will gain me a lot of money. It must be something that will bring me happiness. I know that I want to go to a university and do something good. I want to do something that will help people so I can feel good, so I can come home from doing an honest job, a good day's work.

My parents raised me that way. They're great, really great! I am so lucky to have such a great family. They all believe the same things. We've all gained a sure knowledge of many things for ourselves. My parents have always been church-going people. They raised us all the same way. They attend church regularly and are firm in their beliefs and now I believe the same way. Since I was little they took me to church, but I didn't always feel the same way that I do now. I think I was using their beliefs as a crutch, at first, to support my own feelings. But, of course, I had to find out for myself what was right and what wasn't. And I found that out. My beliefs now are the same as theirs, but that's because I found out for myself.

It was a combination of things that helped me to find out that what they believe is true. I was working in a place that didn't have a good environment. I was working with people who didn't believe the same way I do. I started questioning their beliefs and mine, and of course when I started questioning, I thought I'd better find out what is true.

So I started studying. I was still in this bad environment—working in a restaurant at the time, in the kitchen, and the people there weren't exactly religious in the things that they said or did. So I started reading and studying and praying. Prayer was the biggest one for me.

I prayed for knowledge of the truth, and for feelings that would let me know what was true. The feelings were what did it for me. When I was about fifteen something happened, now that I think back on it. I had been questioning. My cousin was in a serious snowmobile accident. He was in a coma. We were very close friends. I had been going through all this turmoil in my mind about what was right and what was wrong, what was true and what wasn't. I had to find out. And when that accident happened and I found out that my cousin was involved, I was just sick about it.

That night we found out he had been taken by Life Flight to the hospital from the mountains and it was a real humbling experience for me. It brought me to my knees, I guess you could say. I went down to my room and just sobbed because we were so close and he meant so much to me. I didn't want him to die, but that was a definite option. I just remember praying so hard. I was on my knees for a couple of hours, sobbing. I prayed to God: "You'd better let me know what's real and what isn't." And the feelings I received were calm feelings, the most peaceful feelings. It was the best. Then I knew that my prayer to God was answered. I knew that my cousin was going to be okay. It was great. And he is okay!

So I discovered that what I had been taught is true because I knew that there was a God. He had already answered my prayers. I included in my prayers a lot of things that I had always been wondering about, like the books of scripture I was reading, the Bible and The Book of Mormon. I knew from that point on of their truth because I had been reading them and praying about them.

Prayer is essential if we want our questions answered with truth. When other scriptures were given to me—other than the Bible—I thought "Sure, why not?" But I still wasn't sure. I wanted to find out if other books were true or not and the way that I did that was through prayer. Then through studying them out, thinking about them and then going with an open mind. You have to go in with an open mind or you're not going to receive an answer or at least you won't be able to recognize the answer. If you do that you'll be able to feel the influence of the Holy Ghost—that comforting feeling—and you'll know that it's true.

While I was growing up, we were a close family. Oh, there were always the arguments and small things. My parents were always good, but we were kids and had our arguments and things, we had our fights. Sometimes it would cause our home to be a house of contention. But we also had family scripture study and family prayer every night. My parents tried to have it every morning, too. We always gave my parents the rolling eyes and the question "Oh, do we have to have this again?" But they always said "That's right, and we'll have it again, tomorrow." None of us kids wanted to study. At least, we didn't think we did. Now, looking back, I miss studying with my family and I miss praying with them. That is something that I truly am grateful for, you know, because we didn't appreciate it at the time. I look back on it and I know that it did me some good.

My parents are very good people. They wouldn't watch R-rated movies. I didn't agree with them. I was just a kid, a teenager, which I still am, but I didn't see the importance of their decision. I thought that R-rated movies were fine. I thought you just have to not watch all the bad parts. I didn't understand their concern. I remember the one time I rented and brought home an R-rated movie that I really wanted to watch. My parents told me that it wasn't allowed in their house and as long as I was under their roof I couldn't get R-rated movies. I had resentment toward them for that, but I am glad now they set the rules because it was something they believed was correct.

They weren't always perfect. When they would get really angry with us sometimes a cuss word might slip out here and there. But it was nothing super major or bad. When they got angry, we just stayed away from them because they needed a little bit of time to cool down.

My folks really love each other. They are there for each other. I really look up to my dad a lot. Whenever my mom or us kids needed anything—if we didn't have the money, my dad somehow made sure the money was there. He went without things he wanted and gave to us so we could have what we needed. That's how my dad is. He'll do things just for us and if it means going without he does it because it's for his kids and his wife. I really respect my dad a lot. I don't think I fully did, growing up. It's one of those things I can see now, in retrospect. My dad's a perfect example of how I want to be when I grow up.

My mom also has always gone without things she wanted so the rest of the family could have what it needed. She's a teacher's aide at an elementary school and she really likes that. Until four years ago she didn't work but stayed in the home. I think that made a big difference in our lives because we had a mother in the home, someone who loved us, someone who was there for us when we got home from school. Once again, retrospectively, we didn't realize it then, but I'm glad that I had a mom to come home to every day after school, someone to help me with my homework if I needed it, and many other things, too.

I want to be married and have as many children as the Lord wants me to have. In the back of my mind I think about "This is what I want." I want to be able to have a nice house, nothing really big and fancy. I want to have a decent car, just something in which I can take the kids and my wife. Definitely I am going to raise my children the way my parents raised me. Maybe they won't appreciate it at the beginning, either, but I think that they'll eventually understand. People always told me "You'll understand later." It's so true. I do, I really do.

But first of all we need to think of what our Father in Heaven would want us to do. Things aren't always easy in this life and there are many things that stand as obstacles. Of course, to the Savior Jesus Christ the obstacle was a lot bigger than any we will know, but there's going to be obstacles in our lives. We have to do the will of our Father in Heaven and when we do that we are going to get blessings and we're going to see those blessings. We may not see them now, but we'll see them later on, just as I see now the blessings of my family when I read scriptures with them every night, even though I didn't appreciate it then, I appreciate it now.

Even though we may not want to do the things that are necessary for us to do in this life but that our Father in Heaven wants us to do, we should do those things. We may not see the blessings coming from them right away, but when we look back on them later we will see what we learned and the blessings we received from our obedience. I can look back and say "I'm glad that happened." That's how we all can view obstacles in life: We can look back on them and say "I'm glad that happened and I've learned this from that. It may have been a mistake, but I'm grateful for the things that have happened in my life."

It's not like I'm looking forward to more obstacles in life, but I know they'll be there. And I know that I can overcome them. You know, the Lord will never give us anything that we can't overcome. He never will.

As I mentioned before, I am a Christian. Before I got a testimony of Christ I believed in him and in who he is, but I didn't believe in Jesus Christ, with emphasis added. I didn't believe fully in the things he did. I think that being a Christian is more than just saying we believe in Jesus Christ. We have to live that kind of life, too. "What would Jesus Christ do in this situation?" That's the best question we can ask ourselves. When we do that, we're putting our lives in line with his, and we can make him the center of our lives.

We must make it a goal to be like him. Of course, we're never going be completely like him, but I think that we can use him as a goal because he led a perfect life. He was the only person on this earth who ever led a perfect life: He never sinned. He loved all people. I think that is the main ingredient in his life and the things that help us in Christianity. He loved. You have to love people. That's the main thing. That quality is not always practiced in the world and that's why the world is as it is now. When we love people like Jesus Christ did, this world will be a much better place.

Jesus showed his love through service to others. I love it that he healed the sick. We can't be exactly like Jesus Christ in many ways but he was a healer, he made the lame to walk, and most importantly, he died for our sins. He died to help us overcome physical death. That was the most amazing thing that ever happened on this earth. I didn't understand the significance of that resurrection until recently, but it goes deeper than any of us know, or will ever know.

I didn't fully understand the Atonement of Jesus Christ. I didn't and I still don't understand fully what he has done for me, but it's amazing. At the time I was very young, I hardly had a knowledge of it. I don't think I appreciated it but I grew to understand that he is really my Savior because he saved me from that grief. When I prayed to know the truth of things I knew through the influence of the Holy Ghost that everything was going to be okay, and I knew, though it's hard to explain, and it had a saving effect. The word Savior had a new meaning for me. And, of course, it has built from there. It was kind of a spark that started it.

I think about the Atonement of Jesus Christ, when he hung on the cross and died, as he suffered that pain. When I read of his body being laid in the tomb and the tomb sealed, I recall his words to the Jews in the temple: "Destroy this temple and in three days I will raise it up," (John 2:19) And he did arise from the dead. During that time Jesus was resurrected.

Mary Magdalene came to the tomb. The stone was rolled away and she started crying because she thought someone had stolen the body of her Master. A man came up behind her. She thought it was the gardener and said "Sir, if thou have borne him hence, tell me where thou hast laid him, and I will take him away. Jesus saith unto her 'Woman, why weepest thou?'" (John 20:15-16) Jesus Christ was there. He had overcome death. And because Jesus Christ was able to overcome death, all of us will be resurrected and overcome death.

I love the scripture that says "My God, my God, why hast thou forsaken me?" (Mark 15:34) That is when Jesus is on the cross. It had to be done that way. His Father had to leave him for a time and let him suffer the rest of the way so his sacrifice could be of his own free will. I also love him for saying in the Garden of Gethsemane "Father, if thou be willing, remove this cup from me: nevertheless not my will, but thine, be done." (Luke 22:42) Jesus was willing to do what-ever his Father wanted because it was His will, and Jesus would do whatever was necessary. But, of course, it was Father's will and that's what needed to be done.

Resurrection is a free gift that is given to all people, regardless of our evil deeds, even our evil desires. In this life all of us sin and make mistakes. Jesus Christ took that into account. When he was in the Garden of Gethsemane he prayed to his Father in Heaven and took upon himself all the sins of the world. He took upon him the sins of every person on the earth and all the suffering of everyone who has lived or who will live. He did that because he loves us all that much. I think it's amazing that the Lord would show that to me and to everybody. He suffered so much that he bled from every pore of his body. I don't fully comprehend how that could happen. I don't fully comprehend how he could have gone through what he did.

Jesus Christ is very much alive. He lives. When he was resurrected he overcame death. He's a perfect, glorified immortal being and he is perfect. He's very real. He does have a body of flesh and bones, just as he had a body when he was on the earth. He has a body now and he always will. That's something that I look forward to with great anticipation—having a perfect body. Christ overcame death and because he did that I know that when I die I will be resurrected, and that I will be whole and perfect. I look forward to that a lot.

I believe that Christ speaks to us today, very much so. If he did back in Bible times, why wouldn't he now? It just makes sense. Why would he speak only to people anciently? He loves us just as much and he would speak to us the same way. You know, God follows a pattern. I think God chooses witnesses to reveal things to us today because He wants us, in these latter days, to know His will. That's the great thing. We can have that continuing knowledge of Jesus Christ and of the things that our Heavenly Father wants us to know and to do. I know that we can receive that knowledge today and that it will always be that way. He's not going to favor one people over another, because He loves us all. And in order to have that knowledge we need continuing guidance from Him. I know that to be very true.

I know also that He answers our prayers. I know he has answered mine and I know he continues to speak to us, through the Holy Ghost and through the feelings we have. If we go to Him with an open heart and a sincere desire to know something, He answers. I know God deals with specifics. He wants us to be specific, to say "I want to know if it's true." He doesn't want us to say "Bring me a sign." He wants us to make up our minds, study it out, to have an open mind about things and then go to Him and He will answer our prayers. That takes faith, great faith.

Faith is first. There's a scripture in Hebrews, 11:6: "But without faith it is impossible to please him: for he that cometh to God must believe that he is, and that he is a rewarder of them that diligently seek him." We have to have faith. That's the first thing. If we have faith, everything else will fall into place.

My parents taught me to have faith. They told me that I had to find out for myself. They knew that would have to happen, although

I did have a foundation to work from. But I had to believe that He was there and that He was answering me. I think I've always know that there was a God. I just didn't fully comprehend what He wanted me to do or what He wanted me to believe in. I had faith that God would answer my prayer that night my cousin was injured. I knew that God was listening to me. The feelings that I felt...there is just no way that He was not comforting me. It's something I'll always remember. I had faith that God would answer me and He answered me because I had faith.

My faith has grown as I have grown, definitely. And I am sure it will continue to grow. It takes a lot of prayer. And by seeing the love that God has for me, I continue to build my faith in Him. When I pray I know that He will answer me. And that continues to build my faith. As I exercise my faith then I see it growing and then I gain a better knowledge of things. I try to exercise my faith as often as I can, to pray to my Heavenly Father, and I think that shows Him that I believe in Him.

I also try to show Him that I love and believe in Him by the things I do, by the way I lead my life. I'm far from perfect, but I think the way I lead my life shows I love God, by loving all people. That's something that I have to work on. I guess it is one of those things that goes back to having enough faith. I have to continue to do it, and the more I do it the better it'll be. Practice makes perfect!

I think our purpose on this earth is to learn and to grow and to walk by faith because we have to. I think the resources are there and available for us to learn of Jesus Christ and to be better people, but we have to make the first step and to do it we must have faith in Him and in Christ.

One of the other really important things I know we need in this life is to be happy. We have to be happy. There's no point to this life if we are not happy. We're just here, just existing if there's no happiness. There have been times in my life that I wish I had more joy, but I can honestly say that right now I'm happy.

Happiness is the product of living a morally and spiritually clean life. And that involves serious repentance. I've done things before in my life that are not right, but I have repented of them. I have asked for forgiveness from my Father in Heaven and He let me know that I had been forgiven. I know that I was forgiven because I don't think about those things anymore. I don't remember them anymore. They're gone, they're just gone. I don't honor them and have that guilty conscience. When you do things wrong you're going to feel bad for them, or you should feel bad for them. I know that to be true. You can only go so long carrying that heavy load of things you've done wrong before you have to resolve it. I know that repentance and forgiveness brings peace.

When I felt sorry for the things that I had done I took the problem to my Father in Heaven and asked Him for forgiveness, then I made it right with the person that I had wronged and then I went back to my Father in Heaven and told Him that I had repented. I knew that if I did my part, Jesus Christ would make up the rest for me. But I had to do all that I could to make it right. And I knew the rest would be made up for me and that I would receive that forgiveness. I'm grateful for it because all of us are going to make mistakes in this life. I make mistakes all the time. But I know that through repentance we can be happy and we can be forgiven of our sins again.

If we change our lives wherein we can even realize what he did for us and the love that he showed us and the pain that he went through, we can think everything through more clearly, you know. It goes back to that question "What would Jesus Christ do?" And then we must pattern our lives by that. But we'll never be able to catch up to what he did for us. We'll always be in his debt.

I've never really had a major problem that I have had to take to a church official but I think there are things that we can't fully deal with alone—we have to go to others who will love us and help us; maybe our parents or a church official. Someone is going to help us through our problems and they'll help us get back on the path that we need to be on. I think it's important to have parents. I'm lucky that the ones that I have are so understanding. They'll help me through any problems. I may not always be happy with the decision that they make, but they love me regardless of what I do and I know that they will help me to overcome things I need help with.

The Holy Ghost is always available to help us with repentance. I think all of us were born with a conscience. The conscience is the light of Christ in our minds. When we receive the Holy Ghost it's the perfect thing. We feel good. The Holy Ghost is a member of the Godhead that includes God and Jesus Christ and he is united in purpose and works with them, so he knows all things, too. He helps teach us the things we need to know. I like to think it's as you see in the movies; the devil on one side telling you to do this and the little angel sitting on your other shoulder telling you what's good and what isn't.

Through my faith in Jesus Christ and in my Father in Heaven, when I pray and when I need questions answered or I am in pain, as in that experience when I cried for my cousin, I was comforted. I know that I was comforted and that my prayers were answered. All those things are through the power of the Holy Ghost. In John 14:26 it says "But the Comforter, which is the Holy Ghost, whom the Father will send in my name, he shall teach you all things, and bring all things to your remembrance, whatsoever I have said unto you."

I like the part that says "...But the Comforter..." because that is especially true in my life. At that time when I most needed comfort, I had it. I received help from the Holy Ghost and I knew everything would be okay. Because we feel the presence of the Holy Ghost we can know that it's there helping. It's like our conscience. It lets us know when we're doing something right and when we're not. If you're in a store, tempted to take something, and it says "Don't do that," you know that's the Holy Ghost helping you out. It will always let us know the truth of all things if we are attuned.

The Holy Ghost is necessary to our lives because we have to have opposition in all things. If we didn't have opposition we wouldn't know good from bad. We would remain just as we are, not knowing joy or pain or anything, so that's why we have to have opposition. Of course, sometimes we are given painful things to work through. I think that is to help us grow. I know it is to help us grow. Again, we have to look back on it in retrospect. There are a lot of things in our lives we have to do that with. But as we look back we see the reasons for those experiences, the reasons for our trials. They are given to us so we can learn to overcome them, to see how well we will handle our problems. And as we do that we will receive blessings. We may not receive them right then, but eventually, in different ways, on different levels of our lives.

The blessings we receive are not necessarily concerned with material things, but rather we are given knowledge of what our Heavenly Father has for us. We receive better understanding of the things we need to be doing with our lives so we can put our lives in line. It helps us, I think, to really link our lives to Christ and helps us to use him as a constant example because we know that it is through him and through our Father in Heaven that we receive the strength to help overcome the problems we are given.

A lot of our understanding comes from the blessings we get when we are baptized. We definitely need to be baptized in this life. It was commanded that we be baptized. "Then Peter said unto them, 'Repent, and be baptized, every one of you in the name of Jesus Christ for the remission of sins...'" (Acts 2:38), so we have to be baptized for the remission of our sins. This shows our Father in Heaven that we will obey His commandments and we are forgiven of our sins. Baptism means symbolically washing away all of our sins because no unclean thing can dwell in the presence of God. (Alma 19:9 Book of Mormon). And through a remission of our sins we can make ourselves worthy to return to live in His presence.

In order to return to our Heavenly Father all of us will have to die. But death is only a step in this whole scheme of things, so to speak. We go to a place of waiting where we await the day of Resurrection when we will all be resurrected. Our spirits and our bodies will be rejoined and we will be able to be perfected. Then we will live in a place of peace and Christ will reign upon the earth personally during the Millennium. There will be a thousand years of peace. Satan will be bound for that thousand years. After that, we will all be judged by the things we did in this life. That's another reason for this life—it is a test to see how well we can do. We only live once so we have to try to do our best while we're here. After we're judged we have the opportunity to go and live in the presence of God forever. There are three general degrees of glory we can receive. In 1Cor 15 it talks about those three levels. God is a just God. He prepared a way for all of us to receive some type of glory. That shows the love and the mercy that God has for us. Of course, we want to shoot for the highest glory—that's where I hope I go, that's what I'm shooting for.

We need to get back to the presence of our Father, where we came from. I personally believe that we have always lived. It's hard to understand the whole "forever" idea, but I know that we all lived before we were born on this earth. We had spirit bodies. We are all children of God, and just as I want to grow up to be like my dad, we all wanted to be like our Father in Heaven, but God has a body of flesh and bone. He is not just a force. So there was a way prepared for us to be able to come down to earth and receive a body like His.

We have bodies now. We can procreate, like He can. That's sacred. We can exercise our free will, as He can. There are many ways that we are like Him, and there are more things we can become. We can progress much further than we are right now.

When we anchor our lives to the teachings of Jesus Christ we know that we need to become more like him. Of course, then you have the whole world doing one thing and you're living your life another way. Do you know the saying "Eat, drink and be merry, for tomorrow we die?" That's the kind of attitude the world has. If we can change that and do the things that God would have us do, this world will be a much better place. Living in a world of moral decay we need to stand strong in our beliefs because we know our procreative powers are sacred, but they're misused. Look at all the teenage pregnancies that happen in the world, and all the unwed mothers. The family is the center, the block of society and if we don't have that to fall back on, this world's going down the tubes. We need that backbone, that support to help us in our lives.

I have definitely felt the temptation of the flesh, as other teens feel. Temptations are always there but it's what we do with those temptations. It's whether we act upon them, whether we ponder them, sit and think about them. But if we get them out of our mind we're going to be a lot better off, because we tend to act upon the things we think about and ponder on. If we get them out of our head we'll be less apt to act them out.

We have to live the things that Jesus taught. He loved everybody. We have to love everybody. He served them. We have to serve them. We have to go and do the things that he would have us do. We can't just say that we don't have to do our part, because he did so much for us. But this life would be too easy for us if there was nothing to work for. We have our choice, of course. We have to have a desire to serve others, but we also have an obligation. We are definitely commanded to do it. Just like the story of the Good Samaritan. (Luke 10:33-35) This story gives us the example that we must love all people. Christ said we show people that we love them by the things that we do for them, and by the way we live our lives.

Conversely, the things we do in this life and the way we show people we love them shows Jesus Christ that we love him, too. Remember that scripture "And the King shall answer and say unto them, Verily I say unto you, Inasmuch as ye have done it unto one of the least of these my brethren, ye have done it unto me." (Matt 25:40). So it is true that when we do things for people we do it for God, too, and for Jesus Christ. We need to be serving others as much as we possibly can.

There is so much to be grateful for! Look at the earth. Look how beautiful it is. Look at the things He gave us. We just have to look around. Every creature that was ever formed, every thing was created with a reason and a purpose—we may not always understand the purposes, but you just look around. It's great. He prepared a place for us, He prepared the way for us. He gave us Jesus Christ to help us overcome the effects of sin and death and He's going to give us the hope and happiness that we can live forever in His presence if we're worthy. We have to be worthy of it. That's why this life is so important for us to be constantly striving to do what is right.

I know that Jesus Christ lives, that he loves me, and I know that through him I can be saved. He truly is the Savior of the world and I'm grateful for that. I'm grateful that he loved me that much. He didn't have to do it but because he loves me and everyone else, he gave us this great gift. I don't know how to thank him enough for the things that he's done for me.

I'm grateful for the love that Jesus always shows me. Every time I read the account of his crucifixion and resurrection it really makes me think, helps put things into perspective for me. I know that it can help people's lives when they realize the love he has for them. People really are children of God. We are all loved equally because God has no favorites. I know that to be true. I know it is true and I'm so grateful for that.

I like to talk to people about Jesus Christ, to open my mouth. There's nothing to be afraid of. I believe that once we've been given the message we should share it with others. Once we find the happiness we need to share that with others, too, we need to help others to find that same happiness and if we do that we're going to see that joy come into their lives and they're going to help somebody else.

It's a cycle, just like with anything. We can either have a good cycle and help people to find Jesus Christ, help them to find that happiness, or we can help them to start a cycle of hatred. In this life we have the ability to choose, so we can either choose to do the good or the bad. If we choose to do the good then we can show people that we love them and help them. And then just talk to them about it, present them with the idea.

You don't have to be learned in scripture. I'm not. I learn new things every day in the scriptures. I think knowledge of the scriptures is good, but I think that believing first in Jesus Christ is necessary. Scriptures are like a road map in our lives. They help us to know what to do and help us to get where we need to be going. Once we know that we can pattern our lives after the principles we find there, because the scriptures are written by prophets and apostles of old and we can learn from them. But you don't have to be a scriptorian to understand the things they spoke of.

People are often too stubborn to listen. If we have an open enough heart then the Holy Ghost can enter into that. If we honestly want to know things and we pray about them the Holy Ghost will help us to know the truth of all things, like that scripture in John 14:26. He will teach us all things.

I have an uncle who claims he is an atheist and doesn't believe in God, but I know he does. He just puts on that front. I know that he believes in God. He doesn't claim to, but I know that he needs to change that. I'm still worried for him because I know that if he doesn't set his life in line he won't be happy forever. That's what we want; to be happy. We have one shot to do it. We'll be looking back on it—one of those retrospective things again. We'll be hitting ourselves over the head because we didn't make it or we didn't do the best we could, and I think that will be torture for us, to know that we didn't do our best, that we didn't try our hardest.

My message is belief. We have to believe and have faith—try it out. Try it out. Put God to the test. Have an open mind. Go into things with an open mind and put God to the test. I know He'll answer. I know, because He answered my prayers. Remember James 1:5? "If any of you lack wisdom, let him ask of God, that giveth to all men liberally, and upbraideth not; and it shall be given him." Ask in faith. Faith builds—we build off faith.

For my soul delighteth in the scriptures,
and my heart pondereth them, and writeth them
for the learning and the profit of my children.

Behold, my soul delighteth in the things of the Lord;
and my heart pondereth continually upon the things
which I have seen and heard.

My God hath been my support; he hath led me through mine afflictions
in the wilderness; and he hath preserved me
upon the waters of the great deep.

2Nephi 4:15,16,20

GLORIA'S STORY

Born: Edna, Texas   Family Affiliation: Christian
Family: Middle child, two brothers, two sisters   Lifelong Christian
Occupation: Licensed Practitioner, Massage Therapy   Age: 54

MY MOTHER WAS A METHODIST, MY father was a Baptist and they did not attend church with us, so I mainly went to the Methodist church with quite a bit of Baptist thrown in and other churches with friends of other religions. I have always had a great desire to know God and to know Jesus Christ, not just to know about them. I always felt a desire to attend church as a child, even when no one else in my family did. I felt that was the only place I was going to gain the information I needed. That's what people do: they go to church to learn about the Savior and God. I always had a desire to be where I thought they would be

As I grew, I would say the Methodist church was really my affiliation. I was married in the Methodist church. I attended every Sunday all through my high school years. It wasn't until I got married in 1961 that I stopped attending there, because my husband wouldn't attend with me.

I married a very gentle man. He had graduated high school as salutatorian and was very much loved by everyone. He was not pretentious. He was a very dear man and I married him because I was so opposite of him, I guess. I didn't do well scholastically. School was a social thing for me. We were drawn together. I was a senior and he'd already been out of school three years and was going to college. I always desired to marry a man "of the cloth" as we used to say. I wanted to marry a minister because I wanted to be with a man who had very close contact with God and the Savior and I felt that at some point my husband would attain that but that never happened. We never discussed religion or spiritual feelings.

We moved to different places and he went to Korea. That year I did attend the local church. I was one of the sponsors for the youth program there. When he returned from Korea we moved in June 1965 to Texas. He was in the Air Force.

We had been married about four years and we had two little boys, just two and three years old—absolutely adorable, precious. I remember feeling the great desire that it was time to return to church and to take my children. I wanted us to do it as a family. But I didn't know which church to go to. I was open to any church. I was open to anything that God would tell me to do. I was praying about it and asking "Which church is the truth, the one you would you have me go to, Father?"

I remember praying about it and we'd visit one church and meet some really nice people there. Then we visited another church and met very nice people there. I talked with my husband and said "I really feel that our boys are old enough to be going to Sunday School. They need to have religion taught to them and we need guidance with this." I was willing to do whatever he wanted to do. It was his decision and I would support that as far as which church we would go to. But he was kind of apathetic about it. He didn't care one way or the other.

Eventually I received information through two young missionaries who knocked on my door and handed me a new set of scriptures to read. And I really didn't want to hear about it. I had heard a little bit about this particular religion and I really didn't think that it was something that I wanted to be affiliated with. We'd make appointments and then I wouldn't be there. But, bless their hearts, they kept returning to me. When the appointments came I'd be gone because I didn't want to see them. I don't know what I was afraid of. My husband did not want to see them, either.

One day I was so embarrassed because of the way I treated them I did agree. I committed to meeting with them and in my heart I said that I would meet with them one time and then I would have done my duty and they could go and I could be free and clear.

Well, they did come that time and they said they had prayed about visiting me, that this would be the last time they would come by if I was not interested. So we had our first discussion and I was hooked. I couldn't hear what they had to say fast enough. I had to hear it and I knew from the very first moment they opened their mouths that the things they said about Heavenly Father and Jesus Christ and the Holy Ghost—I knew all those things were true. I just knew it. It was something that had been placed in me when I was a small child.

I don't really think it had anything to do with the upbringing I had in the church. I always knew the church I attended as a child was not the true Church for me. Actually, I did not believe there was any true religion. In the third grade I got a fight with a friend over that, because she was of another faith, and I said "Well, there really isn't any true Church on the earth today but the one that I am going to is the best one for me right now." I felt like that encompassed the ideals—I'm saying this and I can't believe I thought that in the third grade: I was five years old. I still had a memory of the first house we lived in before I started the first grade—I don't know if I had a vision or a strong impression, but I was aware that God the Father and Jesus Christ were two separate personages. It was like I could see them in my mind's eye. I just knew and I never doubted that. I knew that one day I would have the opportunity to know other truths.

So, when these young missionaries were telling me these other truths I knew it was correct. There was no way I could deny it. However, I had a struggle with enjoying my new faith because of what my husband and my neighbors and parents would say. They didn't want me to have anything to do with it. However, when I finally got on my knees I prayed differently. Before, in my prayers I would say "Heavenly Father, this really isn't true, is it, this information I've been given?"

It wasn't until I fell to my knees and I asked "Let me know the truth about these teachings" that I received a witness that was one of the most powerful I have ever received in my life. I felt the presence of Christ. I knew it was him because of the love—the love that just literally flowed through me. I felt warm and radiant all around me. I kept my eyes closed but I felt that if I were to open my eyes he'd be standing in front of me. I had never felt anything like that. I have felt similar things since then. So I knew. And I knelt there and cried because it was true. I was filled with joy because it was true but I also cried because now that I knew I had to make a commitment. I couldn't put it off. Didn't make any difference to me what anyone else said, what anyone else did. I had to do that which I had to do.

I don't think that my early church attendance had anything to do with my knowing of Christ. I think it was something I was blessed to know. It was with me when I came to this earth, I believe. I had very little teaching. My parents never sat down and taught me. I did go to Sunday school and vacation bible school and things like that and I loved learning, but it was affirming for me what I already knew. It was like that impression I received when I was a child: I can still see two personages and I knew that one was God and one was Jesus Christ, my Savior. No one ever taught me that.

I say that Christ is my Savior because he teaches me the things that I need to do to make my life better. He teaches me the way I should act. He teaches me the way I should love through things I read in the scriptures, all the scriptures. Impressions that I feel. The hymns that I sing. The spirit I feel when I am talking with my Heavenly Father. I feel a lightness, a strength. I feel love. I feel calmness and peace. The greatest thing I feel is love for my brother, whoever my brother may be. And that's the most important thing. I am a child of God. In that way he is my Savior.

The love of Jesus Christ has taught me how to love mankind. Jesus is my heart's desire. I want to see him. I want not just to know about him. I want to know him. I want to be with him. I don't want to wait until he comes in the Rapture. I want to meet him now. He suffered so for us in the Garden of Gethsemane. I believe that Christ suffered there, and we are told that he bled from every pore because of the agony that he suffered for us and his desire to redeem us that we may return to him. The only way that I can begin to know, to experience what Christ suffered, is when I am suffering to the absolute nth degree of every fiber and cell of my body. When I am in pain and anguish I say to myself "Christ felt worse than I feel when he was in the Garden."

I imagine him there alone in the quiet and the darkness. I have a picture of him leaning against a rock and I know the Spirit was there with him. I know angels attended him. I know angels attend me when

I am in despair. He suffered great grief because of the love he felt—the love he felt for me and for everyone, knowing the sorrow we were going to go through in our own lives because of our own choosing, just as a parent grieves for their child when they make wrong choices or even when they make good choices and it doesn't turn out well for them. I believe Christ suffered many times more so because he loved us so much and he didn't want us to go through the pain. He wanted to take that pain from us and he did at that time. If we could only remember "I don't have to suffer this burden. Christ has already suffered this for me."

Sometimes in my mind's eye I see him on the cross at Golgotha. I feel great love, absolute love and devotion to him. I feel that I would follow him wherever he asked me to go. I know that I would do anything willingly that he asked me to do, as long as I knew it was coming from the Savior. I know also that when I am feeling great spiritual pain, physical pain comes as a release. And I believe it has been give to me to understand that when Christ was on the cross this was a blessing in more ways than one because the physical pain offered him release from his spiritual and emotional pain.

Being baptized was getting in touch with the true vehicle of light in order to be able to continue growing and to express my love for the Savior in this manner. I've had to be very careful because I've been very guilty of feelings of self-righteousness because of the testimony I have of Christ. I love to talk about it, to share it and feel my love for the Savior, to feel that love within me. I become exuberant and gregarious. He has changed my life because he's helped my life to grow and helped me continue to hang in there at times when I've just wanted to throw in the towel and say "The heck with it all."

Jesus has changed my life by teaching me unconditional love, where before I know that love for my fellow man, even for my family members was conditional love. And he did this by giving me other people who demonstrated this unconditional love. By their example I could see how to do it. I used to wonder "How can they love that person?" after that person had been so ugly to them. And they would teach me so I would learn to see the problem from different viewpoints. I asked the Spirit in the name of the Savior to come to me and to help me perceive whatever negative thing may be happening around me that I might see it in truth and in love. Every time my prayer has been answered.

It has not been easy. There have been severe trials in my life. Going through a divorce several years ago I remember the anguish I felt and it lasted many years. I just remember very briefly that the week I filed for divorce I was in the deepest of despair. This was in 1987. I had been married for twenty-five years to the man who was the father of my children. I remember that because of the despair I'd been going through for years but wanting to hang in there. I always felt that if I gave up the next day the Savior would come to me and say 'You should have hung in there one more day. You gave up too soon.' Finally, I had to do what I did. I filed for divorce on a Monday. Darkness, pain. I felt that the Lord had forgotten about me, that he had put me on the back burner and was watching me stew and really didn't care about me during that time. I was distraught. I remember on Saturday night I didn't want to go to church the next morning. Normally I never miss church because I love being there. But I love doing the things that I am asked to do, so I decided to go anyway. I was filled with great grief because of the love I still felt for my husband, though I knew that we could not live together anymore.

After the meetings were over I was called into my leader's office and at that time I was extended a "calling" within this Church. And then I was given a blessing through the power of the priesthood. I immediately felt the love of my Father and my Savior envelop me and hold me up and lift me. And this has brought great joy to me. I felt that great uplifting joy for well over a year. I can't describe the joy that I felt. I knew that everything was going to be all right, that I was loved, that my husband was loved, that I would still have to go through with the divorce but that I would be loved and supported in every way. I just felt so taken care of. I just felt their arms were around me.

Because we are human beings we are weak and we forget what we know and we allow the Adversary to come in and put doubts in our mind, or whatever. I just keep studying. I study the scriptures, I read everything. I keep a prayer journal. I've been keeping a prayer journal now for well over three or four years. I can't remember when I actually started it, I just keep it devoutly. That helps me in so many ways because I can write it out and then, when I'm writing it the Spirit can come upon me. I don't even know what word I'm going to be writing next and then it comes to me as a word that maybe I wouldn't even have thought of, but as I am writing it helps me to be clear about what my choices or decisions are. And the Holy Ghost testifies to the truth of what I read and what revelations are given to me.

I love the Holy Ghost. I am so grateful for the gift of the Holy Ghost that has been given to me. I believe the Holy Ghost has been with me ever since I was born. The Holy Ghost has borne witness to me again and again of the divinity of the Savior. The Holy Ghost has borne witness to me of truths that I may have had doubts about regarding people, places and events. Even when I have thought I had already made a good decision, saying "I am going to choose to do it this way" because I felt like that was the right thing to do—when I got on my knees and prayed about it the Holy Ghost has given witness to me that it was not the correct choice and showed me another way to go. I know it is his influence because I feel light around me. I feel impressions coming into my mind and then feelings of joy and gladness, peace and calmness. Those are usually indications that the road I am traveling or the choice I have made is in concord with what Father in Heaven would want me to do. Whenever I don't choose that I'm usually filled with turmoil. I'm filled with anguish, I'm filled with disturbing things. Because God is peace. The Savior is peace. The purpose of the Holy Ghost is to bear witness of the divinity of the Savior. I love the scripture in The Book of Mormon that tells us about the trials of the great prophet, Alma and how the Lord comforted him in his time of need:

And I will also ease the burdens which are put upon your shoulders, tht even you cannot feel them upon your backs, even while you are in bondage; and this will I do that ye may stand as witnesses for me hereafter, and that ye may know of a surety that I, the Lord God, do visit my people in their afflictions.

Mosiah 24:14

I believe that sometimes we are brought into circumstances to learn from them and they may not be wonderful. We may be brought great trials, great grief, great tribulations. It doesn't mean that we are not loved or even that we are making wrong choices. It can only mean that the Spirit is guiding us into new avenues of learning and growth. We would not seek out answers if we did not have these trials and tribulations that come to us. And we would not grow.

I do believe that Jesus visits the earth from time to time. Not only Jesus but his angels. I believe that Christ is in charge of everything that takes place on this earth, therefore, he can send his emissaries to help in times of crises or times of great anguish or times of joy. But usually it is when we are in our deepest despair that I believe the Savior comes to us.

I believe that he has guided every step of my life. I've tried, even from the time I was a child. I went ahead and I just took what I felt was the best way, not really having full knowledge or certain knowledge. But I know that in the last few years I have seen the events of my life unfold. It's my responsibility to learn the purpose for whatever is coming to me in my life and to find the joy in that purpose. That is the whole reason for going through whatever we're going through, whether we like it or not.

We have to be led by faith. "Faith is the substance of things hoped for, the evidence of things not seen." (Hebrews 11:1) It's that inner knowing, something that, if we trust and go ahead and do all we know to do in a righteous manner, then God is bound. He says "I, the Lord, am bound when ye do what I say; but when ye do not what I say, ye have no promise." (Doctrine and Covenants 82:10)

I think that it is up to us to prove God's promises in every way. That is faith. Sometimes we don't really know but we have the faith and we go ahead and take that step—the leap of faith—and then it all just comes to us and it's beautiful and and we think 'Why did I ever doubt?'

Repentance for me, I believe, is a turning away from doing things that are not in concord with God. Not keeping the laws—and those laws can be anything from the ten commandments to the food we eat to the Beatitudes. When we turn away from them that doesn't mean we're wicked—I don't believe that for a moment because none of us do keep all the laws perfectly—but we can certainly try. To me, sin occurs when we know we have been warned against doing something and we say "Oh, the heck with it, I don't really care," and participate in the event anyway. I think that is a sin against God. We cannot be judging anyone for whatever sins they commit, because God knows what is in our hearts and what's in our minds and what is in our understanding. We also tend to judge the one whose sins are more obvious than our own.

How do we repent of these things? By knowing the Savior and by acknowledging the mistake. We have to admit to God and to the injured party what we have done. I just experienced this yesterday. I was sinning against God because I was angry at someone, being vocal about it. I couldn't believe these things we coming out of my mouth but they were because I was so filled with anger. When I was able to process that and I could go to my Father in Heaven I recognized what I was doing. I called the people I had talked with and apologized to them. They were kind enough to listen to me.

Then I can go to my Father and I can apologize and I can make restitution by extending love to these people, which I have done. You know when you are forgiven—the Spirit sends you a warm and happy feeling and you soon forget about the whole thing. If we are having doubts that must be because we have not forgiven ourselves. I think the hardest part of it is learning to forgive ourselves, which means we have to learn—we want to learn to love ourselves. We need to love ourselves and too many of us don't do that. We may love ourselves in a very egotistical way but we do not love who we are in our relationship with our brother Jesus Christ or with our Father in Heaven. We do not acknowledge that. Once we can do that and recognize who we are we come into touch with our own divinity. "God doesn't make junk." We are all children of God. Jesus Christ is our elder brother as well as our Savior, Redeemer and Judge.

I think baptism is important because it symbolizes our commitment to Christ. And I believe it should come at a time when we can understand that. We should not be baptized as babies, because babies are innocent in the eyes of God. Baptism is right when we can discern between truth and error or discern to make a good moral choice. At that time when we can make a conscious moral choosing, then we can make that choice to be baptized. The opportunity was provided for me to be baptized by authority but it didn't come to me until I was an adult. It was a very difficult choice to make at that time.

When I say "authority," I mean those who have been ordained by God to perform baptisms in the name of Jesus Christ. I believe the Holy Ghost bears witness to you of the truthfulness of that principle and will lead you if you're seeking, to find that particular priesthood. I was seeking way back then and I'm still seeking. I think that when we ask God, He will let us know. It says in James:

If any of you lack wisdom, let him ask of God, that giveth to all men liberally, and upbraideth not; and it shall be given him.

James 1:5

I do believe that and I believe that when I was asking God back in 1965 which church to join I was seeking with pure intent and a sincere heart. He brought it to me. I still had to struggle with it at first because it went against everything I had been previously taught by the traditions of my fathers, so to speak, but then when that opportunity came I made the choice that I knew was correct, but it wasn't an easy choice to make because I was ostracized by my husband and family. But that was a choice I made.

My husband was a very good man but he chose not to believe with me or to attend church with me. I don't know why because we never discussed it. He would have been required to stop smoking cigarettes, coffee and tea and things like that and he didn't think anyone had the right to tell him what he should drink. But for me it was something that I knew I had to do. I do not believe that my husband ever prayed about it, but that's only my perception. God can tell us what to do. God speaks through man. Yes, God can speak through man. We still have that right and privilege to freely discern whether or not that man who says 'I have heard it from God' truly has received it from God. I would like to take it a step further. I believe that any of us have the right to receive information directly from God without having to go through anyone else. Most of us have to go through man in some way because we are not in tune with God enough to know when He tells us something, but the Holy Ghost will bear witness to that effect. It will tell you what is true. We each have the right to receive revelation for ourselves.

I believe there is a prophet on the earth today. I do believe that. There have been prophets on the earth from Adam's time until the apostles of Christ were murdered. Then the greater priesthood was taken from the earth by Heavenly Father until the Restoration in 1830 which produced a modern prophet, Joseph Smith. I always felt we ought to have a prophet. As a child I thought "How come we can't have somebody today that says 'You know, I am speaking for God and for the Savior.'" Those are the things I was searching for, never dreaming that I would find it in my lifetime. However, I did and I do believe that there is a prophet on the earth today that does speak for God for the guidance of Christ's church and who also gives guidance and counsel to those who may be seeking it for themselves.

But divine guidance is no good if it is not listened to and obeyed. The most important thing to know and strive for is to live the teachings of Jesus Christ. I believe in pure religion, as it says in James 1:27:

Pure religion and undefiled before God and the Father is this: To visit the fatherless and widows in their affliction...

And the royal law is to love your neighbor as yourself and do good.

If ye fulfil the royal law according to the scripture, Thou shalt love thy neighbour as thyself, ye do well.

James 2:8

I believe that is truly the purpose of being on this earth. I believe that there have been many people who did keep those laws who haven't heard anything about priesthood and baptism by authority and I believe the Savior knows who they are and that they are worthy of being called up to greet him at any time. I believe if a person truly lives pure religion as Christ has asked us to, earnestly seeking and thirsting after righteousness and to know the Savior, to have that desire to meet him, that they can be caught up before death. I have had the Spirit bear witness to me already.

My first responsibility is to know that I am a child of God, that I have a divine spirit within me, that I can become a god as God is. But in order to do that I have to love my brother, and that's the most important thing I can ever do. Love is healing. Truth is love, love is true and healing, so we can reach out and touch people. We can touch them with the spirit. My prayer every day is that I might be able to radiate love, light, goodness and beauty to all who come into my presence, that I can only touch them with the healing touch of Christ's love. That sounds like a real big order. Who am I to even think that I can be considered such a vehicle of light? But I know that I am and that I can be a vehicle of light. And all this through God's glory, for the glory of God.

I would like to tell of the marvelous ways of God. His helping us, sending his emissaries, teaching us, allowing us to go through all the pain and anguish, allowing us to suffer that we can become like him, because to be like God is to be completely filled with love. Right now another book of beauty come to me, the Odes of Solomon. They are just about the most beautiful lines I have ever read. It tells us that when we try to interpret love, we become that which is interpreted, we literally become love. That is God. He is pure, undefiled love and when we can completely incorporate that in our being, then we can become as God is, filled with the light of intelligence. Light is the power and authority and word of God. The word is within man.

When I can go and find in the sanctuary of my soul the "holy of holies" within me and make that contact with the Higher Power, my Heavenly Father, God within me, then I am the door to everything. I can ask anything and it will be granted unto me, but it must be in righteousness.

I have a situation now where I am not with my new husband whom I love with all my heart, with every fiber and cell of my being. I believe that it is the Lord's intent that we be together for a length of time, a short or long time I don't know. I would like to see that reconciled so that we can serve God together, so that we can help heal the world together. My prayer four years ago was that I would find someone with whom I could heal the world. From all the things that have come to me in the last few years I believe that my purpose on this earth is to be a vehicle of healing to whomever the Savior allows to come into my presence.

And that healing of the world encompasses many great and wonderful things. So I would like to heal the world. I would like to continue teaching my children and my grandchildren. I miss them very much because they live thousands of miles away from me. But the reason we're so far apart is because of the Spirit's guiding me to where I am now. I have been kind of led into wilderness, I guess you could say.

And wilderness is wonderful. Wilderness can bring much truth to us if we are seeking, but we have to be seeking—the wilderness can bring to us the truth of all things. How? By suffering of our sorrows, because usually suffering sorrow in which we seek to know what we need to do brings us enlightenment. If everything is wonderful we might not seek to know what to do. At least I found that for me. I can only speak for myself. When everything is falling into place beautifully, then maybe I don't go to God and say, "What would you have me do?" However, that's not entirely true because before I moved up here almost eight years ago everything was wonderful for the most part, but I knew that I had to seek, so I had to ask my Heavenly Father "What would you have me pray for?"

When I'm confused and don't know what to do I have to say "Let me not ask amiss. Let me know what you would have me pray for," and that's what happened three or four years ago when I was praying to find someone that I could heal with so we could heal the world. Ideals were placed into my mind to pray for, and it has been the hardest time of my life, but I am grateful for it, grateful for trials and tribulations. I am grateful for sorrow because in it I learn what God would have me do and the challenge is "Am I going to love my brother?" It's there. Totally, completely, unconditionally. Do I love my brother, my neighbor, my son, whoever it may be? I have been asked if I am willing to die for what I believe in and my answer is that I am willing to live for these principles.

Healing is a gift of the Spirit. To me, there are the gifts of the spirit and there are the fruits of the spirit. We can be given gifts of the spirit but if we do not use them and apply them in our lives then we are not bringing forth the fruit of the spirit and it avails us nothing.

An important gift or ability the Lord bestows upon some is the gift of discernment, to be able to discern between truth and error. There is the gift of having a testimony. There is the gift of believing on someone else's testimony, there is the gift of prophecy. We can have all these gifts but if we do not have charity—the pure love of Christ for our brother—none of the rest of them is going to get us anywhere.

We can go to the temple, we can serve missions, we can do good works in the eyes of man for our own glory and that looks good because we are out there doing it, but if we don't love our neighbor, if we don't take care of the widows and the orphans, if we don't love ourselves and our brother and truly make an effort to extend this love and light and healing to our brother, the rest of it is not going to do us much good.

The Plan of Salvation is that we come to earth to gain a body, to be tested and tried in all things. Then when God has proven us worthy we will serve Him and love Him no matter what the cost. Then is our election (exaltation) made sure.

There definitely is a pre-existence. That is something that I have always known. There were many spirits that we lived with and many of the people that we live with today are people we knew in the pre-existence. I have no doubt of that whatsoever. Spirit recognition is one of the most beautiful things in the world. And I've had that happen so many times. Instantaneous connection. And it's absolutely a precious, precious gift. I love it. I thank my Heavenly Father for it. How wonderful it is. The veil would be essentially the knowledge we had in our pre-earth life. It's a forgetfulness that is covering up the memories we had of our pre-existence so that we would learn to walk by faith and not by sight and not by the previous knowledge that we brought with us, although sometimes some can see heavenly beings through spiritual eyes. We should learn to test and trust ourselves and to prove God while God is proving us.

Our spirits live forever. Our intelligence, our personality goes on forever, yes, When we are resurrected we have that. So, I believe that the same thoughts and feelings and attitudes we have when we pass from this earth die in our earthly body. We don't just lose them and all of a sudden when we cross through the vail they are returned. We carry our personalities with us. If we have a grudge against some-body when we die, we're going to have that same grudge against them whenever we cross over. This was part of Christ's message to us. I do believe that we can save the world not by believing but by living Christ's message. I recall this wonderful scripture:

Peace I leave with you, my peace I give unto you: not as the world giveth, give I unto you. Let not your heart be troubled, neither let it be afraid.

John 14:27

I believe that God speaks to us today. He speaks to us through the Savior. The Savior gets his message to us when we are open to receiving it. If we are not open we probably are not going to receive it. And so he just comes up against a wall, a closed door. I also believe he speaks through his prophet to the world. And I know the prophet is very open to receive whatever Heavenly Father would have him know in the name of the Savior what is right and good for the world.

By being as Christ was and is we can change the world and I do believe we can change it one at a time. We can change it by living the truth and by teaching it. But I have learned in my experience that very few people want to be taught, so we can't teach with our mouths and with our tongues. In fact, one of the things we're supposed to learn to do is to bridle our tongue and to control our tongue. If we can control our tongue we can control the whole body.

I love 1Ne 3:7 in The Book of Mormon because that sustained me when I was on my way from Texas to Washington and for the first year or so that I was here I would continually read that and ponder it, because of it's perfection. The very young prophet Nephi says:

I will go and do the things which the Lord hath commanded, for I know that the Lord giveth no commandments unto the children of men, save he shall prepare a way for them that they may accomplish the thing which he commandeth them.

Christ teaches us how to meet life successfully. He has proved that to me. And I proved him because he has prompted me to marry, to join the church and to move here, to be a healer and so many more marvelous things that have happened in my life. I knew he'd help me find the way and he did. I proved the Lord by my faith because it was my faith that got me here.

And be not conformed to this world: but be ye transformed by the renewing of your mind, that ye may prove what is that good, and acceptable, and perfect, will of God.

Romans 12:2

Another one that has truly been a transformation for me in many ways has been the prophet Nephi's testimony in 2Ne 4:15-35. When I was going through the divorce many years ago this was my prayer every night and day. I would read it and I would make it my prayer. I put myself there, saying those words. It sustained me and got me to the temple when that way was opened up for me to go.

Remember to open that door of your heart at which the Savior is constantly knocking because it's not opening to him. That is all about truth being like a crown on our heads and bringing forth fruit. Your Lord has prepared for you a feast.

I stand all amazed at the love Jesus offers me,
Confused at the grace that so fully he proffers me.
I tremble to know that for me he was crucified,
That for me, a sinner, he suffered, he bled and died.
I marvel that he would descend from his throne divine
To rescue a soul so rebellious and proud as mine.
That he should extend his great love unto such as I,
Sufficient to own, to redeem, and to justify
I think of his hands pierced and bleeding to pay the debt!
Such mercy, such love, and devotion can I forget?
No, no, I will praise and adore at the mercy seat,
Until at the glorified throne I kneel at his feet.
Oh, it is wonderful that he should care for me
Enough to die for me!
Oh, it is wonderful, wonderful to me!

Text and music: Charles H. Gabriel

CHUCK'S STORY

Born: Oskaloosa, IA   Married with seven children
Family: Middle child of five. Two stepchildren   Lifelong Christian
Employment: Retired physical education, Spanish teacher   Age: 65

I WAS BORN DURING THE DEPRESSION, in 1931. My father started out as
a dairy farmer. He never went past the third grade. His mother and
father died when he was very young and he was raised by his sisters.
He started working when he was ten. Then in 1930 he sold his dairy
cows and put his money in the bank to start a milk processing plant.
The bank went broke and he lost all his money. No one could find
jobs then, but he opened up a little beer and hamburger joint. Just a
little hole in the wall. He sold beer and hamburgers and brain
burgers and soda pop. He never drank alcoholic drinks. Never
swore, anything like that. Sometimes he'd bring home 50 cents a day
to raise a family. We had plenty to eat but no excess.

He influenced me a great deal. His father was an alcoholic. My
father told all his children that he hoped the first drink we took

would kill us, rather than have us turn out to be alcoholics. As a result I have no idea what alcohol tastes like. Even before I joined the Church I didn't taste it. And it was the same way with smoking. He smoked until his first son took up his pipe and then he never smoked again. He was a good man, a hardworking man. It was often said that my father could outwork like ten men. He was tough. You knew he loved you but he never said it a whole lot or hugged us.

My parents got along very well. Never did we hear any harsh words between them. None whatsoever. We came from pretty much a happy family even though there was struggling because it was the depression years.

My father was a righteous man, although we never went to church or talked about God until I was about twelve years old. Neither parent did that. There was no religion in the family until we moved to California and we children started attending a nondenominational Christian church.

Eventually my mother started going with my father and they got "saved." Then they started taking us to church. We heard about God and Jesus Christ and my folks said "Oh, yes, the Bible is true. It is the only true book in the world." So I began to believe that. I began to believe that Jesus Christ is real and that there is a God. I just believed it. I never got "saved" or anything like that when my mother took me to church. They eventually joined the Foursquare church.

They'd take us to church. I always knew in the back of my mind that there was a God but my folks' church and other churches I went to never impressed or moved me, though I believed in the principles that were taught there.

My grandparents, aunts and uncles swore a lot. My brothers and I picked up the swearing habit and I was pretty foul mouthed by the time I got out of the service and got home from Korea. The Korean War started in July of 1950. I joined the Air Force in December of 1950, spending four years in the service. I lived in Korea for a year during the last year of that war. In fact, the Cease Fire was signed while I was over there. But I didn't see any action because I was a telephone man. I strung telephone wires, repaired telephones, things like that. I believe the Lord steered me away from life threatening incidents hundreds of times in my life. I was just steered to the Church.

My conversion happened slowly. A couple of years before I went into the service I met a young lady. First date I ever had was during my first year in junior college. My good friend fixed us up with dates and we went double dating, but we weren't girlfriend and boyfriend.When I met my date, instantly, it just seemed like something jumped in my chest just to be in her presence. She was LDS. She impressed me. She had class. She carried herself well. She had standards. I was just a boy, just wandering, just floating in life, going nowhere. In twelve years of school I never did get an "A", except in physical education and shop. My life was going to waste. Then I met her. I grew up in a little shanty town in northern California, among poor people with poor ways. My dad would always laugh " We're not very smart. We're dumb." I bought into that with the rest of the family. But I met this girl and she changed my life. It was her presence. She was just fine. I had never been around that. I had been around some pretty rough people in my life. Her fineness just impressed me. And then she would talk about her church, and she didn't smoke or drink. She wouldn't go out on Sunday. She and some of her friends who I became acquainted with took me to their church a couple of times. And here again, in that church, there was a feeling, a feeling I couldn't shake. I was impressed to see young people get up in front of 200 to 300 others in Sacrament meeting to give a talk.

This all happened in 1949. The war was over. It was my first year in Junior College. I had a physical education major because halfway through high school I started playing football and getting involved in sports. There I began to associate with people who had gone to college and earned degrees. For the first time, I began associating with people who had some goals in life. I wanted to play football so bad that I was finally able to apply myself. Sports saved me. So I started turning my life around. It was hard. No one should have to struggle to get a degree in college as much as I did. Anyhow, I graduated from high school, went to college and played football. That was where I met this girl. We were friends in college until I went into the service in 1950.

While in the service we'd write to each other, just as good friends. I was stationed in Wyoming where I attended telephone school and I met this young man who became a good buddy of mine. The same thing happened to me almost immediately upon first meeting him. There was something about him I had never seen in anybody. He was different than anyone else. He was LDS. It's uncanny. We became real good friends and I can remember people teasing him because he didn't smoke or swear. I'd even hold some of my swearing back when I was around him. I was writing this girl at the same time.

And then we were transferred to an Air Force base in Utah. And while I was there my first LDS friend married in the LDS temple and invited me to her reception. I went to the temple the day she was married and said I wanted to see my friends. They explained to me that I couldn't go in the temple, as I was not a member of The Church of Jesus Christ of Latter-day Saints. I accepted that. And then my other friend from Wyoming who was in Utah with me married in the temple. I was impressed by that.

I remember a time when we were out on an athletic field. There must have been fifteen or twenty of us and we were on a break from our duties. We were laying out on this field. It was a warm day. He began to tell about eternal marriage and the Plan of Salvation. It was the first I had heard about it. The year was 1951.

It just added up. It was just like he was reminding me of something I had known before. But I didn't hear anything more about the church after that episode. Then we were assigned to Korea. He was stationed in Northern Korea. I was stationed about 100 miles from there. Once or twice a month we'd call each other and talk. He was the only person I knew who didn't smoke or drink or cuss. I watched him. He wouldn't bend. He was moral. I was impressed that the other guys couldn't get him to drink or smoke.

After we left Korea we both were stationed in Oklahoma City. By that time he and his wife had a baby. They invited me to church and I went once or twice with them. I wasn't going to any other church at the time. But I was deeply impressed by him and his wife. He was like a missionary to me, even after we were transferred again to a base in California. I went to church with him two or three times in six or eight months, not paying much attention to any of the doctrine then. He never preached to me but I just knew...

What drew me? A feeling. I decided I wanted to associate myself with that group of people because they seemed to be fine, they seemed to have class, they seemed to have poise, and one of the things that impressed me about their church was its quiet atmosphere. The message was powerful. It's the spoken message, the spiritual or unspoken message, the way people live their lives. I was just a nothing. I'd grown up in a shantytown. I'd never been around fine people like that before. I'd gone to church with my parents before and every Sunday they'd call people forward to be saved. They'd have songs and they'd beat the drum, play the piano and get everybody all fired up. They had pictures of the Christ hanging on the cross to get people emotional. But the LDS Church was so quiet, so peaceful, far more powerful than all of the music and other things.

The day we were discharged from the Air Force my friend, his wife and baby took me down to the bus station. We said farewell and I returned to California. When I returned I told everybody I was going to attend the LDS Church. I didn't know what they taught. I didn't care what they taught. I wanted my future children raised in that environment. In 1955 I went to college for a semester but I ran out of money and sold encyclopedias for the money to stay in school.

There were twelve of us men who took a training class to sell encyclopedias. I became friends with someone there who was a jewel. After our first night of selling we all got together with the trainer who suggested we all get some coffee and donuts and talk over what happened. He started the car, looked at my friend and said "You don't drink coffee or smoke, do you?"

My friend said he didn't because he was a member of the Mormon Church. The trainer noted that I didn't indulge either. I replied: "I decided that I just don't." At the coffee shop my friend offered to send the missionaries to teach me about the Church.

"Sure, send them over," I replied.

The missionaries related to me the story of The First Vision—the story of how Joseph Smith was made a latter day prophet of God. I thought: Wait a minute. You've got to be kidding. I've heard of these people who go out and have visions and the next day they put on robes and they go out, they're prophets, they start up their church and claim to be Christ.

They taught me the First Discussion—a lesson about the Church's beliefs. It was interesting. After they left I thought that all this goodness and all this wholesomeness and power I have felt all these years, it came from that. Suddenly, I didn't see a light, I didn't hear a voice but I knew the First Vision was true. I don't know what happened. It was uncanny the way it happened. I knew that The Church of Jesus Christ of Latter-day Saints is true. I knew that whatever they'd teach me was going to be true. I knew that Joseph

Smith was a prophet of God. That was in April. I was baptized in September 1955.

I was working with the telephone company in the mountains by then. On Friday nights I came home. The missionaries met me there and said "Let's go down and get you baptized." But I put them off for awhile. I wasn't going to make a commitment unless I could commit and never turn back. Like the scripture in the Bible that says to put your hands on the plow. I waited until I was sure, so I wasn't baptized near as soon as they wanted. I told them that if I am baptized I am never going to turn back. I've got to wait until I get to the point where I am willing to do that, otherwise I won't join.

I was baptized on a Friday night. I had never read The Book of Mormon. But they didn't teach me anything. They only reminded me of what I somehow already knew. It's uncanny but I know I learned it in the pre-existence. The missionaries taught from conclusions. They'd make point after point. I would read one thing and it would build to a conclusion. Well, it was obvious to me what the conclusion would be long before they reached it. I was way ahead of them all the time. It was just beautiful. The Plan of Salvation. The fact that everybody will have a chance to accept or reject the Gospel of Jesus Christ. Everybody will have a chance to be baptized.

I was married when I joined the church but two years later I divorced. I was twenty-nine years old. Five years after I joined the Church, the Chruch allowed me to go on a mission. It is very rare for a divorced man of twenty-nine to go on a mission for the Church.

I'm infinitely a better man now than I was forty-some years ago when I joined the church. I'm not perfect but I'm better than I was. I married again, this time for the rest of my life and eternity, and I've been married to my wife for thirty-two years. We've tried to apply the Gospel of Jesus Christ and we have never had a harsh word between us. If I hadn't joined the Church I'd probably be in jail by now, someplace, and I wouldn't have been this kind of a man. I had no purpose in life. I had no structure in my life. I had no goals. I was just wandering, drifting. The Gospel of Christ saved me.

How do I know him? I have read all the standard works several times, also the General Authority talks, the Conference talks. I have listened to the testimonies of others. It was a strong feeling. I had never read The Book of Mormon. I didn't know what the doctrine of the Church was. There was a feeling and it was goodness, whole-someness. It was truthfulness, a secure feeling. It was intelligent and it made sense. I knew it was the right church for me. You don't need a lot of noise and hollering and rolling on the floor. When I was young and living with my parents we'd go to church on Sunday and every Sunday evening service they'd have the altar call. They would play music. Not soft music but music with a beat to it and it would just get people stirred up. They would call out to come down and be saved.

I never went down that aisle. I don't know what held me back. It just didn't seem right to me. I believed what they were teaching. I believed that there must be a God, that Jesus is the Christ and that the Bible is true. But they seemed to make Jesus a sissy, a weakling. I didn't like that. Maybe they didn't do that but I perceived it that way. Prior to joining The Church of Jesus Christ of Latter-day Saints in California a new stake center was being built. I went out and worked side by side with these men. They didn't swear, and they were tough, they were strong. They weren't a bunch of sissies. The next Sunday they'd put on their suits and they'd be doing spiritual things. Gosh, that impressed me.

The Protestant churches we attended looked at it this way: We are here on earth. God, Jesus, the Holy Ghost and other heavenly beings are there in Heaven—two different groups, unconnected. But it isn't that way. We're here on the earth. Our brothers and sisters and Father are there. We're all one group. We just happen to be in sepa-rate places. There's no difference between us. We on earth and those in Heaven are all of one family. We humans just hapen to be here on Earth for awhile. But God is my Heavenly Father. I'm related to him. Jesus is my brother. We're all brothers and sisters. One of these days when I die I'll be on the other side with the rest of "us." Those are some of the things that impress me. It makes sense.

What is a Christian? True Christianity would be pretty hard for a weak mortal like me to ever achieve—but it is the person who is honest, kind, fair, considerate and is obedient to God's command-ments, who accepts Jesus as the Christ, keeps the commandments and serves Him. You don't have to be baptized to be good, to follow Christ's commandments and to accept him as the Savior. Everyone, in order to be saved in the celestial kingdom (1 Cor 15:40-41) must be baptized and must have kept the commandments and endured to the end. But not everyone has to be baptized to be considered good men and women.

All you have to do to go to the celestial kingdom and live with God throughout the eternities is to accept Christ as the Savior, repent of your sins and be baptized. Baptism is a celestial order. That's all you have to do. But to be exalted as Heavenly Father is you must be sealed for time and eternity. In order to do that you must hold the Priesthood if you are a man. You must receive the temple ordinances, the endowments and all those things, and then you must be sealed for eternity. And that is available to everyone if they endure to the end.

Christianity goes back to the Atonement of Jesus. In order to progress more and become like our Heavenly Father we had to go through the things he did, so we had to be sent to an earth. If we were sent to an earth we were going to be influenced by evil forces that would cause us to do things we shouldn't do. Doing those things, we could never return back to Heavenly Father's presence, no matter how much we repented, no matter how good we were after we sinned. It would be impossible. We could not save ourselves. If I go out and steal something I am put in jail for five years. After five years I have paid for that time and I will be forgiven and go on with my life.

But when we are sent to this earth we break the laws of God. We couldn't pay for them. We didn't have the ability. So, one of our brothers named Jesus came to earth and became the Savior, became the Christ. He was willing to pay that price for us. Mercy can't rob justice. There must be a price paid. If we don't repent here in this life we're going to have to suffer. We'll sooner or later be forgiven, but that is after we suffer the same way the Savior has suffered—for our own sins. After we have been forgiven of those sins in the life hereafter we can't repent our way into the celestial kingdom. But if we accept the Savior and accept his Atonement while we are alive he will pay for our sins. We won't have to suffer. We can repent and be eligible for the celestial kingdom.

I know the Holy Ghost was guiding me toward the Church. But I didn't join to receive blessings. Even now people say "Oh, you pay your tithing and you live the Word of Wisdom. You get all these blessings! Well, I don't do it for that reason. I love Heavenly Father. I love the Savior and I like to be obedient because I love them. The blessings don't make any difference at all. I decided I wanted to be honest, to stop swearing and not be immoral. I wanted to be kind and courteous and intelligent and improve my life, without even completely understanding the Atonement. But now that I know it increases my love of Christ and my desire to serve him.

It wasn't until I became a missionary for the Church in Mexico. I had been a member about six years. Marion G. Romney, one of the apostles, was the General Authority over our mission. He came to see us. He gave a masterful discourse on the Plan of Salvation to those Mexican people through a translator. After that I understood the Plan of Salvation like I had never understood it before. That changed my life. I understood the Atonement a lot more and appreciated the Savior more.

People say "What about the Bible? What about these thousands of people in the Old Testament who were killed in these cities? "The Israelites would invade cities and and just wipe people out. I couldn't answer before I learned the full gospel. Now I can answer. I can say, "Look, they're alive, I know it. They live and they're learning the gospel and they can accept or reject the gospel. If they accept it they can be baptized by proxy and have the same privileges we do." Once I heard that talk by Elder Romney things started falling into place. Death isn't as important as some think it is. It is not as serious as some think it is. Usually death isn't a tragedy. It's necessary. There is a Plan. God doesn't make any mistakes.

Though I don't memorize scriptures very well, reading them has greatly increased my understanding. The last time I read The Book of Mormon I used two Book of Mormons and started through them. I'd find something that was strictly doctrine. I'd cut that out and make a third book. So I have a book in there that does not have the writings of the wars, all the contentions and the travels separate. What is left is strictly the gospel of Jesus Christ. Gosh, what an understanding you can get from that. You start reading The Book of Mormon and you see that the stories always return to the gospel. Jesus is the Christ. Then there are wars, contentions, then scripture that Jesus is the Christ and this is the Gospel. It is repeated again and again. I never realized how much it was a testament of Jesus Christ until I read it that way.

The Book of Mormon also deals with the Adversary, Satan. If you have a testimony of Christ and that there is a God, then you must have a testimony that there is an Adversary. He lives. He is real. He is full of hate, envy and despair. His plan wasn't accepted by Heavenly Father. He fought against Heavenly Father. He was rejected. He was sent out, so he wants to punish our Heavenly Father as much as he can. He wants to discredit Him and discredit Jesus Christ and the Holy Ghost. Misery seeks company. He wants to take as many of us as he can. Not that he wants us as his companions, because he'll betray us once he has us. He'll let us die, he'll let us end up drunks and drug addicts, miserable and unhappy and he won't try to save us. He'll just laugh at our Heavenly Father "I've got another one of your children." He wants us. That's the worst way to hurt Heavenly Father.

The longer you're a member of the Church the harder it becomes to follow the Devil. Knowing what we know it is hard not to know when you're doing something wrong. The Holy Ghost is real. You receive the gift of the Holy Ghost. I've heard a lot of people say: "The Holy Ghost will be with you. He'll be your constant companion but if you decide to go into that bar he's not going to go in with you." I think the Holy Ghost will fight. I mean, he'll put up a battle, a struggle and not leave you until there's just no hope any more. I don't think he's going to give up on us. I think that the longer we are members of the Church the stronger our conscience becomes because our association with the Holy Ghost becomes stronger.

We read stories, see movies about the universe and all the different life forms there. I don't know if it's true but I do know a family is there. This family looks just like me and you. This family rules the universe. My Father rules that family. This Father, like I said, looks just like us. We are his children. Whether there are other creatures out there I don't know, but if so, they are all subject to our Heavenly Father. Christianity is the only true religion on the face of the earth. The Church of Jesus Christ of Latter-day Saints is the only church that teaches the correct form of Christianity. Therefore, The Church of Jesus Christ of Latter-day Saints is the only true Church on the face of the earth. Everything it teaches is true. Its doctrine is true. Everything that has been revealed so far is true. I don't claim or think the Church claims that we know everything, but everything we need up to now that we have received is true as it is taught by The Church of Jesus Christ of Latter-day Saints.

I know that Joseph Smith is a prophet of God and that the Church has a living prophet at its head. A lot of people don't realize that every one of the General Authorities, the apostles and the prophet all hold the same keys. The difference is that the prophet holds the keys to preside. If that wasn't the case, when a prophet died Moses would have to come back, Elijah would have to come back, Peter, James and John, to restore the keys again.

I hold the same keys and have the same authority as the bishop of any ward because I am an ordained bishop also, but I can't serve as a bishop again unless I am "set apart" or chosen by the authority of the Priesthood to preside over a specific ward. That's part of the order. The order begins with one God and he rules and there is no confusion. God picks one man to direct all the affairs for the world, all the religious affairs for the world, otherwise there would be just confusion and chaos. So you see, Heavenly Father doesn't run those affairs himself. He lets human beings bring to pass his work. In order for a person to serve God he has to be "called" to that position. No matter how good the man or woman might be, no matter his intentions they can't go out and start making rules and regulations and decisions about God's work without His authority.

It's like a person who sees someone speeding. No matter how good his intentions are and how wrong or how right he might be, this person can't give you a ticket. If he does give you a ticket it means nothing because he hasn't the authority. God needs men and women to bring to pass his work on this earth. He calls them, they don't call themselves. So far He's chosen men to run His church and He gives them His authority. His authority is called the Priesthood. To me that's about as simple as it can be.Men must be worthy of holding the Priesthood. They must keep the commandments of God, have a testimony, be willing to serve Heavenly Father. You serve Him by serving His programs which serve people. The Book of Mormon says that when you are in the service of your fellow being you are only in the service of God. The Priesthood of God is based on charity. We serve wherever we happen to be. I have an obligation to use my Priesthood first and foremost for myself, then for my family and then for the rest of the world. Twenty-four hours of the day I am on call. If someone needs my Priesthood authority I must give it. I have no choice. When I was asked to become an elder I didn't make the commitment for five or six months because I didn't take it lightly, just like my baptism. I wanted to be ready.

I hate to think about what happens if the Priesthood is misused. I guess it would depend on how serious the transgression. Repentance helps us to become better people. I think that true repentance is painful because you have to admit to yourself first of all that you were wrong. You have to face up to the severity of what you do, see its ugliness. That is painful. I have a brother who I'm sure would join the Church but he doesn't want to go through that process.

There are some sins that are so serious our former prophet, President Spencer W. Kimball said that a person who truly repents of these serious sins would cry buckets of tears. Repentance is painful because you have to admit it to the world. You are finally facing it and admitting the wrong. I think that's the important part of it. And what follows that? A lot of peace. A lot of peace. Repentance is a cleansing process. It gets impediments out of the way so you can participate again, be Christlike and progress.

We have to think of what is most important to us. In a Priesthood class I once attended the teacher said "Let's pretend that you're going to die soon. You have about five or ten minutes and you have a chance to write a letter to your family. I want each of you to write in the next few minutes what you would say to them."

This is what I wrote. "Dear family. It has been my work and prayer and purpose in this life to bring to pass the immortality and eternal life of first, myself and then you. I pray that we will all again be reunited in the celestial kingdom. Some of you may come to doubt the truthfulness of the Gospel and the existence of a celestial kingdom but there will come a time when the truthfulness of it will be made known to all of us. I will soon know with sureness of these things. Children, take care of your mother and each other. Be kind and completely honest all the days of your life and you will know true happiness. Hold your heads high and stand above the corruption of the world. Honor your name. My purpose is to be the kind of person that would qualify for Godhood." I want that for the rest of my family, also.

A year or so ago one of my daughters was going astray a little bit. She was just making some wrong choices. I brought her home and I said "It has always been my aim and my work to try to make it possible that all nine of us would live together in the eternities in the celestial kingdom. Daughter, the way you are going there will only be eight of us." Oh, what a difference that made in her life. She changed. Knowing the gospel has really influenced my family to be more righteous.

Much of righteousness has to do with prayer. I never pray for anything except the help to be honest, kind, to keep the commandments, to resist evil, repent of my sins and the help to be better at whatever I do—High Priest group leader, Sunday School teacher, good husband, good father, good grandfather. I thank Heavenly Father for the preservation of my life and that I have lived as long as

I have. At the end of the day I thank Him for the opportunity of having lived another day on the earth. When I get up in the morning I thank Him for the opportunity of living another day. I believe He hears all prayers and that He answers them.

My wife and I pray for things that come into our lives. Things have just worked out. We once thought we needed to buy a new vehicle. I had just graduated from BYU. We had three children. I was starting to teach Spanish in California. We thought we needed a new vehicle. We didn't pray to Heavenly Father for the money so we could get a vehicle, we just prayed to Him to let us know what was right.

We prayed and prayed. We requested a loan from the credit union. One Saturday afternoon we got a call from the credit union representative. He said "We have denied your request for a loan because you have medical bills, you have just started out teaching and we don't think it would be wise."

We got angry. But we finally wised up and repented of the brief tantrums we were throwing. We just looked at each other and we thought "You doggone fools!" We went in and got on our knees and asked forgiveness for acting like that. And ever since we have been very careful. He answered our prayers. The answer was "no." People don't realize that "no" is an answer. They pray for certain specific things and they don't get it and they say "God didn't answer my prayers." That is even the way with life and death: We ask "Heavenly Father, please spare my daughter, or my son, or my wife, or my own life." And Heavenly Father might just not. That doesn't mean the prayer wasn't answered. The answer was "no." It takes faith to accept that. Faith is everything. You just can't live without it. In the long run, after everything is said and done, the most important thing you can do is to resist evil and temptation, to keep God's commandments and serve Him here while you are here. If you do that, everything will work out for the best. It just will. Whether you have a new car here on this earth doesn't make any difference. Whether I die tomorrow or not won't make any difference. But the eternities are what makes the difference. It's important to live your life today in such a way that you are guaranteeing an eternal life.

My wife and I were kind of talking about this the other day. You know, when her brother died, and our parents died over the years, we didn't go into fits of despair and mourning. It was all right because we think we understand the Plan of Salvation, the purpose of life.

Someone once asked me if I would be willing to die for my faith. I'd like to think I would be able to run into a burning building and save somebody but one never knows until one is faced with that choice. I once sold everything and went on a mission for two years. When I finished my mission I had three suitcases. Two of them were full of books, the other was full of old tattered clothes. It was all I had left in the world. Some called me a fool for going on a mission— almost thirty years old. I'd do it again if I was asked, but that is not like giving your life. My mission on earth is to be prepared to return to Heavenly Father. If I can't do that I can't take my family with me and I can't help anybody else.

One of my goals is to be the kind of person that I saw forty-two years ago. I am constantly striving to be that kind of person who can influence somebody. I hope to be to others like the examples I witnessed. To let my light so shine, to be the kind of a person that impresses people so they will want to be better. But neither the Church nor Christianity has a monopoly on goodness. You don't need to be a Christian to be good. You can be a Buddhist or a Jew or whatever. Just be kind and honest and fair, serving and helping people.

If I were to be at the Savior's crucifixion, knowing what I know now, I would think "What a courageous thing to do." Oh, I've hurt, I've had injuries and pain throughout my life and I thought that hurt a lot. Thousands of people suffered pain on the cross—but knowing what he suffered—the fact that he chose to suffer for me. What love he must have for me! A feeling of a lot of love for him, a lot of admiration. What a courageous person.

One thing have I asked of the Lord, that will I seek after,
inquire for and (insistently) require,
that I may dwell in the house of the Lord
(in his presence) all the days of my life, to behold and gaze upon the beauty
(the sweet attractiveness and the delightful loveliness) of the Lord,
and to meditate, consider and inquire in his temple.

Psalm 27:4, The Amplified Bible

SYLVIA'S STORY

Birthplace: Billings, Montana   Divorced, mother of two
Youngest of two children   Lifelong Protestant churchgoer
Profession: RN in a city hospital   Age: 53

I WORSHIP GOD IN PRAYER, BOTH personally and in church and also in the way I live my life and in the way that I serve Him. I am always thanking Heavenly Father for the way He blesses me. I hope my life will be like a fragrance, as in the Old Testament, when there was incense that went into Heaven. That is the ideal way. I want what I think and what I say to bring God pleasure.

I think God is extremely powerful There are so many illustrations in the Old Testament about how He spoke through thunder and lightening, almost like a volcano sort of thing. If He can separate the Red Sea He can do anything. He created the heavens and the earth. He is a genius. When I think of a God as a father image I think of Him having a body of flesh and bone, but it just doesn't matter. He probably has a body, but I picture His character, not His physical body. I think of the Father as being more of a spirit.

He gets to me through His spirit. I am communicating with a spirit. He sits on His throne and when I think of Him He is either in His throne room or, when I am praying to Him and interceding for people, I think of Him as though in a 'War room.' I see a building around Him with something like a strategic military center where orders are issued to angels who pray for us all.

I think of His essence when I think of His character. I think of Him as omnipotent. He's sovereign. He is righteousness and justice, love, eternal life. He is omniscient. He can do anything and control anything. Veracity is characteristic of Him. He's always truthful. He is immutable, always the same.

God wanted a relationship with man and with Adam. He created Adam and put him in the Garden. He must have had a fabulous fellowship with him. They walked and talked in the Garden before the Fall. After the Fall man died spiritually and so he had a chance to repent and a way to bridge the chasm between himself and God. That is the reason for Jesus to come. All through the Old Testament Satan tried to destroy Christ, to bruise his heel. He tried to destroy the lineage. Satan tried to use sinful people, but Jesus came

The way I would describe Christ's life can be found in the Book of John. "In the beginning was the Word and the Word became flesh, full of grace and truth." He did live a sinless life and he was a perfect sacrifice. He died for all of the sins that anybody will ever commit—even Hitler, or other evil people. He was raised at the right hand of the Father and he is preparing a place for us all when our spirits leave our bodies at death. When we die I'm going to see him. I'm going to see a lot of people I have read about in the Old Testament. I'm going to talk to them, ask them questions.

I can hardly wait to meet some of those people—I want to meet John the Baptist and John the beloved, Lazarus and Esther, and so many relatives and friends, my Jewish friends, even many of the patients I have known over the years. The very first thing I want to do—in the Rapture or when I die—I want to run into his arms. I want to see and feel his love, acceptance and forgiveness. If he comes at the Rapture—he's my commander- in-chief and he's going to be on a white horse- but the very first thing I'm going to do is to look into his eyes…

There is a scripture—Mark 16:19—that says Jesus is at His right hand, so I believe Jesus is in Heaven and that the Holy Spirit is here on earth with us, indwelling us and helping us.

I am 53 years old. I was born into a family that had one other child, my brother, who is four years older than myself. He wanted to be a musician. I decided to follow in his footsteps but when I grew up he had gone away to college to pursue a music career. I went to Oregon and I ended up getting into the nursing profession. I also attended a Christian College where I studied scripture and did some work in the Bible there, then moved to Indianapolis where I went to a teaching church for four and one-half years. They taught exegetically from the scriptures, using ancient Greek and Hebrew, extracting original scriptural meanings. Bible scripture was presented on a verse by verse basis. We analyzed one verse each night for an hour's time, either in Greek or in Hebrew, then looked up each word to get a correct impression. So that was where I got my real foundation of who God is, what He is like and how He operates.

Jesus Christ is also very much alive. I know because, first of all, I read it in scripture. And I have prayed to my Father in Heaven to know that truth. In the Book of Mark, 16th chapter, verse 19 it says:

> *So then after the Lord has spoken unto them, he was received up into Heaven and sat on the right hand of God.*

I have a little scriptural card on my wall from my mother, so I know she took me to Sunday School when I was little. My parents joined a church when I was about five or six years old. My father found a Christian church and I went to church with them. I didn't want to go, sometimes, but they took me. We all went. It was the Disciples of Christ Christian church.

When I was a child I was baptized in water and when years later I attended a church service I was baptized again. When I was almost forty years old I was rebaptized a second time. That was a fabulous thing and I remember to this day. I was immersed each time. When I went under the water this last time it was like I was going into a coffin. I was going underground, dying, dead. And when I came up it was just fabulous. It was a wonderful experience, even though I believe I had a valid baptism when I was younger.

Because I grew up in the church I grew up hearing the Word. I always believed it and I have always believed in Jesus. Christ was a visionary. He knew the Plan from eternities past, before he ever came to earth. Yes, he knew exactly what he was doing.

I have always believed that God is love and that He wants to help me. But it has been a gradual process for me to get to know God and to hear the voice of God. I guess I would say it has taken suffering and pain and different situations for me to see what God is like and how He has rescued me. He rescues, just like he came to the rescue of the children of Israel who crossed the Red Sea and then He drowned their enemies.

I think a major impediment in my life is that I grew up in isolation. My mother was forty-two years old when I was born. She did not want me. The only time she ever touched me was to spank me. It was like a Jekyll and Hyde situation. She had been a teacher, so sometimes she would teach me things about nutrition and I learned a lot from her, but she didn't like me until later in my life when I succeeded at things. So I always needed a comfort and a source of security.

My mother could not cope emotionally with me and she was jealous of the aunts and uncles on my father's side of the family, so I grew up around a lot of seeing bitterness and anger. It was just understood that my father could not touch me. I don't know if my mother was abused as a child, but that was the rule. I remember that when I did something wrong I would hide beneath my bed because I was afraid she'd beat up on me.

I think my father always liked me and he always loved to provide for me. In his latter years when he had dementia he'd send me presents every week. He was a very generous person and a caretaker for his family. He had a servant's heart. I learned a lot from watching him. And even though he never told me that he loved me I knew that he did. He was a precious, precious man.

I stole things when I was little. I stole money from my parents but then I said "Oh, God help me not to do this." Once I started the seventh grade and other kids started liking me, that stopped. So it was an emotional thing. God had mercy on me. Though I've made some wrong choices, through doing that and through hurting the heart of God I've come to appreciate His forgiveness all the more. Sinning and making mistakes is not the issue. It's giving up. If you repent and turn to the Lord he turns cursing into blessings. And so I don't stop. I just get up and go on.

I never was really depressed, but I was absolutely terrified when my husband became a drug addict. His addiction, his overdosing on his drugs of choice resulted in seizures and bizarre behavior. But I have this sense of determination or tenacity. I always read the Word, so I kept doing things and always tried to keep some good relationships with my neighbors. I still correspond with them. I guess I have always had at least one person in my life that I could share with. That person has changed. A lot of the people in my life died, as did the three older women who were patients but who were like mother figures to show me what a real mother's heart would be like.

I graduated from high school when I was seventeen. I left home at that time and never returned, except for a few brief visits. The belief that my father loved me has given me a positive attitude toward my Heavenly Father. I married when I was twenty and a sophomore at a Bible college. After graduation I worked for one year so my husband could catch up and graduate. I had started nurse's training because a college professor told me that I could really use nursing in the mission field. I had always wanted to become a missionary, so we had planned a mission together. I became pregnant with my first child, a girl, when I was twenty-six, after graduation from nurse's training. My daughter was born in 1969 in Oregon.

I always believed that if I sought God and His will that eventually things would turn out right. Eventually they did because I married a man I totally loved, although he had problems with the other missionaries in the field who he felt were jealous of him while finding fault with some of his activities. He in time succumbed to the criticism of his peers and became drug addicted. He chose that life style.

I endured that for fifteen years and raised my children basically alone. God was always a source—always rescuing me and always providing—an upholder, a protector. Because of being alone as a child I spent a lot of time alone with Him and I guess that's how I have learned to hear His voice. Through scripture he ministers to me with His word and also through the Holy Spirit. About the time of my divorce people in the church prayed for me. After that I was able to hear God's voice speak to me and that has been the greatest comfort of my whole life.

If I had not found Heavenly Father and Jesus Christ I think I would now be in a mental institution. I really believe I would have. Or I would have killed myself. I did go through some psychological testing as a qualification before going overseas to be a missionary. The psychologist said that if my marriage didn't work out, because I was so barren from my childhood, I probably would never be mentally healthy again. They said my husband was not ready emotionally to go to the mission field so we should stay home and go a psychiatrist. The very fact that I am here and happy now and like what I am doing and love Jesus—is truly a miracle!

Seeing a psychiatrist for counseling never helped us at all. During that time my husband got a year's training in a county hospital in Indianapolis and that was really good for what we had to do out in the "bush" later on. Before our mission trip we traveled around America for a year raising financial support to go overseas.

Finally we ended up in Ethiopia in 1971 through the Disciples of Christ, our missionary church.

We were in the bush, in the middle of Ethiopia. It was only accessible by airplane most of the time, our little station that had a school, a clinic and a church. My husband and I were responsible for the clinic. People came all day, every day. My husband was an excellent diagnostician and several people were saved. As a result, whole families came to the clinic. That was 1970-71. We were in Ethiopia until 1973.

Amharic is the national language of Ethiopia but Galinya was the dialect the people spoke in the station. I was not very good with language. My husband was not either. He could speak well enough to do a physical exam. I think our demeanor and how we took care of people said more to them than learning the language did. If I had it to do over again I would live in their houses with them until I learned their language.

We had a little house next to the clinic. It was fascinating. We had a water tower and a pump for it. Sometimes the water was muddy. I had to use a kerosene refrigerator, and then we had to soak all our vegetables in Clorox. But I never thought twice about it. I have a pioneering spirit and I had always wanted to be a missionary. When I was little I went to church camps and heard all the missionaries speak. Oh, I wanted to be one so much. God gave me the desires of my heart in that way.

All of the other women had a housekeeper who would come in and clean and cook. One man who was on the station gradually started helping me so I utilized him. I had learned about his life. He was the son of a witch doctor and had been a Christian. He was an evangelist, too, on the weekends. He said one time he was going out to preach somewhere and a demon—Satan—came and knocked him off his horse. He made it through that, but his life was quite a testimony to me and he had such a servant's heart that he impressed me. Some people on the compound were just so much fun and so neat. My daughter, who was there during her first few years would always sneak off to the people's houses to eat their food. She loved it because it was really hot and spicy.

Then my husband came down with malaria. He kept taking drugs when we were overseas because he had access to anything he wanted to bring out to the bush. I thought he had Multiple Sclerosis or something because he took sleeping pills and Valium, so he was always falling down. He passed out one time—I thought he was dead. He overdosed and had a *grand mal* seizure. I was totally terrified. I used to just shake in the bed because I was so terrified of what was happening.

Reading scripture helped me a lot. Psalm 27 is probably my favorite scripture and it was the favorite of a patient I had. I grew to love it. I like the whole Psalm, especially the last verse which tells us to "hope and expect the Lord" and I do expect God to do great things for me. The first verse reads "The Lord is my light and my salvation; whom shall I fear? The Lord is the strength of my life; of whom shall I be afraid?" All of those years that I was living on the edge and not knowing what was going to happen... I had a poster with that verse on it. Clouds were on the poster, and I looked at that constantly. Verse four says "One thing have I desired of the Lord, that will I seek after; that I may dwell in the house of the Lord all the days of my life, to behold the beauty of the Lord." That's kind of my theme in life: to worship God and to learn what He's like. A word that comes to mind is "trust." If you think of a word for each letter, it could also mean to Turn and Run Under Savior's Tent.

We were on our station about three years when I became pregnant with my second child, my son. I was five months pregnant when we came home from Ethiopia. We came back to America but my husband continued to take the drugs. My son was born in Indianapolis while my husband worked in the clinic. Then I went to work in hospitals. It was really good for me because I had such a low self esteem I never thought I could do anything and I learned that because I had such excellent training from the School of Nursing I had attended I always succeeded at most of the jobs I had. I was able to work on an open heart surgery floor and I was a patient care manager. I did things I thought I could never do. It was wonderful. Now I work on the Labor and Delivery floor of a hospital and take care of mothers after they have babies. I am pretty good at helping with that. It's very pleasant and I actually have more access to people here than in the mission field.

Eventually I began attending a Bible class where every day I heard a principle of scripture and the next day I would see a positive or a negative illustration of it, so it reinforced everything that I was learning. When you go away to a distant place you have a far greater impact on the people you speak to, just like somebody from Korea came to me and said, "Jesus loves you," it would make me think twice and seem more important. The mission grew tremendously after the Americans left and after the Communists came into that area. The people I was over there with just arrived here a few days ago to visit. They have heard that the Christians have multiplied where our station was.

Many of the other missionary wives were involved in doing things among the local people. I didn't do that as much. I was more into entertaining guests who came to visit. There was another mission family on the station with me and the wife was very good at entertaining. She taught me how to cook for crowds. We would sometimes do that together. The pilots would come and they always wanted to stay at our station because we fed them so well. So the fellowship and the bonding was wonderful. It was interesting to go to church on Sunday. Services were held in the Galinya dialect but I always heard demons speaking through the people. There was a way of deliverance from those spirits, but that is just the way it was. One doesn't think that such things exist, but they do, they're very real. After I came back from Ethiopia I learned how to deal with that spiritual warfare.

I believe that Hell is a place of darkness. It's a very horrible place. I can't imagine it, but I believe it is a place where people go who do not want anything to do with God. I think we all have a choice to make and some people absolutely, deliberately choose not to have anything to do with God. They don't want him. They want other things. I don't think it has anything to do with being worthy. I think it is a free will choice. God created us with a free will.

It's interesting. I believe that when Satan fell out of Heaven many angels went with him and these angels serve him and are his cohorts. There are principalities and powers and there are regions where different demons have control. They have strategies for every person that has ever lived to trip them up and to rob and steal and destroy. Satan is the opposite of God. God is loving and kind and wants to bless us, but Satan wants to take everything from us and out of ignorance we sometimes succumb to that and sometimes because of our own free will we succumb.

I think that the Adversary has schemes but sometimes I defeat Satan by making right choices, so that he thinks up a new scheme. He tries to keep people in bondage and he's very successful at it. Again, knowledge of him and how he works, what to avoid and that kind of thing is very helpful, as is learning the authority that we have over him, because we do have it—but he's cleverer than we are. Without the Holy Spirit we wouldn't really be able to do anything. We would be helpless, but the Holy Spirit has the power to defeat him.

I think that the Holy Spirit has the most colorful personality of all. His personality is so varied. He talks to different people in different ways because they need it, like a good parent would. His personality fits the person. I think he is a lot of fun. I think he is very tender and knows us better than we know ourselves. Absolutely. He knows what is best for us.

He knows our weaknesses, and even though he would implore us to do certain things and acts he never violates our will. He allows us to make our own choices as our Heavenly Father does. No matter how badly we mess up he's always there to restore us, to go on and help us with the consequences of our choices and actions. Sometimes the Holy Ghost helps us to know when we are going wrong. Ignorance is the worst thing. If we understand what he is like and how God operates and it really is very helpful.

The war in Ethiopia came later. When our group went in there we went in with the feeling that we were only going to be there a short time, so our main purpose was to train the local people. We taught them the word of God and how to preach and gave them bibles—Galinya bibles. They had especially printed in their dialect. The school probably closed down after the Americans left. I think we taught enough people how to read, enough of the younger generation that they could read the bibles on their own after we left.

We had translators we'd go teaching with. My ex-husband flew down to the Nile where the people were blue-black. We'd go down there with a pilot and an evangelist and hold a clinic for two days or three days, and once in a while they'd give him a present; chicken or something like that. So it was neat, a wonderful experience. I suppose giving to people without expecting anything in return is really a great thing. But people were giving to us. And people wrote letters and were supporting us. For that reason I support missionaries now. I feel like I'm a part of what they're doing. My missionary message to the world is to trust in God and Jesus as the Savior. In the Old Testament—I'm studying the minor prophets this year—God always wanted people to follow him and to believe in Him and trust in Him. Then He prospered them but they forget about Him and turned their backs and started worshipping idols, so I think having a heart for God and to pursue Him, is to learn of Him. I think we are continually students. Repetition is so important, repeating scripture, repeating principles of doctrine. We just have to hear it over and over and over again. So hearing the word and believing it and being kind to our neighbors is so important. Teaching what we know to others. Frank Laubach, once a missionary in India said, "Each one teach one." Make disciples of all nations. I put stock in the verse in Hebrews 4:12 which reads "the word of God is alive and powerful, sharper than any two-edged sword, piercing to the division of soul and spirit…"

I love all the Psalms. A lot of people read the 23rd Psalm at a funeral but it's been every day of my life that I have thought of that. Psalm 103 is one of my favorites and I like some of the things in the New Testament like the Book of Ephesians. I like Ephesians 1:3 and 2:10. I think in the original Greek it says that 'God runs after me to bless me.' Oh! I have thought of that every time something bad happened to me. When my children were little I'd say "Oh, but you are running after me to bless me." Think of that. In Ephesians 1:17 it talks about how Jesus, when he went into Heaven, handed over authority to me so that I could do what he would do. Jesus prayed that I would be able to understand what my calling is. And I like the Book of Hebrews because it explains who Jesus really is.

The scriptures taught me about being saved. We are saved into the family of God. One of the things I got out of the Bible class in Indianapolis is that we will change genetically. Just like when we are conceived. So at the point of salvation when you believe in Jesus as your Savior you are genetically changed and you become—are born into the family. You can't say, "Well, I don't belong to them anymore. I don't want anything to do with them." You're still a son or a daughter in a particular family. In Greek the given verb tense for being saved is the present tense with the result that the act goes on forever.

I have been so very blessed. My daughter has turned out adoring me and appreciating me. We have a relationship that I never expected. I mean, she blows me away when she says certain things because I can hardly identify with them. She was here at Christmastime to have surgery. I went with her to the procedure and she was so lovely I just said "Oh, gee, you're so lovely, you're so sweet." I took care of her for three days. She could hardly move and she was throwing up. It was just such a wonderful bonding time. So God has restored to me a hundred times over what I was robbed of from the beginning.

That is another thing I would encourage people about. Don't give up too soon. God doesn't do things instantly, sometimes. He does things over a period of time. I never give up, I wait for answers. I don't have to know everything in the beginning. I just trust him to lead me and guide me and to bring blessings.

To those who have thoughts of taking their lives I say no, you would forfeit everything. It would be absolute tragedy, it's so devastating to people who know you. Even if you think nobody knows and nobody cares, that is really not true. I found that to be the case. Every person has a sphere of influence, so suicide is very grievous. People want to help other people. If people are doing terribly and suffering, there are those that want to do anything to help. So it's getting connected with those people. I've learned to be humble and I've learned to ask for help when I need it, to reach out to other people. I think it takes a measure of humility to do that. And it takes a measure of trust and faith. Even if I don't have faith in other people I have faith in God that He will rescue me and He will pursue me with grace. I believe that God has prepared for us certain grace provisions and blessings that he would like to give us and those are forever recorded in eternity and if you kill yourself that memorial is still going to be standing undelivered because you've turned it down by not waiting to receive it.

Repentance is often necessary and it is very important. I can't be out of fellowship with God. It's too painful for me. Repentance is absolutely critical because God is a holy God and He cannot stand sin. I mean, He cannot be in the presence of sin and so the Holy Spirit turns back. It hurts him and it grieves him when we sin. In the scriptures read 1John 1:9 where it says "If we confess our sins, he is faithful and just to forgive us our sins and to cleanse us of all unrighteousness."

I studied the life of Manassah, the eldest son of Joseph in the Bible. He did terrible things. I mean, he became successful and he forgot about God. He put altars of Baal and Ashtarath in the temple of God that David built and he offered his sons to Moloch—had his sons sacrificed! He ordered daily killings in the street. It's recorded. God took him in captivity to Egypt, While Manassah was in captivity he repented from his heart. God took him back and restored him. So if God is merciful like that, anyone can come to Him and repent, which means to turn around, to acknowledge what it is that you have done that is wrong, to change your mind and to stop committing the wrong. One needs to set things right again. But that's what takes humility, making it right with other people. Repentance means moving on. In the Old Testament God always wanted His people just to turn to Him and then He would have blessed them.

God is a god of love. That's why He does everything. God is love. The only reason we know it and can give it away to anyone is because God first loved us and He illustrated that in the Bible and the life of Jesus, through parables and the way He healed people so we would have a picture of what love is, like the Good Samaritan and healing the man who was blind, and things like that. To the day we die we're going to be dependent upon God for guidance and direction. He always brings unexpected things. Crises happen so we never can be independent totally.

I have taught my children about Christ. I would talk to them about Bible class when I came home from my Bible classes years ago in Indianapolis and when my daughter was five or six she was taking notes for an hour, just like I was. I had Bible tapes about Old Testament characters, David and Goliath and so on. I felt that Christian school was the only option for my children and so I worked extra. I worked forty-eight to fifty-two hours a week so that I could have my children in Christian school.

I would just say that Jesus never has ever disappointed me. His heart is so good and he wants me healed. He has so many wonderful attributes that learning about him is a pleasure. He brings pleasure and I like to bring him pleasure by appreciating that. My testimony is my love for God—who He is and what He means to me. And that Jesus is the Savior of the world. If I had to deny Jesus I would die first.

This is not the end of life. Life goes on. I will live forever in Heaven and it will be an exciting place. It will be fabulous. Even though I have a lot of physical things they aren't that important to me. People are more important. Relationships that I have. I guess, just knowing that Jesus is there for me. Living in the present is the best thing to do. Living right now. I can't change the past, anything that has happened or that I have done. I don't know what tomorrow is going to hold so I believe the Bible. I believe every word. I believe every person in there existed the way it was recorded and that these things were recorded so that I would know how to live, what blesses God and what doesn't. Actually, my Bible is my most valuable possession.

Kindness to other people is most important. Know God. Love God with all your heart, mind, mind and soul and love your neighbor as yourself. Then works will flow.

Wherefore, I, Lehi, prophesy according the workings of the Spirit which is
in me,
that there shall none come into this land
save they shall be brought by the hand of the Lord.

Wherefore, this land is consecrated unto him whom he shall bring.
And…it shall be a land of liberty unto them;
wherefore, they shall never be brought down into captivity;
if so, it shall be because of iniquity;
for if iniquity shall abound cursed shall be the land for their sakes,
but unto the righteous it shall be blessed forever.

2Ne 1:6-7 Book of Mormon

JOHN'S STORY

Born: Lucca, Italy, 1920   Married: Three married children
Family: Oldest of three children   Lifelong Christian
Occupation: Retired/Builder   Age: 77

SHORTLY AFTER I WAS BORN MY DAD left us and came to America. My
mother and I stayed in Italy. He was over here for ten years on his
own. Finally, my mother got tired and wrote to him and said "If you
want to ever see us again, send for us or forget about us. You have to
make a choice." My uncle, his brother, was here in America. He said
"That's your family and you owe it to them to send for them." My
father had a girlfriend over here, so he didn't want us here. But he
sent for us and we came here to America. It was bad, terrible. He
didn't want us and he treated us like strangers.

Shortly after we came here from Italy my sister was born and
shortly after that another sister was born, so there's three of us in the
family. My father hadn't seen me for eleven years, so he really didn't
feel like I was his. He treated me like a stepchild and that's the way
I grew up. My father was a mean guy. Beat me up all the time. Beat
my mother up all the time. One time he beat her up, knocked her on
the floor. I was down there holding her head in my lap and he got

mad at me. Pulled me up by the hair and threw me out of the house. I was probably about thirteen.

My mother was religious but she never went to church. She would never change. My dad was an alcoholic and when he got drunk he wanted to beat somebody. He was always beating my mother. That's why my mother moved in with us when he beat her for the last time. I rarely went to church, mainly on holidays, you know. And once in a while we would go to confession and then communion the next day. It was a habit. Everybody did it in Italy. Tell the priest what you did wrong. He'd tell you to say so many Hail Marys. So you said so many Hail Marys and you were forgiven.

I have been a Christian all my life. When I was in Italy, I was a Catholic. Everybody was a Catholic. That was the state religion. I was an altar boy. I lit the candles at the altar for the priest and I helped the priest conduct mass. We had uniforms; white blouses. My cousin and I had already decided we were going to become priests. That was my goal at that time, until we came to America in 1931. In America things changed. We didn't go to church very much. My dad didn't go to church and so we didn't either. I remained a cool Catholic until I met my girlfriend, who I later married. She kept bringing me to the LDS Church up here. She asked me to marry her when I was twenty!

I've been an aircraft mechanic, a test mechanic. Then, when the union went on strike I decided I wanted to drive a bus. So I went down to the bus depot and met a guy there who I knew. He says "What are you doing here?" I said "I though I'd come down here and see if I can drive a bus." "Well, let's try you out." So we got in the bus and I drove it to Georgetown and back and he said "You did pretty good. You're hired."

I drove the bus for about six months. My wife liked it real well. She liked to ride the bus for free. But one day some gal tried to pick me up. After that, my wife found all kind of things wrong with the bus driving. Too much traffic. Odd hours. A friend of mine used to work for the Navy. I got an application and I filled it out. I had ten minutes at the end of the run. The next run I went down there and less than two hours later he hired me. Gave me more money than I was making. Worked my way up to boss of dismantling airplanes. I decided what to take off and what to leave on planes. And I worked there for a long time. It was about 1948. When that ended years later I worked for the Air Force and retired from there at age 58 because I didn't like some of President Carter's hiring policies, which I found too restrictive.

My wife and I married in 1944 when I was twenty-four. Our first son was born with asthma. He was sick all the time. We didn't know what the problem was. Everybody said he had asthma. Finally he had a bad attack when he was about eight. We took him to a specialist. He said "The problem with him is, when he was born the doctor didn't take all the mucous out of his lungs and so it fermented." So they had to take off one of the fermented lobes of his lungs.

While he was in the hospital, my wife was pregnant and she delivered another son who lived a month. I was in debt to the hospital because of my first son. I asked the priest to officiate at the funeral. He wanted $300. I didn't have $300. So I asked my wife. She said "Why don't you let me ask my bishop? He charges nothing."

I couldn't pass up a bargain like that. So he performed the service and he said in that service that if the parents are righteous they'll have a chance to raise them again. That kind of ticked something in my brain. I said "How could that happen?" So I started asking questions. How could you raise a child in Heaven after it has died before your eyes? All I wanted was the answers to my questions. The missionaries who came over wanted to give me the set of lessons. I wasn't interested in that. I just wanted answers to my questions. That's when spiritual feelings really began in my life.

And then another elder came around, a missionary from a town in Utah, with his teaching companion. And he caught my attention right away because he didn't start on religion. He asked me where I was from and I asked him where he was from—from the town "where they grow the largest tomatoes in Utah" and that got my attention.

So the first time we met we didn't talk about religion, we talked about his farm back in Utah. That was interesting. We got along pretty good and before long, why, he was teaching me the Gospel. He slipped it in there. I was baptized by my brother-in-law. That was in 1952. I was thirty-two.

And after that, I was more involved. My wife would go to church and I would follow her. I didn't know much about it but before long I began to study. My testimony kept growing and growing and pretty soon I was given a calling in the Church. I was scoutmaster for sixteen years in the Church. Then I was cubmaster for a certain amount of time, until my older son died. And then I had to quit because every cub scout—my son was a cub scout in my cub pack—every cub scout in the pack looked like my son to me. I had to quit...

I talked about it with my wife. I said "Why do we have to have this?" Sometimes you wonder why. But there's a reason for everything. "Maybe there is something that we weren't doing right. Maybe we weren't humble enough. Maybe we didn't study hard enough. There was something." But to the Lord, death is another birth. We didn't understand that, at first. "Death is the end. It's terrible." We cry, we feel bad, you know. But if you start thinking in terms of the Lord's thinking: we were born from the spirit world onto this earth. When we die we return again to the spirit world onto another earth.

That's the way the Lord works it. Our son died when nine years old. According to the Lord's view, when our son died—I had to do a lot of studying before I recognized this—he didn't have to go through any more trials in the world. He had been tested and tried and he passed the test. Now he's in the celestial kingdom (See 1Cor 15:40-42). Our other son died at one month. He didn't have to go through all these tests. He was such a good spirit the Lord took him back because he needed him to be a missionary—to go out and teach. So once we learned that it was an experience. We felt bad for awhile, but now when we look at it we know that someday we'll meet again and we'll be able to raise him, just like we raised our kids here.

> They are they into whose hands the Father has given all things—
> They are they who are priests and kings, who have received of his
> fulness, and of his glory...and they shall overcome all things...These
> shall dwell in the presence of God and his Christ forever and ever.
>
> Doctrine and Covenants 76:55,56,60,62

It's a challenge to do what the Lord tells us to do but we have two children up in Heaven waiting for us. The night before my son died he knew he was going to die. He asked me to stay with him all night. So I bought a PBY airplane, a Navy airplane kit and I took it to his hospital. We built that airplane together. He at that time had a tube coming out of his chest, where they cut off one of the lobes of his lung. He seemed to pick up. We brought him home and he was active. Then he started to have attacks again, so we took him to a specialist. The specialist said he should take out the other bottom lobe on the other side, because if he didn't my son was going to get worse. The anesthesiologist said the boy's system would become too pure and that his body might not heal. The doctor said if we didn't operate my son would continue to get worse. So we were left with a decision.

We prayed mightily and long that night. We finally decided "Okay, we'll go ahead with it." My son was there for a couple of weeks but he wasn't getting any better. He wasn't healing. He had tubes coming out of his lungs and every time he breathed some of the air would escape out of the bottom of the tube into a gallon half filled with water.

He was really suffering. He asked me to stay with him all night. I said okay, so I went down there to stay with him all night. We built this airplane. About 11 p.m. I thought he was asleep and I kind of dozed off, myself, sitting in the chair next to the bed. All of a sudden, there were no bubbles coming out of the jar. I jumped up and I yelled for the nurse and I shook my son. I said "Start breathing, come on!"

Well, he came back. He started breathing again. "Dad," he says, "I know I'm not going to make it. So I want to die, because I'm not getting any better. I'm tired of staying here."

I said "That's not the way to talk. You're going to get better." All night long, I thought he was asleep. But he wasn't asleep. I kept looking at that jar. The nurse would come in every so often and check it out. I had to go to work that next morning. My wife came in and relieved me. We went in and had breakfast in the hospital restaurant there. I decided I was too sleepy to go to work and I came home. On the way to our son's room the nurse came out and gave my wife a pill to calm her down, and that told her that our son had passed on. The minute I left that bedroom, he had stopped breathing. So when I got home the phone rang. It was the doctor.

He says "Don't do anything drastic." And that's all I heard. I dropped the phone, I jumped in the car and I made it over to the hospital in about fifteen minutes. I got to the hospital and I put the brakes on but the car didn't have any more brakes. It went over the curb and into the bushes. I went into the hospital. I grabbed my son and I said "Come back." I was thinking then that I could call him back like I did the first time. My wife got worried and says "Don't shake him too much." The bishop, who had just arrived, said "That's okay. Leave him alone." So she left me alone with what I was doing, because I was trying to call him back and I was crying.

Anyway, he died and we had the funeral. For about two months, I couldn't work. I couldn't do anything. I'd just sit at my desk and just stare. About two months after he died, I was laying on the bed one night after midnight. All of a sudden I saw my son standing at the foot of the bed.

I grabbed my wife and I shook her and I said "Hey, there's our son." My wife says "Where?" "Right there," I answered. She couldn't see him, but I could. She knew what was going on, but I didn't understand. Finally, my son says "Dad, quit worrying about me. I'm doing what I always wanted to do and I'm happy and I feel good, so don't worry about me any more."

I could see him plain as day, at the bed. Well, that really did something for me. I knew that he was alive. And I knew he was doing what he wanted to do. Probably missionary work. So that kind of completely changed me. From then on, when I went to work I was doing all kinds of things and every minute I've been busy. Never had a question. It was too real. He appeared just like he was when he died, only he was dressed up. White clothing. Good sight, real good.

I know he's alive and waiting for us. I'd rather die than deny that. I think he was sent to tell me those things because I wasn't accomplishing a thing. I wasn't getting ahead. I was losing ground. I was getting behind and moping around. I couldn't carry on a conversation with anybody that meant anything. You know, I lost interest in everything.

I was in the Church, then, but I didn't understand. All I had been doing in the Church was working as a scoutmaster and cubmaster. Never had any job where you had to study to give lessons or anything like that. When you're called to conduct a class you have to study for that. I never did.

Knowledge is very important. You have to keep studying. You can't just go to church and sit there and have somebody tell you something, because as soon as you get out, you forget it. You only retain a very small percentage of what you hear and only a little bit more of what you see. Unless you learn to understand it and mull it over and think about it, you will not really retain very much. I had to study the Atonment to understand how my son could come back to me. That is what the Atonement of Jesus Christ did for my son and for all of us because if he hadn't gone through the Atonement we wouldn't be able to be resurrected. We wouldn't have eternal life.

It was necessary. A person could not have any blemishes in him because our Father in Heaven would only allow a perfect person to go through that. Jesus was going to return to Heavenly Father in the celestial kingdom where all spirits have reached perfection. If the Atonement hadn't taken place we'd be laying in the grave forever, never progressing. We would be subject to the devil. The Atonement of Christ saves us from death and if we are righteous we can live with our family forever in the eternities. Where we go after life on earth depends on what choices we make here. I got two kids there so I've got a special goal, as well as my family's dead. I want to see them all again.

My wife is number one, though. That's understood, she's number one. The only thing above her is God. Then comes the kids. To me, my kids are more important than anything except my wife. I have five of them. My kids are my family. After the children comes the grandchildren. That's it. I can't afford for it to go on and on and on. I can't support any more in this life! This is my policy: if any of my children get into trouble, everything I've got I'll sell if it will help them. I'll give them my house and anything I have to help them. If it goes beyond that, you're on your own. Because when you get to the grandkids their granddad is supposed to help them. I can only go so far and my assets aren't that much that I can continue on down the line. I have worked very hard for what I have. I've always worked to make my family happy. And we thank God for what we have. My wife and I have a set time every night for our evening prayers. You'll always find us on our knees at 10 p.m. And then, whenever the idea comes into my head, I pray. And we always ask a blessing on our meals.

My wife's always thinking about me. She knows me better than I know myself. She does things to please me, to keep me happy. And she never gets mad. I never met a person who doesn't get mad. She is my friend, my best friend. I talk to her like I would never talk to anybody else. I just can't imagine being without her. Sometimes I go to our other house for a week or so to work on it. I can hardly wait to get back, because I don't have anybody to talk to, to confide in. I confide in her a lot and I joke with her and we laugh together. I tell her jokes that I would never tell anybody else. It's just that when I'm with her I feel free to say or do whatever I want. I don't insult her or anything like that. She's just one special person to me. Paul said it best:

> So men ought to love their wives as their own bodies...for this cause shall a man leave his father and mother, and shall be joined unto his wife, and they two shall be one flesh.

Ephesians 5:28,31

You have to support your family in lots of ways. You gotta let them know that if they get into trouble or a jam or whatever, they know where to come to for help. A lot of times they call me the Godfather. A joke, you know. They do it with kindness and when they do get into trouble—my two boys got in a jam and they had to come to me and ask for help. I helped them. I never asked for my money back. I don't want to get paid back. If it's a legitimate problem that they run into, what I have is theirs. I'll never ask them to pay it back. And they know that. They never ask unless they absolutely need it. One of them was going to lose his house and he came to me. I went over there and we had a family meeting. We sat down with him and his wife and I, and we went over his finances, figured out how much he needed and then how many credit cards he had. He sat right there and he cut them all. We bailed him out. He kept his house. I told him "Don't worry about paying me back. Just get out of the hole." And he did. He got out of the hole, he's on his feet and he's doing real well. This is one of my favorite scriptures:

> And, ye fathers, provoke not your children to wrath: but bring them up in the nurture and admonition of the Lord.

> Ephesians 6:4

I was lucky. I married my childhood sweetheart. I should have married her four years sooner. She asked me four years sooner but my dad had me so upset I couldn't make a decision. Finally, she got mad and started going out with other guys. I couldn't stand that, so we decided to get married. And I'm happy with her. She's sick now but she's going to get better. We raised a good family. All my kids, they all get along. They're all good kids. I give that credit to her. I could be a lot richer but I just like to do what I like to do. I like to build houses. I like to keep busy. I've built three houses since I retired. I'm busier now that I ever was. I don't know how I ever had time to go to work!

Spiritual growth is very important, too. I know I can learn a lot more. I think I know the gospel pretty well but I'd like to learn a lot more, the history of the Church, for example. I am very hard of hearing, but if I could hear better I'd be a lot more active.

I am grateful for the way the knowledge of the gospel has changed my life. It was a gradual change. It wasn't an overnight deal. I used to be hot tempered. A hot tempered wop, they used to call me. And I'd fly off the handle over a little thing, you know. But the more spiritual I became the less off the handle I'd fly. I became quieter, more calm. I think my wife helped out a lot on that because she never flies off the handle. And whenever I flew off the handle, she just retired to a "cocoon." She wouldn't speak for a week.

Oh, I'm sure the Lord brought her to me. If it wasn't for her I would never have joined the church. She never pushed it on me, she just set the example. She used to go to church and if I wanted to go I'd have to follow her or stay home by myself. So I'd follow right along behind her, like a little sheep, you know. I learned all about the Plan of Salvation.

As I understand it, we were spirit children with our Father in Heaven. And when we got a body and were born here we took a body for our spirit. A soul and a spirit joined together. That's the way I understand it. And when we die the spirit leaves the body and goes back to the spirit world. I know the spirit goes to the spirit world, the body goes to the grave. At the resurrection they'll be joined again, in a body with flesh and bone.

Sometimes I think the soul is the conscience. But I'm not positive. When you die the body goes into the grave and the spirit goes back to Heaven and your conscience stops because the spirit knows all about everything up there. The body doesn't know anything. It goes back to dirt. So when the spirit and the body are resurrected you get your conscience back again—the Spirit of Christ, they used to call it. Everybody is born with that. That is different from the Holy Ghost.

The Holy Ghost tells us what is true. I had the right to have the Holy Ghost after I was baptized, but that's not a guarantee. You may not get it, because if you don't follow the covenants that you made at your baptism, you will be unworthy of the Holy Ghost's companionship. You are given the right to have the Holy Ghost but that doesn't mean it's forced on you. You have to earn it. You have to follow the commandments and if you do the right things and don't break your covenants when you're baptized the Holy Ghost will help to guide you, help make your decisions, so you will know the difference between right and wrong.

If I make a good decision I have a good feeling. If I make a bad decision, I worry about it: "Did I do that right or did I do that wrong? Doesn't seem right. Wonder if I missed something." Questions come up.

Satan wants to make our decisions for us, but he wants all the credit. Satan's cruel. And he deceives a lot of people. He's very tricky. He'll have the same kind of Plan that the Lord has. And he'll slip in a little untruth, little lies. But he's forgetting that we're all different and they're going to force their will to make us peaceful and happy, no matter what we want. The Lord's Plan says "You've got your free agency. I'll tell you what's right and you make the choice. If you choose wrong you're going to pay the penalty. If you choose right, you'll be happy. You'll have joy." Well, the Lord's Plan is giving us the opportunity to decide what's good for us. There's a difference.

That's why the Lord put us here, to have joy. Satan doesn't work that way. It's just like the comment that was made by one of the leaders of the New World Order. He said "we want to force the stupid masses to do what's good for them." In other words, they'll make the decisions as to what is good for us.

I love my country and I try in my way to protect it against evil, because it has blessed me tremendously. I have the freedom to make my own choices. I've never gone for want of anything, whereas in Italy, many times I went to bed hungry. In America I've never gone to bed hungry.

There are millions who do go to bed hungry, and in part, that's their choice. The parents make the wrong choices. Either they don't work, maybe they do drugs—that's Satan's plan—to bring drugs into the country. As long as we obey the Lord's Plan—and those are the righteous people in the United States—we won't have homeless people. We won't have so many doing bad things—immorality, unrighteousness, crime and everything else. We've had evil organizations in America since 1776, that's when Satan started his plan. I like America because it lets me be free. It gives me the right to own property through the federal Constitution.

I think the Constitution was inspired of God, but I think it has been torn to shreds by the politicians. The American people are misled because they think it will never happen here, that we'll never lose our freedoms; we'll always be free. But we're losing it every day, a little bit at a time. And our poor kids. I don't know what they're going to do, how they're going to pay that debt. They'll never pay it. I think that soon America is going to fall flat on its face. Most American people are going to wonder "What happened? What happened? We didn't think it would ever happen here." If I had my way, anybody who murders would pay for it with his life so he wouldn't kill anybody else. If I had my way, I'd eliminate ninety-nine percent of the politicians and go back to the Constitution. I don't have much patience with people like that.

I am not short on faults, though. I'm not very tolerable of some people when they don't seem to understand the right way or the wrong way. I don't have much patience, sometimes. I know that Heavenly Father and Jesus Christ exist and they're alive and well and thinking of my best—hoping that I make the right decisions so I can join them up there. I know that they were human beings at one time and now they're perfected human beings. They're perfect, and that's my goal, to be like them. I'm kind of weak sometimes, but there are several things I love to do.

I always like to build things. I'm different from most people. And, sometimes, I stand on my deck up at my other home and look at the lake and the beautiful mountains. I say, "Boy, the Lord knows how to landscape the earth." And, sometimes I think "I can't wait to get up to Heaven so I can do the same things, to build an earth and put mountains there and streams and trees and fruit and all that stuff, see. "He's just really having a good time building the earth. That's what I want to do. I think He has just done a beautiful job. In Hawaii, Heavenly Father put fruit trees, palm trees and islands and blue water. I'd be a little different. I haven't grown to His status. I wouldn't want people to come in and pollute it. I'd want to keep it beautiful, pristine, like He had it. It might sound silly, but that's what I like. In fact, I can hardly wait to build my own world and landscape it like I want to!

The Gospel plan is about progression through life. If you study the Gospel it makes sense that there was a pre-existence. We came down and we were born here and we live so many years here and we pass on. There has to be an existence forever. It doesn't end. There has to be a beginning and a continuation, a whole plan. I believe strongly in the Plan of Salvation. I know that when you die your body goes in the grave, but your spirit goes up to another world, alive. Jesus Christ arranged for us to be resurrected and to have a body after we are resurrected. Everybody, whether they are good, bad or indifferent or crooks or murderers. We're all going to be resurrected. And maybe I won't be so forgetful, like I am now. So I'm not worried about that.

You will be able to see and hear and all knowledge that you had in the pre-existence comes back. That's the spirit world with our Father in Heaven. We were there with him before we came to earth. I believe people born at this time were held back especially for this critical period in Earth's history because in the pre-existence we were stronger in the faith than many others who came before us. We were held back on purpose because He wants to have special spirits on the earth in the last days. We're going to be tested more than anyone ever was.

If the time comes where somebody says "You either deny the Gospel or lose your life," I'd say "Shoot away. Let's get it over with."

Jesus taught us the whole Plan, how we can return to our Father in Heaven. It was Heavenly Father's Plan and Jesus said that he would follow what our Father in Heaven wanted and he also said "I'll do anything that is required to implement your Plan and You get all the glory." Satan says "I've got a different plan. I'm going to save everybody and I want the glory for that. I want to be just like you, God." Now that wipes out all free agency, free choice. No one can progress. If you're forced to do things, you don't learn. We learn by experience, by doing. If you're forced to do certain things, it's backwards. That's why a lot of countries are backwards. The Communist nations never progress because they're told what to do. China is that way. They won't progress unless they open the doors and let people in. They need to learn to love Heavenly Father and our Savior, Jesus Christ.

> *But unto every one of us is given grace according to the measure of the gift of Christ. Till we all come in the unity of the faith, and of the knowledge of the Son of God, unto a perfect man, until the measure of the stature of the fulness of Christ.*
>
> *Ephesians 4:7,13*

I love Jesus Christ because he showed me the way. He showed me how I can become better—how I can become worthy to go to the celestial kingdom to raise my two kids. He showed me how to be a lot happier by following his ideas and his instructions. I'm a lot happier than I ever was. Reading the scriptures helped me to know him. I read them all the time. I read The Book of Mormon. As a matter of fact, I read it quite a bit. I have one next to my chair in my other home and I have another here in my desk here. Oh, it's a true book. It is what it says: the most correct book on the earth. When there are discrepancies between that and the Bible, The Book of Mormon comes first. That's what I think. I know it's true.

I really didn't start reading it deeply until I was called on the High Council. Then I was forced to read it. Sometimes, when you get busy during the day you forget to take time off to read it. When I got called to the High Council I had to do a lot of research. That's when I learned the gospel, because the talks I had to give every month forced me to do things that I would never take time to do otherwise.

Well, I think people ought to read The Book of Mormon with an open mind and begin to realize if they look at reality they should look at the last five or six thousand years. The population has been growing more and more. In the beginning it was a brand new world. And yet by looking at the population growth I have to say there was a beginning and there's going to be an end to this earth. You follow me? The population has been increasing in the world. Progressing. So that alone should tell people that there was a beginning and that ought to start them thinking "What started this whole thing?" If they have an open mind and start thinking about it they can begin to learn what the Gospel plan is all about.

And after having received the record of the Nephites,
yea, even my servant Joseph Smith, Jun.,
might have power to translate through the mercy of God,
by the power of God, the Book of Mormon.

And also those to whom these commandments were given,
might have power to lay the foundation of this church,
and it bring it forth out of obscurity and outr of darkness,
the only true and living church upon the face of the whole earth,
with which I, the Lord, am well pleased,
speaking unto the church collectively and not individually

Doctrine and Covenants 1:29-30

DANA'S STORY

Born: Redwood City, California	Lifelong Christian
Youngest of five siblings	Divorced mother of two
Occupation: Secretary	Age: 31

JESUS CHRIST HAS CHANGED MY LIFE. I moved here from California and things were going okay. I was hanging out with a fast crowd, going to Happy Hour, having friends over and drinking wine. I didn't drink a lot, just during Happy Hour. I also took drugs. That was something I thought was really important. When I lived in California I got in with a fast crowd there and started doing those things. This was before I moved to Oregon. Then I met someone. He was the most beautiful man I had ever seen. I really started to feel affection for him. It wasn't appropriate because he was married, but it didn't change the way I felt.

We were working on a project together and we had to spend two days in a city in northern California. We went to dinner. Afterward we went to a night club in the same facility. I stayed up that whole time just drinking. We were just talking about life and he was telling me about friends, how important they are. The things he was saying were going right through me. I thought they were the most beautiful things I had ever heard. I had never related to a man on that level without having a physical relationship, but nothing physical was going on. It was religious talk. The desires I had became even stronger. It was really strange. He walked me to the hotel room. There were two beds. He sat on one. I had had a few drinks, I was tired. He kept talking to me but I started to feel bad. He said "Well, I am going to leave." I said "Just wait until I go to sleep and then you can leave." He must have sat with me until two or three in the morning. When I went to sleep he was gone.

The next afternoon we were at lunch. He was saying that there was something far beyond a physical relationship. He was talking about friends and how a true friendship should last forever. It is not like a relationship between a man and a woman that is here today and gone tomorrow. Suddenly I felt energy that started at the top of my head and went through my body. Then I just started bawling. I just couldn't stop. I felt that he loved me so much. I knew it then and to this day I know it. We still talk. He is in California and I am here. That was the end of the drugs. I could not stop using, but after that day the desire was gone. I still don't know what happened that day.

His love for me was something like the love of Christ. It was pure and innocent, totally selfless. Then my search really accelerated. That's when I was studying with another religious group. So he told me all these things—what about this, what about this? And then I just started thinking about all that had gone on in my life and I thought "I can't go back to them. That's not right." He showed me something bigger. The way he was explaining it to me it was like every church that I have been to so far is not "big enough." They don't encompass what God really is. I had no idea what it might be but I just knew that these other things were too small in focus. So I stopped going there. Then probably six to eight months later I got a job and came to Oregon.

I have always believed in God. I know He's there. I've always believed that. But it wasn't enough for me. I used to talk to God all the time, especially when I wanted something. As a general rule I used to say 'You know how much I want something. Please help me.'

I would say "Dear God, I promise that I will do this. If you will let me have this I promise I'll do this, this and this." He always answered my prayers. I remember when I wanted a horse really badly and my mother said I couldn't get it. I talked to God and told him I wanted it so badly. Well, I got it. It was really funny, because I talked to my mother a year ago about it and she said "You know, I had no plans of ever getting you that horse. The money I used to get it I was saving to buy myself a car." It's amazing but I have always talked to Him. Once my grandmother was sick. I asked Him "Please don't take my grandmother. I need her too badly." He let her live. I was eight then. That has always been very real to me.

When I was looking for something more to believe in I went into a laundromat and saw a Christian magazine. I read the first paragraph of an article and thought it was good. Then I read the second paragraph and said "This is wrong."

I asked someone else at work. She said "Oh, yes I joined the church that this manager belongs to and its just fantastic. We have this great program." So I asked "Can you get me some literature on that church? I'd like to know about it."

She said "Oh, I might be able to dig out this little flyer. I'll see what I can do."

It was so callous. I thought "That didn't feel very nice." She never said 'Well, why don't you come to our service? Our service is at 9 or 10 o'clock.' Nothing. I was turned off by that.

I remember reading all the literature at the Baptist Sunday school about God speaking to the prophets. I remember crying when I was eight or nine years old "Why don't You talk to us any more? Why did you tell them the ancient prophets what they needed to know but don't talk to us anymore?" That just puzzled me. It was never enough. I was looking for something.

When I moved here there weren't many other black people. Just three guys. In my place of employment black people are about 2% of the population, so out of 4,000 there are only about forty. I told them "You know, we all gotta get together. Why don't we have a potluck?" I put on a potluck for everybody. Somebody donated the house, opened it up and I invited these two people. I knew one of them was a member of The Church of Jesus Christ of Latter-day Saints because of the talk around. They'd say "Yeah, this black man's a Mormon. That's the only reason he is in the position he's in." I really didn't think much of it then.

So we get to the potluck and we're all having a good time. Twenty or thirty show up and it's really a lot of fun, kids running around from a big family there. The men are downstairs and the women are upstairs. A lady is talking about her church. She says "We're having this barbecue at my place." It was a Relief Society event they were having.

She said "You know, its a missionary church. Don't worry, they're not going to try to convert you. We just want you to come over and have a good time." She invited me and said "You gotta come, you gotta come." I said okay. The night before I was stressing over it. I'm not going to feel comfortable around all those white people, I thought. So I told her the truth and she said "Okay."

So that went by. Then she invited me to a lunch one day. I went to lunch. And that was fine. I thought she was a very nice woman, very direct, opinionated. I found that a little odd, but I really liked her and I thought "That's just her personality and I can accept that," where before I couldn't.

One night after that I was in my bed. This was 10:30 or 11:00 at night and I just felt horrible. I had a good job, I was paying the rent, my kids were happy, they're in a good school. Life was okay and I was bawling. I was so unhappy. I was praying to God to help me. I said "I know You are out there somewhere. I feel so disconnected. Everything that I have ever come across is too small. It's not real. How do I find the way? Please help me to find You."

I called my mom and told her what happened. I had already told her about this woman and the Church. "You know, Mom, a black woman in the Mormon Church, ha, ha, ha. I feel so awful. I don't know what's wrong."

"Dana," she said, "you know what it is." My mom said "You should call that lady."

"What? Mom, I told you what church she belongs to."

She said "Dana, give her a call."

I said, "All right." So I called her and said "You know, I don't want to commit to anything; all I would like to know is if you can give me some literature on your church." That was on a Sunday.

She says "We have this thing called Family Home Evening where the family gets together. Sometimes we play a game—it's not real formal. And then we have dessert afterward. So, if you and your family want to come for that, why don't you come by? And I will try to get a couple of things together for you."

I said okay and went over there for Family Home Evening. I was incredibly impressed with the interaction between the children and the parents. Teenagers, interacting. When they said something the parents listened. It mattered. I had not seen that before. I just thought "Wow, the level of respect they all have for each other, and the love." You could feel it. They gave me a Book of Mormon, they gave me a tape and they gave me something else and I took it to work to show this woman I was working with but the bag disappeared. I don't know to this day what happened to it. I had never even opened the book. I just had this little sack I was excited about.

So I didn't say anything. How was I going to tell those people I'd lost it? How careless of me. They would think "We took all this time to get this stuff ready for this woman and look what she did with it." So I didn't tell her until she asked me "Have you read it yet?" and I said "I am so sorry but somebody took it. It's gone." I was so afraid.

"Oh, I can't believe it. We'll get you another one. Why don't you come over for the next Family Home Evening? This time we have a couple of ladies who are missionaries and they can explain it to you and answer any questions you might have a lot better than we could because this is what they do."

I said okay and before I knew it I had the First Discussion of the six that LDS missionaries normally teach investigators of the Church. They asked me "Will you read these things?" I said okay. I remember reading the introduction to The Book of Mormon: "This is good, this is really good." When I was reading a section in Nephi I thought: It's not like anybody ever told me. How has this been hidden all this time? I have known Mormons. No one's ever told me about this.

I finished the rest of the lessons in two or three weeks. I remember that when I was attending a Baptist church, all you do is raise your hand to get baptized. When I was there, there were probably ten who came down the aisle. "Do we have anyone who wants to get baptized tonight?" You raise your hand and go up to the front. There is no real commitment made.

And the other group I was studying with—you have to go through two or three books. And they have to feel that you're committed and prepared to be baptized. I studied with them on and off for twelve years. The first seven or eight years no one ever even asked me, which was pretty interesting. It was something that never even came up. I never was baptized in that church because they never felt I was committed enough. I thought I understood them, then. I am talking about the level of knowledge that is available within that organization.

The last four years I studied with them I was married and had my children, so I took them with me. I must say that was the best thing for me at the time. It really was, because it was like boot camp. It was so rigid I think it was really good. For example, children were required to sit still. That's why I have never had a problem with my kids and I'd been taking them to church with me since they've been around. I could take them to a movie theater and never have a problem because they were accustomed to sitting for two hours at a time.

So when the Mormon missionaries asked me at the second or third discussion if I would commit to baptism I said "I've been doing what I believe, living as I want. I can't get baptized." But what stuck in my head was the story of Peter, traveling through Damascus, who runs across a man who says "Can you baptize me right now?" They go to the side of a little river or a pool of water and Peter baptizes him right there. Then why do I have to wait? That never jived with me. I was just waiting for the truth. I made that choice.

It was always my choice about getting off of cocaine. God always left those things up to me. And when I chose the right way He was right there to help me carry it off. To have a fulfilling life we should start out with the world. Everyone wants to be the best, they want something. When we come here to earth we want to be successful. We want to be popular. We want to be with our families, we want to go to school. Some people want to have a good job. We have an internal desire and we facilitate that. Some of us smoke, some drink, some use sex. There's many different addictions that we get to try to fulfill this internal desire, this longing. Mine was sex and drugs. First it was friends. I had one best friend. Then I found out what boys were. Then it was sex and drugs and I had to have it. I had to have a lot because I was never happy. That was another reason the other religious group never baptized me. I was always breaking that moral code. So the one thing the LDS Church did for me was to give my self respect back. That raised my self esteem. I realized it wasn't sex that I wanted. I wanted companionship. I wanted understanding. I wanted compassion. All of these things I get from the members of the Church. Love. I get love from my brothers and my sisters. And that is complete. What I recognize through reading scripture is that we don't need physical things. We don't need a new car, we don't need a new house, we don't need things.

The reason we are here is to learn, not to see how much we can buy. There is a scripture that says "Lay up for yourselves treasures in heaven, where neither moth nor rust doth corrupt...." (Matt 6:20). This life is so temporary. We are supposed to work on getting home to Heavenly Father because that lasts forever. This life is a fleeting thing. We need to work hard on the spiritual needs. Christ can help us do that because he is the way, he is the life. He holds that light. That spiritual light. If you keep following that you'll get wherever you want to go. The scriptures are a road map. Everything that we need is there. And the wonderful thing about it is that it is true— even for non-members.

Jesus was a visionary. His nature is half spirit or godlike man and the other half mortal. Having an immortal father and a mortal mother, he had the ability to see beyond what we as humans see. He saw the causes and long term benefits of life, death and the Plan of Salvation.

The laws that are operative in the Bible, they go far beyond our earth life. It is something that is applicable to the eternities. They never change. Christ's atonement accomplished that. He died to make way for the rest of us who come here, that we may be cleansed through the shedding of his blood so we can return to our Heavenly Father. Now that is an earthly act, however it has eternal and spiritual implications and applications. Not just the act itself, but the true significance behind it.

It is very clear to me that these laws are a requirement. In The Book of Mormon and the King James Version of the Bible there isn't anything like our civil laws. A law that works for one state isn't applicable to another. It's not applicable in Canada or Japan. That is short term thinking. People are very short term thinkers. If we all were to follow the laws of the gospel we would not have communicable diseases. We wouldn't have a lot of social problems. Laws aren't only for our benefit here. They are eternal laws. The laws of Christ and Heavenly Father are so far reaching that we mortals do not understand them.

The Old Testament and New Testament scriptures show this. What latter day scripture did for me was to bring the other testaments of Jesus Christ alive, instead of looking at a history book. It now is a moving part of life. One of the major differences is that latter-day scripture, of course, is so recent. It just brings Christ to life. He's portrayed accurately as far as we as mortals can portray him. I don't believe that there's anything absolute or perfect in this mortal world—but I think any variances are not significant. I am not visionary. I don't have the ability of a broad view of things. So if there are any variances they are through mortal error.

My mother and grandmother have all these old sayings they have passed to our generation. My grandmother says "Man can't stop you from getting a blessing from God. Nobody can stop it. When you're due, you get yours." And that goes back to the black member of the LDS Church who they talked about at work. They said the only reason he is where he is: he is a member of that Church. Well, probably so, because when you are doing the right thing and you get a blessing there's nothing on earth that can stop it. When Heavenly Father wants to give you a blessing and the Holy Spirit says "This is yours," it's yours.

Now the Adversary is like the jealous stepson. He knows his place but he always wants to cause problems for us because of his jealousy. Because we made the right choices and he made the wrong choices. He recognizes that, so he is very bitter, very, very angry. He doesn't want us to get back to God. He tried to keep me away from the Church. Oh, he would bring people—bad people into my life. I believe things were taken away from me by the Adversary to try and get me to turn my back on God and not trust Him. But one thing. No matter how bad anything ever got, I was angry. I was hurt and I would tell God that I didn't understand why He would let this happen. And I believe that God does let things happen, good and bad. When bad things happen He can prevent them. There isn't anything on this earth that God can't do. But it is for our own benefit. When we go through tragedy it's for our good. That is one thing that I still don't think Satan really understands. God has the ability—and this is what I love most—God has the ability to take the worst thing that someone can do to someone else and turn it into a benefit. He did it with me.

Everyone should seek to know Christ. Everyone. Because it puts everything in perspective. Through Christ we have a better understanding of the world. You gain a better understanding of yourself. People who have a hard time relating to a certain god or religion—they are not going to get in touch with the part that makes them who they are. Get in touch with your spirit. What is your spirit telling you? What is it that you need? What really happens when you die? What has happened to those who have been close to you who have died? Why does the sun come up at a certain time? Why does it go down at a certain time year after year after year? You have to understand that everything God does has a purpose. There is a purpose in the seasons. There is a purpose in having plant life on this earth. There is a purpose in having water. Why should we be any less? What is our purpose? Christ will help you find your purpose in life. It's not just that we are here to raise a family, go to school, work or be someone's friend. We have to have a personal Savior. I have found a one-on one relationship with the Savior through prayer.

The only thing I can equate a personal religion with would be an adopted child looking for his real parents. All I know is I knew He was there but He hadn't talked to me. I wanted to know where He was and why He had left me alone. I asked him "Don't you love me any more?" I became a member of the Church and learned that He does love me and He says 'I never left you. I've been watching you the whole time. I remember letting you sweat a few times, but I knew you could do it.'

I always knew that I have a Father in Heaven who loves me, who really wants to see me, just like I want to see my children succeed in this life. He wants to see me succeed. He wants me to get to the highest level of mortality that I can. He wants me to do all the things that I can in my power to help those around me and the best way that I can help myself is, I think, through other people because—and this is a big life lesson that I just learned recently and I love to learn these big life lessons because once I learn them it means I don't have to repeat them and I can go on to something greater. If I put others first, truly first, and if I can remove pride out of the equation of life, not only am I happy but I make other people happy around me. People I may not even know. People come in and out of my life. Sometimes I may not even get their names, faces or anything else. But I am going to touch their life. And I think we all do that for each other every single day.

Every time we walk out of our front door we touch somebody's life. I am grateful that my Father in Heaven is there and that He uses the Holy Ghost to teach me, to help me, and that He's always there for me. Also Jesus Christ. I know he lives, I know he died for each and every one of us that we can all live and we can experience—I call it exquisite joy.

Because the joy that I experience today is far different than the good times that I thought I was having before. Exquisite joy is just the most incredible feeling—I go to work and I feel the presence of the Spirit. I don't want it to go away so I don't even turn on the radio. I am just driving to work on another level. It's beautiful and I'm grateful because I know that he's real. He's real to a lot of people of all kinds and all beliefs.

We members of The Church of Jesus Christ of Latter-day Saints have active temples on this earth. They are visited by members from the 'other' side, beyond the vail. They visit for their ordinances which they didn't perform when they were here. And I think they are there to assure people at different stages in their lives that they are okay, that they need to keep doing what they are doing. Some people need more tangible evidence than others. One of the sisters in the ward talks about the country she is from where they have a lot of very vivid manifestations. The acts we do are for our benefit, so the manifestations are for their benefit. Maybe somehow their faith is wavering. Maybe they need something more tangible to keep them going. And Heavenly Father sees that we get what we need. We need to worship Him through our acts. Acts of worship are constant. They are what I think, what I do, how I treat others.

I am extremely happy in my life. I know of God and I know of Christ, who Christ is. More importantly, I know who I am through Christ. Since I joined The Church of Jesus Christ of Latter-day Saints it has really expanded my awareness of my spirituality. It has been a beautiful thing to experience more of myself on a spiritual level. Christ is my personal Savior. He is my oldest brother who died on behalf of myself and my brothers and sisters that we may all go home to our Father in Heaven.

I truly believe that many of the ordinances we carry out in the physical world are spiritual in nature, but we need them because we are physical beings. Not just the acts themselves. We need to associate something that we want with something physical—something that we learn but can never see or touch. I went to a movie and saw the film "Mask." The boy is blind. His mother said "What are clouds and what is ice?" He said "This is blue" and he gave her an ice cube. He was trying to describe to her something she could feel, trying to describe to her what a cloud is and he gave her a wad of cotton balls so she could understand In reality we are the same. We don't know the things we need to know, so we need something we can touch, feel, see and experience so that we can truly observe. The act of baptism itself, the sacrament, going to the sacrament every week, prayer, basically going through the humility of being humble, of repentance, these are ways we can experience what is spiritual.

Repentance isn't a matter of cleaning up our past sins. Looking back isn't necessary. That is similar to guilt and the Church does not desire to make you feel guilty. They endeavor to make you feel sorrowful so that you will not trespass again, but not to make you feel guilty so you will constantly belittle yourself. When you go through the waters of baptism it means "That life is over, it's gone." You are now a new cleansed person. In some cases not everybody is really going to have something to repent of.

Not everybody is going to have lived a sinful life or be the kind of child who has heavily sinned. So I don't think that is appropriate. Repentance doesn't have to fall in that category. However, if you are in a situation where you did do something wrong then you need to experience repentance—to recall how you felt when you did it and how you feel now. It's coming to an accurate knowledge of right and wrong. I no longer feel the need to be promiscuous. I am not without desire but I know that I will keep my covenants. It's no longer an issue. If I can do it, anybody can do it. I did those things because I didn't understand. But when I have a realization of why it's wrong I can stop. Being on drugs hinders me from feeling the Spirit and prevents me from experiencing my spirituality. It prevents me from spiritually progressing. That's why I shouldn't "do" drugs. It affects chemicals in my brain that I need to think and make rational decisions, to use those God-given choices that I have.

I go back to the foresight and the wisdom and Jesus being a visionary. He understood that life is going to be changing rapidly for us, especially in these latter days. New things are popping up, new distractions. And I don't think they are just distractions. Satan and his band of demons are working harder and harder because they know the time is drawing closer and closer. I believe that Jesus Christ will impress or manipulate the minds of individuals to help them, give them more knowledge. Satan and his demons are on the other side doing the same thing. But God has the ability to turn anything that Satan does into something good.

Today I would be willing to die for the things I believe in. In the past I wasn't. I hate pain. If it doesn't hurt there's no problem. I ask God to help me keep progressing. I don't want to ever become comfortable or stagnant. I always want to be reaching out of my comfort zone. Then I know I am growing. There's no doubt in my mind that I have chosen the right thing because I asked Him. I asked people for help and I was so disappointed, but when I asked Him— he put me and the lady together. He put me with the right people. Attending all the other churches, I was always longing for something. This is the most completely fulfilling organization on this earth. It doesn't matter who you are, where you are. He's got you covered.

The Gospel of Jesus Christ has truly changed my children for the better, too. They are so much better. It's easier for them to trust themselves, their own instincts. They pray when they need something. Sometimes I have to remind them but they know they can ask Heavenly Father. They have raised their self esteem. They recognize that when things are said which come from The Book of Mormon and the Bible, they can believe it. They tell me "Mommy, I thought this, or, Brother or Sister said that." They are learning to trust others but at the same time I'm trying to teach them "Don't trust what I say, don't trust what they say. Read it for yourself." When they read the scriptures I ask them "What does that mean to you?"

There are things that are beyond their comprehension. Being pre-teens, that's understandable. The LDS Church truly has drawn us closer together. We say our prayers in the morning and in the evening. It's nice, especially for young girls. It teaches them that they don't have to give their respect or dignity to anyone. It's theirs and no one can take it away. The Church teaches them how to make better choices. Along with that the Church stresses knowledge, going to school, but that's another more formal avenue. We can teach ourselves. I think that we need to read and not just read our books or what is published by the Church but read other books using our knowledge and the Spirit for discernment.

The Holy Ghost prompts you. Sometimes it's very vivid—like when I was at the temple. It's like a voice in my head. It spoke to me. When I am out and about—like when I am looking for my keys—I pray for little things. I pray for anything. Mom always said God can move mountains. I believe it. I have come to realize that it is okay to ask for little things. Nothing is too small for God. He's there for us.

I know the Savior has a spiritual body. But it is in another dimension. Yes, it has another substance, too. He will appear with a body when he comes back but I don't think everybody will say

"That's Jesus." He will appear to his faithful followers only and I think that includes people outside the LDS Church, all who truly love and follow him.

There's nothing in this world today to look forward to like his coming back to us. In the last two weeks I've started to recognize that is the most important thing. That's why these scriptures mean so much to me. He is coming back. We don't know when but the most important thing is to let other people know. When I think of Jesus Christ upon the cross at Golgotha I feel his strength, his courage and his sorrow, a lot of sorrow for all those who won't get back to him.

I have not always been aware of these broad happenings outside myself. It goes back to my membership in the Church. It has taken my spirituality to a new level. My parents have taken me to churches of one kind or another since I was small. I was immersed with religion but never immersed in spirituality. That's where I find that the Church is not a religion. I do not see it as a religion. It is a spiritual vehicle we get behind the wheel of and drive, but we're not driving it by ourselves. There's one big pattern. I can't see it but I know that it exists. There is one universal pattern that Jesus is the source of and it goes beyond this universe. That's what keeps the plants alive. I can't conceive of it but it's there. Everything has its time and has its season. It goes far beyond the universe as we know it. Our focus at this level is to be taught. It frustrates me that we spend money on Star Wars, space wars, and all the things that are out there. What we need to do is to use this class time focusing on our current lesson: life, love, charity, caring, the fruits of the Spirit.

I would like to tell the world not to ever let anything or anyone on this earth or out of this world come between them and the Savior and our Heavenly Father because no one is more committed to each life than the Savior. He was that committed to my happiness. He died showing us that.

I believe also that God speaks to us today. I know that he speaks to me because some of the choices I have made in my life I would not have made without being prompted by the Spirit through a strong feeling inside. I think "This is crazy," but things happen that myself or any other person could not have manipulated and they have a positive outcome. That happens quite often. If I leave things up to my Heavenly Father through thinking and praying, knowing where my limitations are, that's where miracles take place.

Come unto Jesus, ye heavy laden, Careworn and fainting, by sin oppressed.
He'll safely guide you unto that haven
Where all who trust him may rest, may rest.

Come unto Jesus; He'll ever heed you, Though in the darkness you've gone
astray.
His love will find you and gently lead you
From darkest night into day, to day.

Come unto Jesus; He'll surely hear you, If you in meekness plead for his
love.
Oh, know you not that angels are near you
From brightest mansions above, above?

Come unto Jesus from every nation, From ev'ry land and isle of the sea.
Unto the high and lowly in station, Ever he calls "Come to me, to me."

Text and music: Orson Pratt Huish

FRED'S STORY

Birthplace: Seattle, Washington   Single, never married
Family background: One older sister   Lifelong Christian
Occupation: Production Worker   Age: 46

I CAN ALWAYS REMEMBER BELIEVING IN Jesus, in the Church and in The Book of Mormon, pretty much all my life, because I went to Church as a little kid and I tried to keep the commandments and I tried to do the things I was supposed to. I was constantly trying to live the gospel. Even as a child I believed in Christ. You know, when you are a little kid you don't have the same knowledge you do when you're an adult, but you still believe and know those things. My mother was LDS, but not my father. They have both passed away.

We went to Church every week when I was young, but as an adult living away from home I did not attend for about two years. When you are a young child, you don't want to go to Church that much and at that time religion doesn't have a lot of meaning for a child, but I'm glad I did go because it gave me a foundation for having a deeper belief in the Savior today. My father always encouraged us to go to church, though he attended only a couple of times. There were many times I didn't want to, but he told me to go and he made sure that I went. My sister is a firm believer, also, and she attended with us.

I think it was just my faith as a child that kept me believing. I tried to keep Heavenly Father's commandments. I can't recall that I ever did anything really bad. Little boys always do goofy things, but nothing really out of the ordinary and I built my testimony on faith. I have experienced little things that helped me build upon my knowledge of the Savior. I think I really believed that the Gospel was true pretty much all my life because I studied the scriptures and I would pray, probably not as much as I do now. I know the scriptures well, though I'm sure there are some who know them better than I. I have a love for the scriptures and I read them as often as I can.

I think when the Savior really became effectual in my life was at a point in time when I found out that I needed to make major changes in my life and I really wanted the Savior's love and his influence.

When I was young, for many years, I lived a terrible life but at the same time I tried to live as a Christian and as a follower of the Savior. I just lived a double standard. I did things that were hideous and abhorrent to God and man and I did that for more than twenty years of my life. I have always tried to change, to do those things that were right and stop doing what I know to be wrong, but it seemed I was always attracted to the old habits.

One day the bishop called me in the office, and with tears in his eyes he asked if anything was wrong. I knew right then I had to make a decision to change. I could hide some of my activities. I could lie about why I couldn't go to the temple or why I couldn't do a number of things that I wanted to do. Did I really want to continue living that double standard? Did I want to bluff the bishop or did I just want to change my life? I had to make that decision at that time. This happened only a short time ago.

Within a matter of a few seconds I decided it was time to tell the bishop and that changed my entire life. It was one of the greatest things that I have ever done. I knew what I was doing was wrong because it was an abomination before God and man and I didn't like those feelings within myself because my life was in a state of limbo.

I wasn't good or bad, but I had no direction. I wanted some kind of direction in my life. I wasn't accomplishing anything. I wanted to have peace in my life. I wanted forgiveness. I wanted to be able to go to the temple. And none of those things I could do. I could kind of lie about them but I didn't want to. Being worthy enough to attend the temple was especially important to me. I felt that sooner or later, my evasions would be found out. I didn't want that. I wanted peace in my heart and conviction that I could have the Holy Ghost to be my constant companion because at that time he wasn't a part of my life, not because he didn't want to be, but because I had lived a life such that I drove him away. I didn't want that situation anymore.

I felt better when I confessed to the bishop. I didn't feel forgiven right then, but I knew I was now on the right course. I didn't feel that I was forgiven at that time because I had to prove to the Lord that I really was trying to keep his commandments. It was over a number of months that soon I began to slowly feel better within myself and slowly I felt forgiven. It was over the course of a long period of time.

Repentance and forgiveness are true principles of the Gospel. Forgiveness is one of the greatest things that our Heavenly Father has devised because it is a way by which one can completely cleanse one's life. We can't be forgiven in a few words, as some people in some Christian religions think. That cannot be. It's true that we can change our activities the moment we say that we're going to change, but to truly feel that inner conviction takes time, because we need to prove to our Father in Heaven that we are willing to keep on the right course and to keep His commandments. We not only need to prove to the Lord that we are changing but to ourselves as well. Our actions must prove our words. And what other way can there be? A scripture from The Book of Mormon comes to mind here:

> O all ye that are spared because ye were more righteous than they, will ye not now return unto me, and repent of your sins, and be converted, that I may heal you?

> *3Ne 9:13*

Now, of course our Father's forgiveness is dependent upon the degree of our sins, and mine were much worse than others, so it took time. Today I'm a worthy temple goer. I pay tithing and I keep God's commandments. I feel forgiven but I still have remorse for the things that I've done and I'll probably have that all my life. I know I'll have to keep the commandments to the best of my ability all my life. It's what I want to do. I can remember the bishop telling me of a talk that President Boyd K. Packer gave about life being a treasure box and whether or not we put in good treasures or bad omens depends upon the destination of our lives.

This whole experience has helped me to know my Savior better. I believe that it has because since I have been filled with remorse I can really feel how much he had to suffer and atone for me. I don't know how much my sins have caused the Savior to suffer but all I can say is just that I'm really grateful for his Atonement and I want to try to do those things that would help heal some of those wounds he suffered. I had to give up my sins to know him.

There is a beautiful scripture in Mosiah 4:2,3, which expresses the great peace we can know when we ask for and receive forgiveness through the Atonement. King Benjamin speaks:

> And they had viewed themselves in their own carnal state, even less than the dust of the earth. And they all cried aloud with one voice, saying: O have mercy, and apply the atoning blood of Christ that we may receive forgiveness of our sins, and our hearts may be purified; for we believe in Jesus Christ, the Son of God...

> And...the Spirit of the Lord came upon them, and they were filled with joy, having received a remission of their sins, and having peace of conscience, because of the exceeding faith which they had in Jesus Christ...

We should all care about the Atonement because the Savior did suffer for each of our sins. If it wasn't for the Savior's Atonement we would all be subject eventually to Satan and be ruled by Satan. We would have no chance to come back into our Father's presence. We'd have no chance of forgiveness, no matter what we try to do—there would be no hope in our lives. Because of the Atonement, at least we can see there is hope inside of us. It's more than hope. It's a goal we have. We can know that our bodies will be reunited with our spirits. We can know that if we keep the commandments as fully as possible that through the Savior's Atonement we can come back into our Father 's presence.

And I think that's the essence of the Atonement. It is true that we can look at the scriptures and we can see exactly what the Savior did, who he atoned for. If it were not for the Atonement we would have no hope in this life or in eternal life with him. Through the Atonement of Christ we gain that hope. Our bodies could never be united with their spirit without the Atonement of Christ. I wouldn't be able to look forward to having a perfect body, one without disease. I think our main purpose here is to gain a body and to keep our Father in Heaven's commandments. We are here primarily for our own salvation.

Without hope there is Hell. Hell can be something like I have experienced. It can be terrible. Your life is confused. You have no direction. Some people may not recognize that as a hell, but in a sense it is, because you flounder, with no sense of purpose. The scriptures tell us that after death we can know what Hell is really like. It is to be trapped by confusion. It is the absence of our Father in Heaven, Jesus Christ and the Holy Ghost, and that, to me, is unfathomable.

On one occasion, after talking with my bishop and making a full confession, the Bishop' Council decided to make certain decisions regarding my church standing. As I sat with the congregation that Sunday morning a few months later I was asked to participate in the blessing of a baby. My name was read over the pulpit I knew I could not take part. I just sat there and felt shame and embarrassment overcome me, because twenty years of supposed fun and sin had cost me this precious opportunity. That was to me the closest encounter with Hell that I have experienced. I resolved at that time never to put myself in that position again.

Satan is everywhere. His influence is everywhere. We can see it so much on television, in the media. We can see it everywhere. It seems that so many people just don't recognize it until it is too late. I am so grateful that the Savior has come, not for my sins alone, even if I hadn't done so many of the things I have done in the past. Grateful doesn't begin to tell how I feel. I am grateful to have the opportunity to be back in our Father in Heaven's presence. I want to be able to go on keeping my Father in Heaven's commandments, to learn how to be in compliance and obedience to Him that I can have the Holy Ghost as my constant companion, because in these troubled times I need his companionship to tell me right from wrong. Sometimes there are so many gray areas in life that it is hard to make the right decisions.

Of course, we need the influence of the Holy Ghost to help us make the right decisions. I feel now that he works in my life in that he has given me peace, because I don't feel any more confusion. I try to let him direct my life. He is essentially my friend. Without the Holy Ghost we can be more easily led astray. Now we can be influenced by the Holy Ghost but without constant companionship we cannot be sure we are doing our Father in Heaven's will. Christ's essential message was to keep one's life so in order that we can return to our Father in Heaven's presence.

The ways of God are marvelous. It's hard to focus in on that, but not hard for Him. I think He's with us in every aspect of our lives. He's everywhere. What is important is how much we're willing to listen to our Father in Heaven's commands. Our rewards will be great. One of the greatest is that after our death on earth our spirits will continue on. We will be able to feel and experience new things, and they will be coupled with our ability to have eternal glory. I think our senses will be heightened because they will be clearer. Our bodies will be without disease. No matter which eternal kingdom (celestial, terrestrial, telestial) we are assigned to, it will be glorious there, even if we are in the lowest kingdom we will no longer be subject to disease and the frailties of our bodies.

Prayer is very important. When I pray I first like to thank my Father in Heaven for a number of things, for the basic things of life. And then there are things I ask him about, everyday things in life; my job, the basic sort of things. And I always ask for His forgiveness and to know in what ways I can live a fuller life. I believe he answers all our prayers. Perhaps not in the way we expect him to; but He can answer prayers through experiences in life. He can answer prayers through our friends as we help one another. He answers prayers by the still, small voice of the Holy Ghost. He can answer them in many ways: even a 'No' answer is an answer.

Prayer is necessary for us on earth because life can be very hard. It seems that we are given hardship because we're dumb. We bring problems upon ourselves. If I put my hand on the burning stove and if I know better but I want to do it anyway, I'm going to suffer the consequences. If I want to dart across the street in front of a truck I'm going to get hurt, and I will know that it is my fault, I brought on those hardships. If I abuse my body in various ways and it becomes diseased because of the things I have chosen to do to it, I'll reap the consequences of those past actions. But sometimes through no fault of our own, hardships come about. We get diseased, we get sick, we lose our jobs. Any number of things happen. And certain physical effects of those events happen, even though we may not see them. But these experiences help us to gain and to grow. By facing hardship and being able to endure them we can have the greater presence of our Father in Heaven to be with us because we mastered a certain hardship and it was a growing experience.

The Savior said it best—There's a scripture in John 17:3:

And this is life eternal, that they might know thee, the only true God, and Jesus Christ, whom thou hast sent.

I think that is essentially what the Savior wanted us to know. There are important things to strive for in our lives. We need to know our Father in Heaven, and I think to know someone we have to become like them. We cannot be exactly like our Father in Heaven or Jesus Christ because we cannot be perfect in this life, but what we can do is to conduct our lives that we can every day have a little better life, closer and closer to the Savior as much as we can.

I think there is a beautiful scripture that tells about knowing our Father in Heaven.

For how knoweth a man the master whom he has not served, and who is a stranger unto him, and is far from the thoughts and intents of his heart?

Mosiah 5:13

And it came to pass that I, Nephi, said unto my father: I will go and do the things which the Lord hath commanded, for I know that the Lord giveth no commandments unto the children of men, save he shall prepare a way for them that they may accomplish the thing which he commandeth them.

1Ne 3:7

I believe in the basic principles of my faith: to be baptized by one having the proper authority, to keep the commandments of our Father in Heaven as much as we possibly can and to take upon ourselves those sacred covenants that will lead us back into His presence. For a man, it would be to receive the priesthood and to attend God's temples where he can perform saving ordinances in accordance with Christ's direction as stated in the Bible and in the

Doctrine and Covenants. For members of the Church to be worthy to attend the temple is necessary because there we make everlasting covenants by which families can be together forever. We cannot become a family unit without these obligations and sacred promises between man and God. In Malachi it states that we need to perform certain ordinances to return back to our Father in Heaven's presence. It is necessary to make and keep these ordinances so after this life we can pass by the angels of Heaven, giving them the information that will lead us back to our Father in Heaven's presence.

Generally, in the temple we learn about man's salvation and take upon ourselves special responsibilities through sacred covenants which are binding that we make with our Father in Heaven. We can also do baptisms and other work for the living, and for the dead by proxy, and through these actions families can insure that throughout eternity they will never be separated and will have eternal lives together, if they live or have lived worthy earthly lives and if they accept (on earth or afterward) the full Gospel of Jesus Christ through membership in his Church. Since the dead cannot perform these ordinances for themselves, by searching out our genealogy we can get the information and do this essential work for them. In the spirit world those who have passed on can accept or decline those ordinances which have been performed in their behalf. We can also be married in the temple for time and throughout all eternity by keeping the commandments. The blessings of eternal marriage in the celestial kingdom include great promises and the gift of increase in many ways. While there are grave consequences from our Father in Heaven for the violation of the promises we make in the temple, the blessings we receive for keeping our covenants and living by the commandments are immeasurable and worth the price of self-discipline. I know that we can have tremendous joy in our lives. I love this scripture:

> ...prove me now herewith, saith the Lord of hosts, if I will not open you the windows of heaven, and pour you out a blessing, that there shall not be room enough to receive it.

> *Malachi 3:10*

One of those great blessings is that of the temples of God. The temple is a clean, a holy place. It is a place where the Spirit resides, if we are worthy enough to enter into the temple, because not just anyone can enter. We have to observe certain rules that have been stated by the

Church and obtain a Recommend each year. Living by these rules don't make one better than another, but adhering to strict guidelines prompts people to find the best within themselves. A few of these guidelines include our promise to pay tithing, to keep the Word of Wisdom, to live a morally chaste life. When we accept these parameters for ourselves we become obligated to make a yearly accounting to our bishop and our stake president. These are some of the standards that qualify us to enter into the Lord's sacred temples. Saving principles make one's life cleaner, more receptive to the Holy Ghost, and by doing so we can feel peace, because in the temple everyone is dressed in white as a symbol of cleanliness and purity, reverence and respect.

I am grateful that we have temples and that we have a living prophet upon the earth today. I believe a prophet is a good idea and necessary because he is the voicepiece of the Savior. If the Savior were here the prophet and the Savior would say essentially the same things. Jesus Christ would be telling us to keep the commandments. We can find out essentially what the Savior wants us to know indirectly from him every six months at General Conference and we can also find out each month what the Savior wants us to know by reading in the Ensign (magazine of The Church of Jesus Christ of LDS) the message from the First Presidency. The Prophet has told us many things he wants us to do over the years. One very important thing is to have a number of things stored up for times of need, also to get out of debt. There are other things the Savior would be telling his prophet who then asks us: what are you doing to promote my name? What are you doing to expand the growth of the Church? What are you doing for the salvation of those who have died before?

Jesus himself said it best. I am referring to Section 1:38-39 of the Doctrine and Covenants:

> What I the Lord have spoken, I have spoken, and I excuse not myself; and though the heavens and the earth pass away, my word shall not pass away, but shall all be fulfilled, whether by mine own voice or by the voice of my servants, it is the same. For behold, and lo, the Lord is God, and the spirit beareth record, and the record is true, and the truth abideth forever and ever. Amen.

We can know about the Savior by listening to what his prophets tell us. We can also know the Savior by reading about him through the scriptures. That is the most obvious way. But most importantly, we can know about the Savior by trying to make our lives perfect. I think man's purpose in life is to gain a body, to keep the commandments of our Father in Heaven, and to live in such a way that we can return to His presence.

I believe that there are harder times coming soon, but they're still a little way off. We can always see things coming. Some of the signs I see are terrible. Things that you should never see on TV. Sex, for example. You'd never see sex openly displayed on television a few years ago. Abortion is another area where God's word has been denied. Abortion is becoming so acceptable. Some people feel that it's wrong but many feel that it's getting rid of a mistake.

The world will be changed when Christ is our leader. It will be during the Millenium. There will be no war, no bloodshed. People will want to live their lives such that they will want to do the best for their brethren, even though there probably will be many different churches in the world. There will be many different opinions but there won't be the strife there is today. I envision Jesus Christ as a glorified person who will look much the same as you and me, except his countenance is white and radiant because of his glory and you will be able to see all of his essence. He has a body like ours but his is glorified and we will see that no one is like him. We will know him because we will have that witness from the Holy Ghost that he is the Savior.

I have thought about being willing to die for my faith. That's a tough question. It seems right now that everything is nice. There are anti-Mormons, but those are just little things. But there probably will come a time when we will have to put up our lives for our Church and for our Father in Heaven. I know it will come soon. If I were put in that position I'd want to feel that I could die and go back to the Savior right now. I want to feel it's my goal. I think dying for the Savior now would be more like this: Are we killing sin in our lives? Are we willing to commit our lives to the Savior as much as we possibly can? To me, that would be dying for the Savior: by our words, by our deeds, by living the Gospel.

The life of Christ and his Atonement for us has meaning for all people. There are many who don't believe in Christ. For them, obviously, he is not going to have any direct meaning, but for those who really do believe, no matter what faith they embrace, his Atonement is effectual in their lives.

There are a number of things that in the past have helped and inspired me, but they would be too long and too laborious to go into. I think I have a good story because I have lived a most debauched type of a life and I have changed. The Savior has made atonement for those sins that I have committed and he can do the same for anyone. There is no sin that the Savior has not atoned for, except for those sons of perdition, and to me that is the greatest story in the world.

O God, Aaron hath told me that there is a God; and if there is a God, and if thou art God, wilt thou make thyself known unto me, and I will give away all my sins to know thee, and that I may be raised from the dead, and be saved at the last day.

Alma 22:18

For I have received of the Lord that which also I delivered unto you, That
the Lord Jesus the same night in which he was betrayed took bread:
And when he had given thanks, he brake it, and said,
Take, eat: this is my body,
which is broken for you: this do in remembrance of me.
After the same manner also he took the cup, when he had supped, saying,
This cup is the new testament in my blood: this do ye, as oft as ye drink it,
in remembrance of me.
For as often as ye eat this bread, and drink this cup,
ye do shew the Lord's death till he come.

I Corinthians 11:23-26

DAVID'S STORY

Born: Boise, Idaho	Christian since age of ten
Family: Oldest of three	Family Affiliation: Church going
Occupation: Hospital Chaplain	Age: 44

MY MOTHER'S SIDE OF THE FAMILY IS Mormon. On my dad's side are Baptists and Nazarenes. Through a series of circumstances my mother left the Mormon Church. When she was sixteen she met my dad. Two years later and they married after graduating from high school. They both wanted to find a church, so they decided on a Christian church in Boise, and so that's where I grew up—going to the First Christian Church of Boise.

I always liked education and learning. After I graduated from high school I went right to college. My first two years were spent at a state university. After my sophomore year I transferred to a Christian college where I finished my Bachelor's degree. I also took classes at another state university, then, because I was interested in psychology. After getting my B.A. in Biblical Studies I went right to seminary in 1976, obtaining a Master of Divinity degree three years later. I was still interested in psychology and counseling so I also earned a Master's in Counseling by 1981. I had ten years in a row of higher education and I was ready to stop that for awhile, so I went to work. It's really only been since 1981 that I have been employed full time! Three years ago, I decided I wanted to work on my doctorate and am currently finishing that project.

I served for two years as associate minister in my church and fourteen more years in the Dean of Students position at a Christian college. I have been a hospital chaplain for only the past year.

I don't have any question that I would still be a Christian if I hadn't had all that education. I would be active in a church somewhere, but I know that my undergraduate training in biblical studies and seminary training have had a major impact on how I view faith, the church, the Bible, all those things. You can't study intensively for all those years and not be changed somewhat on several levels. To be what I would call biblically literate, that is to be able to read the Bible, to look beyond the words on the page and to understand the context, the history, the people and how they lived when the various books were being written is very deepening. I never get tired of it. I mean, I always will be a student of the Bible because I can read a text over and over again and learn something new about it. My education transforms the whole thing and I can go back to a verse almost like it was new to me.

Graduate school and seminary changed me in another way. It broadened my perspective of faith. Through studying other denominations, other religions, I think I look at faith from a much more global perspective than I would if I hadn't studied what other people believe. It helps me to understand where there are some limitations, both in my own faith and in the faith of others.

I don't plan to stay in chaplaincy. Once I finish my doctorate I plan to go back into higher education, and certainly my first preference is to go back into church related education. That's what I'm training to continue to do, since I've done that for a decade and a half already. But I don't know. The only thing I'm fairly certain of at this point is that God opened the door for me to work in the hospital as another way to prepare me for the rest of my life. I don't know what that is going to be, but I know that I will be able to use those lessons in ways that prepare me to be better at what I am called to do next.

I believe very strongly in free will. We're always given choices. God is not closing things off, but I think God sometimes opens several doors for us at once and then says "Pick one and go for it." At this point I don't know what's behind any of those doors. I just know the doors are there.

Being a parent I have to admit I'm looking for material and spiritual comfort. I don't find that a major conflict because I think we're given instructions in the New Testament to be very responsible with both the material and spiritual blessings God has given us. I have a daughter who's just entering her teenage years and in five years she is going to want to go to college. She's very bright and maybe will be able to go to good colleges, even private colleges. My wife and I are going to want to give her the best opportunity possible, so in terms of materiality there is a sense of a standard. But we never lose sight of who is the real source of our material life.

I guess I'm looking for a balance between the physical nature of living and the spiritual nature of living and trying to find ways to make them both as effective as possible. Somebody has called it "the extreme middle." Balance. It's not a life of compromise. Rather than trying to be extremist on what we might call the left and the right, either in liberalism or conservatism—I know there's lots of definitions for those words. I don't care to be a liberal or a conservative. I think both philosophies have major problems when they reach certain points. I look for a balance in my spiritual and material beliefs.

To put it another way, it's the quest for how to be as fully human as possible, because I think that's what God created us to be, to develop our potential. When we sin, that's where we compromise our potential. It not only lessens our humanity, it also opens the door to evil.

Certainly, the first thing I'd go back to is wisdom: to better understand how to relate to people, how to become more compassionate, to resist the temptation to look at our society and just become despondent or cynical about it. I don't think those are the things that God calls us to do. I'm at a point in my life, because of this career change, where I don't really know what lies ahead for me. I just know there will be change. It isn't, however, change with no purpose. I have to be attentive to grow as a person in the process of the change.

My view of God has changed a lot over the years. For me it has been a developmental process. I know that my understanding and my views about God now are much different than, for instance, when I was eighteen. I believe I've grown and matured in my faith, and I think that all Christians who take their faith sincerely go through that maturation process. I think it's built into the system, part of that potential God created within us.

Hardship plays a big role in the maturation process, too. When I left the Christian college it was not at all a happy parting. It has been the worst spiritual crisis I've ever had. In fact, it was the first real spiritual crisis for me. I felt cut off, exiled. I have been processing what hardship means over the last year and a half and my perspective has literally flip-flopped. Working in the hospital has helped and I think one of the lessons I've learned has contributed to this new understanding. I would have said a year or two ago that God's will for us is to have continuously fulfilling and happy lives and to have strength to deal with the occasional crisis.

I now look at suffering from the opposite perspective. Hardship is the result of the human condition. It is something we have created. So many of the diseases that we see have been created by humans inadvertently over the years, but nevertheless, we're responsible in one way or another for most of those illnesses. Now the more I look at it I think faith gives us the strength to get through the hardships that life is going to continue to throw at us. There's going to be very few people who live an idyllic kind of life without hardship. That doesn't mean our lives have to be terrible, horrible and torturous all the time, but, in fact, there are several hundreds of millions of people who deal with extreme hardship on a daily basis and yet those people can and do come to faith. That is the connection.

Does God give us hardship? Does God create natural disasters? Does God create wars and holocausts? No. God does not do that. The earth can be a dangerous place to live, and we have few defenses against such geological events like storms, earthquakes and volcanoes. Humans, too, have developed weapons which are far too powerful to control. Politics, and sometimes religion makes pawns out of innocents. So, it's what we used to call—when I was studying sociology in college and graduate school back in the 70's—"man's inhumanity to man." We create our own hardships.

Now there's another force at work in the universe. Let's say that there's a pervasive presence of evil. I'm talking about a force far more insidious than the popular image of the devil with a pitchfork. It seems to me some things happen that appear to be so evil, human acts by a person, group or nation that are so counter to what God wishes, evil has to be looked on as a reality in the midst of the human condition. And it does not represent God's wish for the world.

When we find evil, sometimes we can do really simple things to counter it, like being kind to a person who has been depressed for one reason or another. Sometimes we have to do much more complex things, like working politically to change an injustice, to rid a South Africa of apartheid, as an example.

On a personal basis, the best way to confront evil is to use the Golden Rule. That can sound like a cliché, but behind it is the reality of the Spirit of God saying "Not only treat another as you want to be treated, but treat another as I have taught you to treat others" and do it as brothers and sisters in the gospel, putting off the "natural man," as Paul teaches us in Romans 12:1-2. The Golden Rule is really like a beacon in the darkest night helping us find our way back to the human potential God creates in us.

There are common forces to life. But there's a distinctive force given by God that makes us human. You could start out by saying that as *homo sapiens* we are just the latest species of hominid. We could be very biological about it. That's not really what I'm talking about. What I'm talking about is that there's a distinctiveness about being human that sets us apart from the other species, to begin with. That story is told in Genesis in the Creation story. From my perspective it doesn't make any difference whether you accept Genesis, chapters one and two as historical reality—God kneeling by the side of a stream bank and forming the man, or if you put that into an evolutionary context. It's the lessons you learn that matter. We are human. There is something distinctive about being human. We either have to resign ourselves to saying "Well, we're just a freak of nature," or it's an act of God that humans are here.

If you look at us from a purely secular perspective humans are just another accident of the evolutionary process. But I don't believe we are an accident (even though I think that evolution is, in fact, an accurate way to describe the appearance and disappearance of species found in the fossil record). And the reason I see us as distinctive is that there's a clue given in the Genesis creation stories in chapters 1 and 2. God wanted to make sure that we knew we are not an accident.

How do we lead a fulfilling life, then? In some ways that's the second most important question a Christian can ask. The older I get the more strongly I believe that there's no such thing as a Christian hermit. To be Christian means that you are not only in a relationship with God but you are also in a relationship within the covenantal community which is the "church", with those who will say at least that "Jesus is the Christ, the Son of the living God." This public confession has defined that relationship between the Christian and the church from its very beginning.(See Acts 2)

In our society, despite all its technology and all the things that compete for our attention, we are no different than when Jesus was walking on the earth two thousand years ago. We come to understand that there are things which are completely mundane and which have no transcendent or eternal application. The core of meaning in our lives is found in our faith in the One who died on Calvary and who rose from the dead. Just as Paul wrote in 1Cor 2 "For I decided to know nothing among you except Jesus Christ and him crucified." (New Standard Revised Version Bible) And the world is going to laugh at us, the world's going to poo-poo us, the world's going to discriminate against us and sometimes the world's even going to kill us. It doesn't change that center or that core, however. History's been split down the middle with the crucifixion and resurrection of Jesus Christ. Everything is different because of that.

God wants to have a relationship with us now, during our earthly life and through eternity, to restore our relationship with Him that has been broken. The relationship was broken by human action against God. Humanity made the choice to sin. We see that in the story of Adam and Eve, in the Fall and the expulsion from the Garden. The fall from grace.

A scripture I have loved for a long, long time is in Paul's letter to the Ephesians, Eph 3:20-21, his doxology:

> Now to him who by the power at work within us is able to accomplish abundantly far more than we can ask or imagine, to him be glory in the church and in Christ Jesus to all generations, forever and ever. (NSRV)

For me this scripture epitomizes the relationship between Christ and the church and Christ's commitment to the church, as well as the power and mission that the church derives from Christ. All that in two verses. I think it means the body of Christ and the kingdom of God on earth. Paul is not talking about any one particular denomination. He's talking about the whole church. It's a witness to Paul's genius and inspiration that he was able to write that and get so much in so few words.

There is a "covenantal community." Christ established his church. And even though we have, through human failing, split up that church, there's still only one church. "One Lord, one faith, one baptism,..." (Eph 4:5). That seems pretty clear to me.

We can't literally live a life like Christ lived. There is too much history between him and us in terms of the person of Jesus. But, I'm talking about a Christlike life epitomized by the risen Lord. That incorporates the fruits of the Spirit, the gifts of the Spirit, being involved in Christian community and working on growing in our faith. Jesus taught us to treat others with compassion; he taught us to be kind to those who have less and to those who have more. He taught us to put away some of our assumptions about humanity. He says to turn the other cheek, go the extra mile. These are counterintuitive to what we want to do if we look at ourselves simply as biological beings. We need to put off the natural man. Social justice is just as important as personal justice.

I think the gospel of John reflects a sense of community that grows. In the synoptic gospels of Matthew, Mark and Luke, there is a great deal of time and effort—and rightly so—describing people coming to a decision about joining Christ. In the gospel of John you see people making decisions, but it's not just to come in from the cold. They're already in the community in one way or another and at a certain point they mature and realize that they have made that decision and that that is indeed what God is calling them to do.

I believe very strongly, as well, in the inspiration of the scriptures in that God's message written there is, in fact, truth. Where I make the distinction is in the understanding of which events are historical (in the sense of you and I sitting here having this conversation), and which events are metaphorical. The best example of that and the most controversial are the Creation stories.

The Book of Job also is, in a sense a drama, a very powerful drama, one which calls all believers of the Judeo-Christian tradition to examine their beliefs about cause and effect. Even though it's metaphorical it still conveys spiritual truth. We read the Bible in order to understand the revelations of God. We make a choice to accept that what has been written and collected in the Bible reveals God's truths about life, about salvation. Every other claim for what I would call "canonicity" has to meet that same historical criteria. From my perspective, no other writings meet that criteria. They do not survive what I call the "razor of history."

Some of the things in the Bible are very hard to understand. I've never felt like I should pray to know the truth. But I think that Solomon had the best idea—to pray for wisdom. I pray for wisdom when I come across something that I don't understand and there are lots of different points of view and contradictions. Often, I do receive answers. Because of what is recorded in Acts regarding the Pentecost and the giving of the Spirit, I am confident that God speaks to us today. Where I differ with some other groups is that from the perspective of completing the covenants and meeting the historical criteria of faith, I believe the testament is complete.

These are the hard questions of faith. I work on those questions. The other part of it is whatever context God gives me to live in, to work in. I try to help myself and others grow. We'll see what happens. I come out of a tradition which tends to look at what is essential to faith from a very simple but not simplistic, perspective. In my faith tradition we have just one statement, and that is we believe that "Jesus is the Christ, the Son of the living God and he is our personal Savior, our Lord and the Savior of the world." All other creedal statements made by the various churches may be accurate and instructive but for us they are not necessary for being a Christian. I believe that what is essential to be a Christian is to confess that Jesus is the Christ and then to live life in obedience to what he taught. Our faith rests upon the crucifixion and resurrection of Christ. Everything else adds understanding to that.

Prayer is very important, too. What God has done is to teach us how to pray. I think God teaches—and this is interesting—so many different cultures over so many thousands of years have prayed—so I think it's something that's created in the system. It gives us a way to verbalize, to focus on communicating with God, so He knows what we want. But prayer is not magic. We cannot use prayer to manipulate God because He sees into our hearts and knows our motivation.

Christianity is a religion that is founded on historical criteria and that criteria is that Jesus was a man. He lived in Palestine at a given point in time. As Christians we are faced with a choice! If the life and death and resurrection of Jesus was not historical, then we as Christians are fools. Paul said that in 1Cor 1:18-25, especially verse 18:

> For the message about the cross is foolishness to those who are perishing, but to us who are being saved, it is the power of God. (NSRV)

So we are either absolutely correct in asserting that Jesus is the

Christ, the risen Lord, or we are perpetrators of the biggest deception in all of history.

Certainly the risen Christ is the focus of my entire being.

I think, throughout human history there's been the story of two kinds of messiahs. I use the word messiah in the general sense of the term. People have tended to like one and not like the other. The one they like is the messiah who rides in on the horse and conquers whomsoever is their current enemy. A messiah can be a very localized event. The standard messianic model is the knight in shining armor, like an Alexander the Great or St. George. There are clues throughout all the Jewish scriptures, both the canonical and the extra-canonical scriptures. But you notice, none of those so-called messiahs are around any more. They're all dead. And most of them ended up being killed by somebody else.

The other model for the messiah is the unexpected Messiah. He shows up in Bible stories as well but he tends to have a much different impact. I think that what God was preparing humanity for was an unexpected messiah who would split history in half.

The unexpected messiah comes from a place that no one expects. He doesn't fit the model. This true Messiah is going to be different. Throughout the history of the Israelites, as the Jewish religion developed over time, the people were not observing their various covenants even though they were given the covenants and revelations from God.

But God was preparing history to be cleaved in two, to use an old phrase. God knew He had to prepare history—that is, humanity—in a certain way. I don't know the mind of God. I can't say, "Well, God decided to do it this way because of XYZ," but that's what's revealed in the scriptures. God is attempting to move human understanding, through the Chosen people with all their frailties and failings, all their faith and strength, to the point where, when God said "Now is the time; this child is born." That child would grow and someone would understand the reasons behind it and they would recognize him as The Messiah.

In fact, that's what happened, though not everybody would come to the understanding that this was God's chosen one and through him everything was going to be different throughout eternity. But as Christians we believe that Christ fulfilled the Mosaic Law and therefore he is the one true "unexpected" Messiah.

The Atonement of Christ in the crucifixion has helped me, also. For me, that act splits history right in two. Obviously, there are some things about it I don't understand at all and can't in this life. But, for God to manifest himself in such a way that he says to this group of people he's created and who have, by and large, rejected him, "Even though you reject me, I'm still going to show that I love you with one perfect act " it becomes the penultimate act of reality, and for me it grows in importance.

I know, for some Christians, that what science has discovered about the universe has been very threatening. They feel God has been pushed farther and farther away. It's exactly the opposite. The larger we discover the universe is the more astounded I am at what God is able to do. It's His universe. For God to set those things in motion and then, on one tiny planet, to have this relationship of salvation in the midst of death boggles my mind. It continues to grow in importance, in incomprehensibility.

Jesus Christ has certainly helped me to mature in my faith. I think the most important thing that Jesus has done for me in terms of my faith development has been through the process of facing choices. He has helped me to understand the implications of those choices, from very mundane things to very universal things.

The scripture which has the biggest impact on my personal faith is the Prologue of John: John 1:1-18. The thing I like about it is that it goes from the universal to the personal, from creating into being.

And the Word was made flesh, and dwelt among us, and we beheld his glory, the glory as of the only begotten of the Father, full of grace and truth.

(John 1:14, RSV)

The core of Jesus' teaching was, essentially, "You shall love the Lord your God with all your heart and mind and strength and love your neighbor as yourself." (Matt 22:37-38, RSV) In a sense we can maybe condense that. I think he is saying to us "In the midst of a world in which death is reigning, choose life." If we believe in Christ's message we need to act on it. Then God will use us to save the world.

I love the scripture in 1John 4:20:

If anyone says 'I love God,' and hates his brother, he is a liar; for he who does not love his brother whom he has seen, cannot love god whom he has not seen. (RSV)

The commandment we have from him is this: Those who love God must love their brothers and sisters, also. That's one of those distilling verses from the New Testament. There it is. It tells you.

Before I came to this hospital as a chaplain my faith was really tested. The situation had to do with myself and another person who had quite different perspectives on the same thing. I thought that my perspective was the better because of the way I was holding to the policy of the institution we worked for. The other person wanted to make some short cuts that not only played fast with the institution's policy but also set us up for some real problems in the future. Politically, he won. It reached a point of conflict where I went to my boss. A few days later he called me back into his office and said "I'm going to go with the second person's opinion." I was asked to leave.

There are times I feel really mad at God. This past year, with everything that's gone on, I've been mad at God a lot because of the injustices at work. I believe so deeply that I was the innocent party. I decided to take the high moral ground. Not to backbite. I was not going to tear down this other person, though I thought he was very wrong. The more I heard from what others had experienced from this person the more I realized that he was wrong.

It took me a while to integrate it all. Now, when I look at people who are in a medical crisis, I realize I have gone through a crisis of faith and meaning, just as they're going through a similar crisis. Only the particular of our experiences differ. The dynamics are identical. It took several months to work through my own grieving process, my consternation, my indignation.

I reached the point where I was able to, in a sense, make a resolution: I was going to try to gain as much, grow as much, learn as much as possible from my experience at the hospital. At the same time, I committed myself to do the very best job I was capable of with the gifts I have been given, to help those people in the hospital with their crises. I really feel I have grown. I can feel it in my attitudes, in the way I respond to other people. I can feel it in my actions, my desires, in the way I treat others.

I can tell I've grown in my counseling ability when a person who I'm working with comes to a clearer understanding of what they need to understand. That might be something at the level of comprehension, or something only at the level of behavior. The more I grow in my counseling I see that counseling is a part of my faith. I'm trying to help the individual find meaning and growth in his or her life.

Probably the most important gift I have been given is my ability to sit and listen and to find ways to identify empathetically with people without being patronizing or feeling superior to them: I want to feel like a friend, a pastor, the one that can perhaps help that person to find meaning and comfort in the midst of illness.

And a sense of grace. I think it's a sense of "let your light shine." The people who are in the bed—since they don't have to remember me—my role is to help them find meaning. That helps them come to terms with whatever the illness is, what it's doing to them and how they are going to live the rest of their lives. Now, for some, that's a really short time. Some of them are going to die in a day or so. Some of them will die that afternoon or that morning. But the challenge is still there.

When I was in seminary I thought about doing hospital ministry. But that really wasn't my highest priority. I felt God was opening some other doors and in fact, that is what He did. But now, here I am in this setting where I am working in a hospital and I'm grateful to be here, even when I don't like it. The intensity is almost over-whelming. What keeps me going? Well, I guess two things. One, a belief that the Spirit is going to give me the strength to get through it. I'm not there in the room by myself. And the second thing is a commitment to help the person who is ill process what is important for that individual.

When I decided to go for ordination, I knew there were some things I was going to give up. One of those was probably a large, lucrative income. But I knew the trade-offs. I decided the trade-offs were worth it. And they are, they are. It has to do with that covenantal relationship. There's one level of that when you accept Christ and you become a Christian. But when God asks you to be set apart in a particular way for service, to do his work, that's a gigantic decision to make. And I take that covenant seriously.

A key verse for me is 1John 4:7-12, which is the "God is love" passage. I think when he uses the term "passion" that is one of the manifestations of love, recognizing that divine love and human love connect in a sense of the divine.

Beloved, let us love another, because love is from God. Everyone who loves is born of God and knows God.

1Jn 4:7 NSRV

It's like what Paul says in 1Cor 13.

If I speak with the tongues of mortals and of angels, but do not have love, I am a noisy gong or a clanging cymbal. Love is patient; love is kind... love never ends.

1Cor 13:1,4,8 NSRV

I think this is one of those places where the Bible is very consistent. Jesus talks about loving one another, loving our neighbor as ourself. In John 17, the prayer for unity, Jesus talks about teaching the disciples to love one another as they love the Father. Our actions, in a sense, are just meaningless, just noise in the world, if they are not founded upon and flowing out of Christ's love for us. The Spirit helps us to love. And that is again consistent with what John is saying in the first epistle, 1John 4:7.

I am willing, if necessary, even to die for my faith. You see, that issue was resolved, in one sense, when I accepted the chance to be ordained, because I knew that one of the things I was giving up was as much earthly control as anybody can have over their destiny. And, that in fact, I knew I might be called at some point in my life, whether young or old, to walk into a situation on behalf of God and to die doing His work. That was one thing I had to come to terms with before I knelt down and had hands laid upon my head.

If, in defense of my faith I were to be asked to declare in few words the essence of my life and deepest beliefs I might just say "I believe that Jesus is the Christ, the Son of the living God and he is the Lord and Savior of the World. What do you believe?"

And after him was Shamgar the son of Anath,
which slew of the Philistines six hundred men
with an ox goad:
and he also delivered Israel.

Judges 3:31

BILL'S STORY

Birthplace: Coos Bay, Oregon   Married, three children
Family Background: Only child   Christian since age 17
Occupation: Wholesale lumber salesman, teacher   Age: 54

I THINK THE MAJOR THING CHRIST accomplished is that he was sent here
to die on the cross for our sins and to be raised up. As we talk about
accomplishments one of the things that we don't emphasize enough is
the resurrection. Without the resurrection we don't have anything. We
spend a lot of time talking about Christ on the cross, but the real thing
is the resurrection and Christ being alive. I think that's number one.
That's the big thing he accomplished here, doing that. Then you have
to go back and look at how he led his life. I think he led his life very
forthrightly. He was honest about what he did. He was very compassionate. But the other thing he did was not necessarily try to be around
only the righteous or the people who thought they were righteous. He
gave his life to those who needed help. He went out and mixed with
the public—you know—the tax collector, the Samaritan woman at the
well, Nicodemus, the man at the pool of Siloam. To me, those were the
things that he accomplished in his life. The work for us is to realize
that we're not supposed to be only in church. We're supposed to be
out mixing among people, sharing lives.

Are works necessary? I don't like to look at it as works. I see the
answer as sharing your life like Christ did. He went out to do good
things with those people who needed reaching. We need to make
sure that we spend time with people who need help. And that can be
in many, many forms. The one thing I believe about works—in the
Book of James 2:20 it says "Faith without works is dead." But the
reason for being charitable is not that we need to be: we want to be.

171

Christ was very obedient. In fact, in the Garden he asked if he could be spared, but he completed his task anyway. Obedience is very important. I do believe in obedience. Like I said, there is the caring, comforting, being out amongst the people. Jesus was obedient to what he had to do. Some of the new charismatic groups spend much time on love and not necessarily enough time on being obedient, because there are times when you need to do things when you don't feel like doing them. That's one of the other things that I've learned: I'll do it anyway, even if I don't feel like it. Sometimes I don't feel like going and teaching my class. But I find that if I submit to God and say "Hey, take me over and help me to teach," it turns out better. It's amazing how that works. So obedience and caring—Jesus was always forthright, he was truthful with people, good or bad, even though there were times he expressed his anger. So I think that the life he led was a sample of what all our lives are, other than the fact that he led a perfect life and we can't.

What does being a Christian mean to me? When I accepted Christ into my life to be my personal savior I became a Christian. I haven't always walked the Christian life. I actually accepted the Lord in 1960, so I consider myself a Christian from that time, even though I didn't walk the Christian life. I was a freshman at the University of Oregon. One of the dorm counselors had gotten me involved with the college program at the First Baptist Church locally and started introducing me to the fact that one needs a personal relationship with Christ and to be immersed in water. I remember kneeling in a room and we prayed together and after that I was baptized into that church.

I had a wonderful feeling and I got very involved with the Youth program there. I was also quite involved with the Campus Crusade for Christ for some time most of the years during school. It is a missionary youth program that is run by Campus Crusade which is still very active. They have outreach programs all over the nation and do work on campus. It's primarily a bible study program where groups gather in homes or dorm rooms or frat houses and have meetings.

I don't consider that I received much religious training at home. My mother, a long time member of the Lutheran church was a religious woman, my dad wasn't. Her father was a lay pastor who helped start several churches. My mother was quite active in her church. She taught Sunday school, she did a lot of grade school activities. She was involved in the ladies' committee and made sure I went to church every Sunday as well as to Sunday school. I was a part of the youth program there. I did that more out of a desire to please her because she wanted me to go, than because it had much meaning to me.

My father was different. I knew him very well. He lived a long time and we used to spend a lot of time together but I wouldn't say he influenced me. I watched him at his bible study and prayer and was a part of that.

I don't really feel like I learned much from them about being a Christian because I never was really exposed to the fact that you need to accept Christ as your savior, although in later years I found out my mother had done that. It just wasn't shown.

College was very productive for me. I was married during my senior year, 1964. I played football in Oregon and so I had a lot of media exposure. Because the gal I married was Lutheran we married in the Lutheran church.

When I graduated I started teaching right away and completed my Master's degree in Physical Education by 1967. My doctoral work was in anatomy and physiology. I'm a dissertation short of a Ph.D. My undergraduate major was Physical Education with a minor in science. I went on to get a Master's degree in Physical Ed and then my doctoral work was all done in anatomy and physiology. For the next seven years I taught high school physical education, but my goal in life was to be a football coach, so the last two years that I was involved in education I was back in school coaching as a graduate assistant. At the time I held a visiting professor's position in the PE department I was also doing graduate work!

Anyway, I became very active in the Lutheran church. Actually at 21 years old I was a church elder; I sat on their board. I was actually teaching confirmation classes, too but I was too young. I was not mature in my Christianity at that point to be able to handle all that I had. I wasn't happy with the life I had so I began looking around for change. I've never considered myself wanting a normal marriage routine where you each go off to your work, you come home, you sit and watch TV and this and that. I got started into that when I was really young, twenty years old but I felt thrown into all that activity. We were married seven years and we had one child together, then I went off and was coaching at the University while finishing my degree, trying to do a lot of different things.

There were a lot of things I shouldn't have done (but none were against the law). I have experimented with drugs but very little. I have always had a good moral sense in terms of how I treated people and how I lived my life. I did live it on the edge for a little while during those post-college years, drinking too much, trying to find myself. We had a house with a double car garage, two cars and a boat. We were young and all of a sudden life was too far ahead, so I suggested that we sell everything and go to Mexico for awhile, find each other and just enjoy life for a bit.

But she was too insecure. The marriage was in trouble and eventually we divorced. I did take off for awhile when I lived in my pickup and boat. I might have stayed a little more fancy free but my college advisor cornered me and said "Well, I've got a job for you. Do you want it?"

I was raised with a strong work ethic. You work and you work hard. So I couldn't say no. I always have had kind of a sense of responsibility but I didn't want a new position to be that immediate because I felt too young to be tied down.

When my wife and I divorced I really separated myself from the church because that church pretty well disowned me and it really burned me out on "the church." I didn't want anything to do with churches at all for about a fifteen year period.

When I really started coming back it was through involvement in martial arts. What really brought me back was the sense of humbleness that they teach. Martial arts helped me to understand that I was okay. Once I got started with that I began thinking seriously again but still not going to church. We moved a short distance north about that time. We had some neighbors who were active in the Christian church there and before long I was again attending church. But it didn't last long because I lost my new job. That turned into a real disaster. Eventually I was offered a good job in the city we lived in formerly and we had to return there. In the meantime I'd been visiting some churches and I ended up at this little Baptist church. I didn't really like it there because they were all older people but it has turned out that this is where I was supposed to be. It's where the Lord wanted me. It happened when we returned to our former city about seven years ago, so it's really the last seven years of my life that I have become dynamic as a Christian.

I was attending this little church but at the same time I was going through financial difficulties like you couldn't believe. We didn't know where our food would come from. We lived six months without a refrigerator—just couldn't afford it. All this time I was going to this church and all I'm doing is giving of myself, teaching, holding it together. I was needed there but from the church I never got much in return except for an elderly couple who saw me through some financial times that made a huge impact in my life. All of this has God's impact on me. Being there, what I've done for the church, what this couple did for me, have been the biggest changes in my life.

My security in life has always been money. There were times in my life when I had lots of it. In 1980 there were three of us in a partnership and we had 5 million dollars in assets. I lost all that. When I moved to northern Oregon I started to recoup all those assets but lost it all again. But my security and point was always "When I get this money then I can do these other things." I've always been a self-sufficient person. I can do whatever has to be done. But the Lord was trying to teach me that I needed to be kind of broken of those things.

It's kind of like what happened to Moses. I always look at Moses' life. He was rescued—raised in the Pharaoh's court, and if you read of his early life, he had all the comforts. The Bible tells about him being a handsome, well educated man. What does he do? He goes out and sees the Egyptian fighting with a poor worker and Moses kills him.

So what happens? He gets shoved off into the desert with his father-in-law re-educating him. Then God came to him in the bush. Moses said then "How can I do anything? I'm slow of speech." He had to get to the point where he trusted God to do what had to be done. And that's what has happened in my life. I had to get to the point where I relied on God to do for me what needed to be done.

In the last seven years that has been my story. And as I realized that and trust in that, my life has blossomed. I'm happier than I have ever been. I'm more secure, I have more peace. I may not be successful by the world's standards. My success now is what I can do for people. If I can do something for somebody, if I am able to comfort somebody…that's what matters. We are helping a couple we've recently met. He's fighting Agent Orange. She has cancer. We take them meals, and that's the biggest blessing of my life. My whole success in life now is being able to reach out and do for people. And the other thing that has changed dramatically in my life—I've been a highly competitive person. I'm still a competitive person but it doesn't matter now to me if I lose. I'm not just talking about sport activities.

I'm different in my business dealings now, in that what matters to me are the ethics of the business that I am in. I try to be honest about everything that I do. I tell people what they need to know about what they're going to buy from me. Good or bad, I try to represent it for what it is instead of trying to sell them something faulty and then dealing with it. I would rather they think of me as always being honest with them and trusting that when they get something they will know exactly what they're getting. I will make a fair profit but I don't want to gauge anybody, either.

The biggest change in my life came once I realized that I have to depend for everything I have on my Heavenly Father and my Savior, to see me through every day. I'm still struggling with the idea of making money. It's still a struggle in my life but I try to deal with that every day, because we have to survive, but my security is now in God and in Christ.

And I give great thanks to the Holy Spirit because I think that's where all of our communication comes from, the Holy Spirit. If we're filled every day and ask that we have the Holy Spirit with us, that's were our communication with God comes from. Every day. Whether it be through prayer that is answered, whether it comes from reading scripture or out of discussions with people, or from church service, it's the Holy Spirit's working through us that makes all good things happen. And the more in tune you are with that Spirit the more you're able to gain from it by being obedient, by prayer. For me, it's mostly prayer, meditation and Bible study.

A couple of scriptures come to mind: Judges 3:31 (see page preceding this chapter) has been very important to me, helping me to realize that with my tools—my talents—I still have an impact upon the lives of others for good. There are many scriptures in the book of James that I am quite fond of. One is "…faith without works is dead" (James 2:20), a controversial scripture. For me it has great meaning because I feel like I can fulfill that.

But my life has been full of trials. I vividly remember going through trials and being very angry at God. Why me? Why me? What did I ever do to deserve all this? I always led what I thought was a pretty good life, though there were periods when I just drank too much, spent too much time in the bars. But I've always taken care of my family first. When finally I started coming back to the right path I began trying to regain and renew my faith, my spirit, but that's when I got attacked the worst. That's when things really went haywire. Satan was after me all the time. He put me into bad situations. I got into a bad business situation here that was just awful. It took us down. We had the car repossessed. We had to sell our house. Things kept getting worse and I got angrier. There were times I felt so lost and alone that I just wanted to bail out.

Once you start becoming active in the gospel you really get pounded by the Adversary. I find I still get pounded because I still go through a real sense of anxiety over finances, because I work in a commission sales job, so I'm not guaranteed any money at all. I have to sell every month to generate an income and I go through a real sense of anxiety at times and that comes directly from him.

Satan didn't want me to do what I am doing now. I have been effective in my life. I've been able to help a number of people and kind of halfway hold this church together to the point that we have another church outgrowth here and I'm working with a youth group program. I did a Bible study in the jail for awhile. Being instrumental is doing all of those things.

There are some that Satan directly uses for evil. He really wants to create lots of apathy in the atmosphere, to create attitudes like "It's okay, it doesn't matter" toward right and wrong, so that people become sympathetic to things that are going on around them. Living the gospel of Christ is a matter of standing up and trying to help somebody, or influencing the legislature to be more Christian-like. Satan wants apathy in the country. You don't find him down in the taverns. His activity level is where people are trying to accomplish something for Christ.

The first thing that comes to mind when I think of my Savior is that he died on the cross so I can be saved. That is what is deep down in my heart; undying gratitude. My gratitude to him for that act lies at the bottom of my heart. From there its being able to understand that the best I can. In terms of what it means to have eternal life I don't know that I'll ever understand that until I get to that point. I'm not sure that I need to. I've gradually grown a full peace so that whatever happens in my life—it has importance but they can't take away the fact that when I die, I'm saved. That grows with me in importance every day.

Now when you think about what that means, it just means that I want to give back to be able to respond to that. I don't really feel anything else. I don't feel like I have to do anything. I want to do whatever I do. I want to do. And so in my heart, I have this sense of serving—I find it growing year by year and as I submit myself, as I become more obedient to what I read and get out of the scriptures I want to become more serving. You know, I want to do more things and my personal life, my personal needs are not as important as the needs of others. And it's not important that I go down there to church and that people take care of me. It's important that I take care of them, because as I take care of them I am getting filled.

It's like I said: It goes back to Moses. You have to trust that you're going to be taken care of. I have to tell you one interesting story. When I was going through what I thought was a lot of serious financial problems I got a call from an old friend. He'd gone to the church here. He's in the lumber business. We'd traded off and on. He called me and said "Why don't you come on down and have some pie, Bill?" He's a fair amount older than I am.

So I went out to the mill and we went out and had a piece of pie. He asked me how I was doing. I was going through my "woe is me" sad routine and here he is, seventy years old, still working, and he's saying "You know, Bill, I'm going to tell you something."

He had raised four kids. When the kids were gone, he said "It was my goal to give 40% of my income away to the Lord. I didn't ever quite reach that but I was giving a lot of it away." He had years where he made bonuses of $200,000. He's this rough, gruff guy, but he's got a heart for the Lord like you can't believe. He cries when people accept the Lord. "You know," he said. "When I came up here I got involved in investments. It was all legal. Five years after I invested the IRS reversed their procedure and came after me for a million and one half dollars in back taxes.

"All I had left was an office building here. The economy here in 1980 was very bad. People laughed at me. 'If you think you're going to sell this building, let alone sell it for cash,' they said, 'you're nuts.'

"In thirty days they were going to take away my house. The days passed. One night I just rolled out of bed, fell on the floor and said

'Lord, I give this up to you. I can't deal with it anymore.'" Here's a man who is nearly seventy years old at the time; retirement age.

Within the next two weeks the property sold and he paid his debt. But he had nothing left. He ended up working more. His wife was not in good health. I believe the Lord led me to him and to hear that story. It was an amazing lesson to me. The point is that this man was being obedient because he was giving that kind of money to the church with his heart in the right place. The most important thing to him was to lead somebody else to the Lord. It shamed me because I was worried about myself. It was just a real testimony to me to hear about that experience. But all those things kind of just contribute to who you are, contribute to strengthening your commitment, strengthening your faith and preparing you for the things that are going to happen to you or not happen to you depending on where your priorities are and what you are doing.

I know it is true that Christ died on the cross and I have put my faith in him and asked him into my life. If somebody's going to shoot me, I have that knowledge. I have looked down the face of a gun. In 1980 I was running a little lumber company. It was the last day there. Three men came in the door—we didn't deal in cash. We were fortunate that we had about $50 in petty cash in the safe, but they came in and actually laid us on the floor. They were going to tape us up. They shot the gun off. But you know, I never was in fear. I was worried about what might happen to people but I didn't have a sense of fear that I was going to die. I'm not afraid to face whatever it is when I die. I don't have any regrets. I'm not—I'm not finished with my mission here. I just have that sense that something's going to happen and I'm still in training…

I go back to that passage in Judges 3:31. I feel like no matter what I do, God is using me. It doesn't have to be for great things. I don't have to do great things. There was a time in my life where I felt like I wanted to do great things, but that was for my benefit. I mean, my sense of whatever I do always comes from what God does through me. I feel like my greatest sense of mission is to just do for people, find people and try to help them as a family, as we're doing now.

We do all we can for others, like this one family, for example. The father doesn't get around very well, the mother is going to be hobbled up. They have two teenage boys. They need some help with food, somebody to help cook and to help them around the house.

We've helped them move. We also make sure that they know that we're praying for them. They know that. We give spiritual support. I think part of my mission in life is to deal with kids. Sometimes it's most frustrating for me because they do test my patience but I do think that that's part of what I'm supposed to be doing.

I also envision myself being able to be involved in a life skills class. Being able to help people with life skills. Understanding what they've been through and how they're dealing with a lot of problems, because one of the things that we're faced with in our country and are going to be faced with increasingly is the difficulty for young people to make enough money to survive. So, you know, and in a lot of cases they don't know how to deal with that. There are a lot of people out there like that and I guess I just have a real sense of how people need help and somehow we've got to get them through their hard times.

Probably my favorite quote is from Isaiah 40:28-31:

> Hast thou not known? hast thou not heard, that the everlasting god, the Lord, the Creator of the ends of the earth, fainteth not, neither is weary? there is no searching of his understanding.
>
> He giveth power to the faint; and to them that have no might he increaseth strength.
>
> Even the young shall faint and be weary, and the young men shall utterly fall:
>
> But they that wait upon the Lord shall renew their strength; they shall mount up with wings as eagles; they shall run, and not be weary; and they shall walk, and not faint.

The important thing is—and I've used this again and again with the older people in our church—you can't grow tired, because you always have the strength to do whatever you need to do. It's real interesting. There is a period when I was in Portland, for example. I never had enough time in the day. I opened the weight room and I work and I do volunteer activities, and I always feel like I have a lot of time. I come back to this passage. "Those who hope in the Lord will renew their strength."

Once you get that trust He'll take care of you. It's a fact!

I try to do the best I can with my children. My kids are in a period of growth. They don't go to church all the time. My daughter is fourteen and has been baptized. My son is sixteen, not yet baptized, but I know that he's a Christian and he's accepted Christ. I have very good children. They are good people. They have good values. We spend a lot of time together. I mean we talk and share and do things. It's a lot of work but they treat people correctly. They're sensitive about people.

One of the things I try to tell people now is that we need to have a trust in God so we can survive. Trust not only gives us survival but becomes a huge blessing in our lives, granting peace and joy at being able to live life. Turn it into a Christlike banner—giving of yourself, being a servant.

We were talking about scriptures earlier and I think one of the greatest things is when Jesus washed the disciples' feet. The blessing there was teaching them to be able to receive what Christ could do for them. Because we worship this awesome God who has all of this power we can't comprehend. It is difficult for us to think we as individuals are worthy of being able to accept all that God has—all that there is.

When I talk to a youth group I tell them: if I can only get you to the level of faith in God which I have now you wouldn't have to go through what I did to get there. That's the one thing I would wish them to get out of what I do or through a book, through my testimony or through my teaching—if they could grasp that commitment to the Lord and learn obedience at a young age and not have to make all the mistakes.

I think they should go through trials but if they learn to accept the Lord and are obedient to him—I was not obedient for a long time. Many people are that way. They're either raised that way or they live a wild life—then all of a sudden they reach a point where they go out and experiment with the wrong things, or they become questioning of God—if they still understand deep down that Christ died for them and they need to live their lives according to his will they'll come back eventually to the fold, and that's okay to do— you're going to wander, you're going to go off, but you gotta remember that you also need to repent and get back to obedience to Christ, not fooling around any more.

I know there was a point in my life where I wasn't very mature and if it came down to being a strong witness I would be shy and I would do exactly what Peter did. Now I am at the point where—I'm very close. I'll stand up for my faith and take whatever I have to because God has been so good to me in the last few years.

I would have to say right now my favorite character in the Bible is Moses, followed by David. I think David gives us such a reason to understand the Lord's "mercy," because you have to remember that even though he 'messed up' he was God's chosen. David had probably as big a heart for God as anybody in biblical times. The thing that's so neat about David is that it gives us hope, because we're going to mess up, too, and it gives us hope that we can still accomplish all of God's work and be God's chosen.

Peter became the head of the Christian church in Jerusalem, the main church, and if you remember, he and Paul got into it. Paul wasn't teaching all the right rituals and it was real difficult for him. You think about the times and how those people were raised, particularly the Jewish people and how difficult it was for them to accept Christ, to leave the teaching of Moses. That would have been really tough because they had so many laws and this brash young Peter comes out doing all the contrary things.

You know, many times I have struggled with this. I wonder if it would have been easier to have accepted Jesus when he was there, to have watched him do all his miracles and see him in action for that short period of time. Or, is it easier for us today, after two thousand years of history, though he's not here in person. We have testimonies down through time—I almost think it's easier for us today to accept. It's difficult because of the way that we're raised.

I pray for some material things. I do pray for the ability to make enough money to survive. In our country our wants are far greater than our needs. That's a fine point that you have to be careful with. But primarily now I pray that the Lord keep me on the right track— that he fill me up and uses me for His work each day. And then I pray for others. I have a list of people that I try to pray for each day. But my primary purpose in life now is that I be used by the Lord.

In the book of Habbukuk 3:17-19 I love the scripture. Let me say it for you:

Although the fig tree shall not blossom, neither shall fruit be in the vines; the labour of the olive shall fail, and the fields shall yield no meat; the flock shall be cut off from the fold, and there shall be no herd in the stalls: Yet I will rejoice in the LORD. I will joy in the god of my salvation. The LORD God is my strength, and he will make my feet like hinds' feet, and he will make me to walk up on mine high places…

Now there is a book called "The Hind's Feet." The author writes of walking above the valley of doom, walking above your problems. The Lord gives me hind's feet. like deer being able to cross high, craggy mountains, keeping above it all, in other words, above all of our earthly problems down below. Please give me the hind's feet to be able to walk above all of that.—even though there's nothing produced I'll be joyful in the Lord because I walk above all of that in my life. The important things are in the Lord and not necessarily in the circumstances of my life.

There are so many things to remember. Read James 1.2-4.

My brethren, count it all joy when ye fall into divers temptations; Knowing this, that the trying of your faith worketh patience. But let patience have her perfect work, that ye may be perfect and entire, wanting nothing.

In other words you have got to go through this and you have to persevere and become mature. There may be times you don't feel like it, but you've gotta do it because you have to get things done so that you can become mature and complete, not lacking anything. If we continue on with that scripture, James tell us further:

If any of you lack of wisdom, let him ask of God, that giveth to all men liberally, and upbraideth not; and it shall be given him. But let him ask in faith, nothing wavering. For he that wavereth is like a wave of the sea driven with the wind and tossed. For let not that man think that he shall receive any thing of the Lord. A double minded man is unstable in all his ways.

James 1:5-8

We have choices. You take somebody who is going to cut firewood, but he doesn't know much about felling trees. A tree is lying on the ground but he goes out and fells a tree and gets killed. He's made a bad choice because he didn't know much about what he was doing. He didn't have to die. He could have cut the tree that was on the ground. I think we get ourselves in trouble when we do things we don't know much about or that we know are dangerous. We make some choices in our lives that are not right because we just choose to do that. I know there are some things that I've chosen to do in my life that have not been right. But I've repented and changed.

I don't look at it as turning around. We're always moving forward but once in a while we get off the road, taking the wrong path. We have to come back onto the right road because it leads us to Heaven…it leads us right into Heaven!

Trust in the Lord with all thine heart;
and lean not unto thine own understanding.
In all thy ways acknowledge him
and he shall direct thy paths.

Proverbs 3:5

GREG'S STORY

Birthplace: Indiana
Family Affiliation: Oldest of four sons
Occupation: Electrical Engineer

How long a Christian: Lifelong
Married, four children
Age: 39

MY CHILDHOOD WAS HAPPY for the most part. But I've always been very shy and that did give me some difficulty growing up. I was raised in a good family. They loved us. My father was gone at work a lot but my mother stayed home with the boys. Being the oldest of four boys I was responsible for them, too. My youngest brother is twelve years my junior, so I definitely had a part in caring for him as a baby.

When I was young it was very difficult for me to speak to people. My shyness was due to a natural inclination, I think, and I have always continued that. Often I felt unhappy because of that or because I wasn't communicating well with others. I wanted to communicate more, but I didn't feel accepted many times. I had difficulty with being teased. But I always knew there was a God. That's one thing I can always be thankful for because it helped support me a lot prior to the time of gaining full testimony. I didn't really put that knowledge into practice. I was very selfish, if you will. The main problem I had to overcome was just trying to think of others more and to not worry about being accepted. I was often unhappy with my social situation. I was depressed often because I felt I wasn't accepted. Being shy, you're often pushed of to the side and forgotten about. I was often forgotten. Because of my lack of self-confidence I had trouble taking advantage of the talents and abilities I had. Gaining a testimony has helped give me confidence and to know I can do things.

Verily I say unto you, Whosoever shall not receive the kingdom of God as a little child, he shall not enter therein.

Mark 10:15

The teenaged years are not easy, anyway. After I did seek out and gain a testimony it made a big difference. I was comfortable with myself after that, not worried as much about everything that went on around me. I was more secure in what I did and I knew that regardless, I had a Heavenly Father and an elder brother in Jesus Christ who loved me, so I was able to communicate much better after that. I was able to gain confidence in myself.

It took a couple of years before I really gained a testimony. I started at about fourteen years of age. It took study on my part. I wasn't real consistent at first, but as I became more consistent I was able to solidify it and receive my testimony. I actually felt the Holy Ghost speaking to me of the truth of the Gospel; that The Book of Mormon was true, that Christ lives and that Joseph Smith was a prophet. The Spirit was speaking in my heart and mind.

The Gospel made a change in my life. I definitely did things I wish I hadn't done and I had to overcome those things because they inhibited my growth. My main problem was not being at peace with myself, I think. I prayed and ask for it. I studied the scriptures and it wasn't until I did that that I started to make progress. Before that time I was left on my own and, of course, made all the mistakes. But directly receiving a testimony of the truth of the Gospel in my mind and heart, I knew. It gave me calm and peaceful feeling that sustained me while I built upon that. And after gaining a testimony I was able to keep that peace and move on.

I've had friends who have had some severe problems with drugs and other such things and they can really turn their lives around. All they have to do is start searching for truth and start caring about what answer they get and being willing to accept it.

I tried to teach my brothers that and it did make a difference, I think. If nothing else, I did share by example. My parents have commented on the difference it made in my brothers; my going on a mission for the Church when I was nineteen. My parents were converted when I was about a year old. Missionaries from The Church of Jesus Christ of Latter-day Saints contacted them. It took a year of study before they joined the Church.

I grew up in a smaller area where the Church is not real strong. The radius of our ward was approximately sixty miles, so we had people traveling over an hour to get to church. Locally, there was not a lot of membership to associate with on a daily basis.

When I was fifteen my family moved to Poughkeepsie, New York and I was quite influenced by one of the leaders in the Church—a Young Men's advisor. I was drawn to him because, more than anything else, he accepted us and had love for us. He cared for all the youth he worked with and that made a difference. He encouraged us, not by pushing, and he helped me in particular to feel I was doing okay so I could continue to move on.

That experience really helped. I mentioned earlier that I served a mission. I served in Thailand and in the Philippines. Prior to that time I had always said I would not serve a mission. I gave people various reasons but what it really it came down to was that I was afraid of going through two years in a foreign environment. But I had constant knowledge that it was what I was supposed to do. I couldn't deny it. It was made clear to me through the Spirit that I had to serve a mission.

My reliance on the Spirit of the Lord is very strong. I make a lot of mistakes on my own. I know that God wants to help us, guide us. Just like with my children. I want to guide them the right way and help them avoid mistakes and errors. I know that God is there for them and willing. It has given me comfort to receive that. Sometimes the answer is that I need to make my own decision and that is okay. That is how I came to believe The Church of Jesus Christ of Latter-day Saints is God's Church. I have a testimony. I have prayed and asked. I didn't accept blindly. When I was fourteen my seminary teacher told us that everyone is entitled to have a spiritual experience and to know of the truthfulness of the Gospel, whether it's true or false. Then you need to seek that out. I was going to church with my family and had normal rebelliousness here and there. My brothers and I found it hard to sit still, just as my nine year old son does. It's easy to say "Oh, this is boring, I don't want to be here," so I didn't accept the Gospel just on the teachings of my family. I started to look at it and to prove to myself whether it was true or false, fully willing to accept whatever answer I got. And the answer was very clear: This is God's Church. This is the organization that Christ has set up, the prophets speak for Christ and he communicates with them.

How did I get the answers? I was stubborn. Even when trying to deal with my children. My wife lets me know that. It took a couple of years. At first I took the opinion that I should be told right now if this is true or false, giving prayer with no thought or pondering ahead of time. But that way you don't communicate, though that, in itself, is a communication to let you know that to communicate with God your heart must be right. You've got to be willing to listen. And you can't just expect it to happen. You've gotta work at it.

> *Wherefore he that prayeth, whose spirit is contrite, the same is accepted of me if he obey mine ordinances.*

> *Doctrine and Covenants 52:15*

I'm of course here to gain experience and to prove to myself whether I will do what is right. That has been mainly the learning experience for me. But I have been able to help people in other ways various times through service. I think service is so important. We need to not care about ourselves but to care about others. One of the things we need to do is to share our talents, abilities and time to help others in whatever ways we can to help them overcome suffering. My wife contracted cancer a few years ago. When she went through chemotherapy we had many from the Church who helped lighten the load: They helped get the children to school, brought in food when things were most difficult. I can't thank them enough. I owe Christ service to others in the same way. That's one of the things we learned early on in my wife's treatment. Our bishop told us that we need to let others serve, too.

I'm happy with my life now. I know that I am doing what's right and that I have followed the commandments. I don't have regrets and guilt weighing me down each day and that makes such a big difference. One of the biggest blessings in my life has been repentance. Nothing of a real serious nature, but the gift of repentance takes the burdens off. And because of that I am able to have peace. Repentance allows me to get a fresh start, to move ahead, to take the lessons I have learned from my mistakes and put that behind me. Christ has suffered for us. We don't have to suffer all that all the time. Even though repentance is not easy it leaves you with a new birth afterward. The healing it provides helps to move us along in the right direction.

Faith and reality are not separate issues. There are many things we have today that were just not thought of back one hundred years ago and I know that many great things are still to come. When my parents were my age they knew things that we have just taken for granted, and my children will take for granted things that don't exist now, so I know there are things that we have not been given to understand yet. But that doesn't diminish their truth. The existence of God is there and I know that because I've felt it in communication and prayer. I've felt His presence. But you can't know that unless you experience it for yourself.

You've got to seek, you've got to pray, you've got to have faith and be receptive, not carry pride and all the things that just pull you back, hold you back. Faith is a kind of trust, trust in God and it's defined in The Book of Mormon as a hope for things that are true but are not seen. I think that describes it better than anything I could say. I work with people who are educated. They want to look at things philosophically. There comes a point where you've got to believe because there are things that we just cannot explain by knowledge. It's got to be by faith.

I have a friend in the Church who told me of the difference faith made in his life. He had previously been into drugs and attempted suicide several times. I can't remember how he was exposed originally. As he was taught he gave those things up. He was able to turn his life around. He is not a rich man. He struggles financially in many ways but he knows. He's got that faith. He knows that the Gospel is true. That can be felt by all of us reading this Book of Mormon. I hope they keep this in mind. It doesn't matter what they have done, they can turn around. God loves us and he wants us to be happy. I know another man who is not a member of the Church who I worked with. He was an alcoholic. Many things in his life were just wrong. In turning to Christianity he was able to totally leave that behind. He stopped smoking and drinking immediately. Once he knew Christ he turned his life around.

Jesus had his trials with the Adversary. He recognized him. He didn't flaunt the devil. He knew the power of the devil. If he had not been worthy he could not have performed the miracles he did. He could not have cast out devils and other miracles. When he fasted for forty days and nights, then was tempted by the devil, Jesus' responses are the best example of how to deal with him.

He received basically the temptations we all receive; first, weakness of the body. He could have made bread out of stones. He had the power to do so, but that would have been succumbing to the temptations and weaknesses of the flesh. And Satan tempted him to use his power, to cast himself from the pinnacle to prove he was the Son of God, but it finally got to the point where he said "Satan, get behind me. Leave me alone." That's what we have to do, too. It's very clear. We know when things that are wrong come into our minds or come before us. We have to draw the line and say "I don't want any part of that." I found it effective in my own life. I recognize the wrong of things and I just say "Go away." It goes away because I just close the door. It's almost as easy as it sounds but it takes a lot of patience. I have learned self-discipline doing that.

Humility is also a necessary ingredient in fighting evil. Christ taught that constantly. He said "...become as little children..." (Matt 18:3) Children are teachable and that is what humility really brings. We need to be teachable. Lack of humility is concern for self, I think, and that is one of the things I had to understand. My shyness was having too much concern for myself. There's a lot of people I know who are educated. They base everything on what they learn out of books, but that is pretty limited. Limited by believing in only what men know. God knows everything. He created the world. He created us. We've got to have that humility of willingness to exercise faith.

I think we've got to prove our faith. The story of Job is a good example. He was a man who was perfect in many ways. But he was tempted and made to suffer many things to see if he would still follow God. I have had trials in my life that were difficult. It takes faith to get through that. And I know it could have gone either way. My wife's problems have tested us. Fortunately, she's still here. She has no risk factors in any way. The cancer just popped up. It took a year of surgery, chemotherapy and the works. Faith has strengthened me so I can't say I'm sorry, because it has been good for our family. It helps focus us better. As difficult as it was and still is because it is something that never completely is cured, we know what needs to be done. I appreciate every day with my wife. I appreciate that she is here to help our children because I couldn't do it all myself.

Now faith is the substance of things hoped for, the evidence of things not seen.

Hebrews 11:1

A lot of the pain and unhappiness we have we bring on ourselves by our choices and by the way we look at things. I could have easily have blamed God for my wife's experiences with cancer and have been miserable but I chose not to do that. By choosing we reach make or break points where we either progress or fall behind and lose what progression we have made. I know that God loves us and that is why He provided the Savior for us and all the ways to come back to Him. Having children of my own—well, you want to do everything for them, but if you do that they're not going to learn. So you do what you can, provide them with the way and make sure that they know where true happiness is.

Christ had to go through the same pains and difficulties that we all do, that's why he came into the world as he did, as an infant, and not as an adult. He had to learn to walk and talk, and he had to learn step by step who he was, then what his mission was, what he had to accomplish and how to do that and to communicate with our Father in Heaven. Of course, he got to the point, though he was the Son of God, that he was able to draw upon that full power. He knew his mission was to take upon himself the sins of the world that we can all overcome them. Without that we're trapped. Being imperfect, there's no way to meet the entrance requirements for Heaven, which is to live with our Father in Heaven. We essentially strive to become perfect, and Christ taught us by his example how to be perfect, the things that we should do. He suffered on the cross and died so he could be resurrected and all mankind could be resurrected to receive immortality as a gift from him.

He taught as he thought was needed. He taught parables so people who were there could understand. Many times it takes analogies for us to see clearly what something means. He spoke through stories many could understand. He also spoke the Gospel in parables sometimes because those who were not prepared to follow him, were not ready to understand everything he said. Until they were able to understand they would not be fully accountable for those principles. I see it as comparable to children, who have to go through steps in their progression and learning. So do we, in the Gospel. We have to train our spirits just as we train our minds and bodies. There are many things I am coming to understand better now than I did when I was a missionary.

My mother has always had a strong spirit about her. She gave everything. She did not care about her personal needs much. She did everything for her sons. She continues to care and provide for us to let us know of that love. My mother always believed in me and encouraged me. She let me know that I was capable of doing what I wanted to do. She helped support me in doing that. She didn't know what I needed to do, but there is support and strength there. She has done that for my brothers and she does that today, to support my father in his righteous endeavors and the callings that he has had. She is very special in my life because of that. She bore her testimony to us to let us know of her beliefs and that helped me.

My dad was a challenge to me, sometimes. I have been very close to my father, too. But the biggest problem I had was not spending enough time with him as a child. I would feel jealous of him. He spent a lot of time away at work and my brother, the one youngest after myself, was more dominant and his interests were more along my father's lines in some ways and that was difficult for me, one of the things I had to overcome, not to have jealousy. I know that my parents love me for who I am and they love my brothers for who they are and it is going to be different for each of us. But that doesn't make any of us worth less. We do what we can. I see many people who don't have the capabilities to do what the world is going to bless them for, but they do so many other things. They care for others and they help. Just being able to make people happy sometimes is a great gift.

I am not sure how to formulate it, but I know that everyone needs to be happy. The only way to be happy is to forget about the world, about things. Forget about pride. What you really have to do is to gain a relationship with God and build from that. He will show you. He will help us overcome our problems, take us from what step we're at right now and help us to move on, to grow. Things that we will face are not always going to be easy. Sometimes he'll put things before us to make us grow and we think "Oh, why do I have to go through that?" But you've gotta do it. And you'll be helped as needed. God loves us and he'll help us if we ask. So the main thing I would say to people is "Don't keep God out of your life."

To people who say there's no togetherness after this life, no families in the eternities, I'd tell them to look at themselves and see where their true happiness and joy is. For me, it is in my family. The experiences you really cherish are with your loved ones, your parents, your siblings, your wife and children. I can't imagine having full happiness in the eternities without a family, in that association. God Himself is our Heavenly Father. That is a family association. We're taught that Christ is our elder brother and we are all linked together. We need that link with families. It is something that brings and keeps you closer.

I was about 24 when I married. She was the first woman I cared for that deeply. I had dated somewhat. There were others that I thought I cared for but I didn't know them that well. When you're young your mind is clouded many times by the physical feelings you have and the attractions. We have to get beyond that. My wife is someone I love and respect and it's reciprocated. That's the wonderful thing. I knew my wife for close to a year before I even dated her. She can tell you some of the frustrations she had that I didn't give her enough attention during that time but she had patience with me and in going through dating others I finally went to her and gave her a chance. Once we really spent time with each other we felt each other's spirits and there wasn't much more to be said. We did wait for probably another year before we got married and we have a temple marriage. Our patriarchal blessings are complementary. Her blessing was that she would have a mate of her choice and mine that it would be someone of the Lord's choosing, so basically she made her choice and it took me a while to come around.

I think her problems with cancer have made her more spiritual. There is a definite difference. When we first started treating the cancer and things were getting worse each step we went, I felt it might be fatal. After turning the problem away from just ourselves to the families and the ward and letting the people in the Church know, through those prayers everything was changed. The progression from that point was like the difference between night and day.

Love makes the difference. Love is caring without really concern for yourself. It's caring about an individual with no conditions. Charity is also defined as the true love of Christ and he showed that many times, loving the sinners. He suffered for us. He didn't have to suffer on the cross. He didn't have to go through the suffering in the Garden of Gethsemane. It was because of his love for us. Heavenly Father strengthened him as He could because God knew that His Son had to go through the suffering. He sent the Holy Ghost to strengthen him in the Garden. Jesus had to go through these things. That was charity, to help lessen his suffering. But that was his choice, also. He put it before his Father and said "If it be thy will, remove the cup from me." It was the will of the Father to continue on with His sacrifice.

Jesus answered them, and said, My doctrine is not mine, but his that sent me. If any man will do his will, he shall know of the doctrine, whether it be of God, or whether I speak of myself.

John 7:17

Sometimes God takes someone from us we deeply love. That's something that is very difficult for people. But we all have to die. It's made very clear in the scriptures, too, that things are better with God and Christ. You don't have to suffer the pains in daily life that we do here. You've got peace there. You've got the presence of God and the experiences of some of the prophets and their visions of seeing Christ and feeling the closeness of his love. We're selfish to try to keep all of our close loved ones here with us. Where they go they're not unhappy. They go to live with God. If they're righteous they'll go to a place called Paradise and wait for the Resurrection. As they wait there they have support of others who believe as they do. It's a wonderful place, although they miss having the experience of their bodies, also. That will be the blessing we'll have after the Resurrection, that of immortality. That means never dying again, never having the pains we now have. Our bodies will be perfected and reunited with our spirits. I believe that will allow us to perfect our spirits more, also.

The Bible has many answers but the other answers are in the latter-day scriptures that have come forth. The Book of Mormon is a particular help to me and the other scriptures that have come forth through our Church have clear answers to our questions.

God loves everyone and I feel that he wouldn't isolate people based solely on their heritage or their location. The Book of Mormon is a record of people who lived on the American continent. There were people on the Asian continent and in many parts of the world in Jesus' time. The Book of Mormon is a record of the prophets and their experiences and prophecies. I know it's true because I prayed about it and received a strong witness. It fact, that is really what brought a turnaround in me and directed me toward living a life following after Christ, not seeking after things of the world.

The Doctrine and Covenants gives all the directions for restoring the Church and that's important from an administrative standpoint. It contains a record of many experiences of the Saints, too. We can see how people grew and learned. The Prophet Joseph Smith was not trying to hide his errors and mistakes. He was rebuked many times and the Doctrine and Covenants recorded the mistakes he made and showed him what he needed to do to overcome them. So that's also instructive in my life, to see that there are things that need to be done universally.

And now as I said concerning faith— faith is not to have a perfect knowledge of things; therefore if ye have faith ye hope for things which are not seen, which are true.

Alma 32:21

Believe in Christ, seek him out. Lay aside your pride and go for it. It's not worth it to seek the things of this world. We're not going to have it beyond this. It won't make a difference. But seek out Christ and count on him as a friend. Not as a friend that you go and goof around with, but someone who is a mentor and a teacher. Someone you can count on unconditionally for all his love. You can look at the structure of the authority that has been restored. I've had that experience. I lived on the East Coast and I've seen the places—where the priesthood was restored to Joseph Smith. I felt the Spirit there. It is a wonderful thing.

God saw mankind was ready as to begin receiving that authority again—that it could be reestablished on earth. I can't imagine how bleak it must have been after all those years of apostasy to the time it was finally restored. The programs are inspired. They are there to help us in so many ways. The unique thing about the Church is that we are given responsibility. Everyone has responsibility and we have to follow through and take our responsibilities to lead and teach. As we do that we teach ourselves—we learn a whole lot more. We don't depend on someone who has ministerial training. There are no professionals. We are all dependent on our backgrounds, our experiences and most of all, upon the Spirit. When people attend with an open mind they can feel the Spirit. Everything is done through love. It's not done with force. The purpose is not to gain from the people in the Church except to grow together, to overcome whatever we need to, together. Looking at it, it helped bring people in our ward unit here closer together to do that service—holding a fast as a whole ward really made a difference.

I know this Church is of God. In the scriptures it says "By their fruits ye shall know them." (Matt 7:16; Luke 6:44; 3Ne 14:16,20) And I know just by looking I can see definitely that to follow Christ through this church is the right direction, that good has come from following Christ's Gospel.

Christ said basically to repent and follow him. He gave us the way to follow, showed us and taught us what we need to do. Follow all the commandments he's given us. Essentially, love God, follow God. When Jesus was asked what the greatest commandment was, he said it was to love God and then to love your fellow man, the second great commandment. Then you've got the Ten Commandments, which were given to Moses, which are very simple and basic to my belief. Those are things you must have ingrained in you: for instance, respect for life. If you have that already ingrained in your personality you won't be tempted or have to overcome your problems with it. That is true with all things. I have made a choice and now I know what is right and wrong and I know what I'll do in a given situation, so it's not as difficult to make decisions.

Master, which is the great commandment in the law? Jesus said unto him, Thou shall love the Lord thy God with all thy heart, and with all thy soul, And with all thy mind. This is the first and great commandment. And the second is like unto it,

Thou shalt love thy neighbour as thyself. On these two commandments hang all the law and the prophets.

Matthew 22:36-40

Making decisions because I know the Gospel has made life easier for me. Going through school was difficult for me. Getting my education was not easy, but putting my faith and trust in God and asking for His help helped me get through that. It was a long process. It took me longer than some people to get through, but again it was putting my faith in God and my children. You don't know what to do with your children sometimes. Just constant prayer for guidance, inspirations, they help me do what's right for the children. Each child gets a different personality, but they get to the point where sometimes you just don't know what to do to help them. Without the guidance of God I would really be at a loss for that.

We have daily scripture study and prayer and that's been the biggest teacher of anything for our children. We teach them the Articles of Faith. When our children were younger we weren't in the habit of studying the scriptures with them each day. We just prayed with them each day. But it made such a difference to study the scriptures with them every day. It's helped them to be better readers. We've worked with our children as son as they could talk. When they find words that are difficult to say, they learn how to say them. I think teaching them to read has been one of the biggest teaching tools for our children. They understand things so much more than when I was a child. We had prayer in my family. It wasn't as regular as my wife and children have had it, but we didn't have the daily scripture study when I was a child, and that would have made a big difference because it brings the words of Christ into your life every day and helps keep minds focused upon him.

Tithing is something I have a testimony of, also. It takes faith to pay tithing. If you try to analyze it and look ahead, I don't think I could afford everything I need to take care of my family, but yet in paying tithing everything works out. More important than that I am giving back some of what has been given me and it helps me from keeping my thoughts entirely upon the world. We can get so caught up in our possessions. It takes away from the Spirit when you do that. They are necessary, there's nothing wrong with that. That's one of the things we have to learn here, the right balance. Tithing helps do that, helps teach you that balance you need to get back to Father in Heaven and He'll just continue blessing you more and more when you do that.

The greater law is to give everything to God and your fellow man. To live in total harmony and not seek after worldly pride and possessions but to have what we need and to continue to move on and to progress in what we need to do instead of accumulation of worldly things is the benchmark of whether we are successful or not. Christ told his apostles to come follow him and to not give thought for their daily bread and that they would be provided for, just as the flowers of the field and the animals are provided for. We are told to come to Christ with a broken heart and a contrite spirit. That makes a big difference because you can't communicate with God in pride.

I feel much closer to God in His temples. The temple is a wonderful place. You feel the spirit of God. You don't have the worries of the world. There you are relieved from those worries and that strengthens you and it helps in many ways. When my wife got cancer I was working at the temple as an ordinance worker and so was she. I think that helped. We were there often and it helped prepare us. You don't have to worry about the stress of daily life, of trying to support your physical needs, dealing with all the hatred and attacks you may get in the normal world. People trying to take advantage of you and such. You are there and you're dealing with God, instructing you, teaching you, and you feel the Spirit so strongly.

It can be a beautiful day outside. The sounds of the world are out there. When you enter the temple there's the sound of the Spirit. I can't explain it. Your worries are lifted, you know that everyone in your family is taken care of okay. You're there to perform a service for others. Clear, more purified without the normal more worldly things around you. It just helps you to think in a higher plane. I've gotten many answers in going to the temple. My mind has been relieved from those normal burdens. I can think more clearly and be what God wants me to be.

Happiness can be very temporary. You eat a food that you really like. That makes you happy for a short time. Joy is a peace and a feeling that you have. It's like when you walk in the temple. You experience joy and it is just a peace. You feel the love of God. You live that time in the Spirit. You just feel it within your soul. You know the difference. It's different than just knowing the answer to a question, to a math problem or some other such educational pursuit. You feel it at a different level. It's not just in your mind but in your whole body. Until you experience that you really cannot describe it. You get a tingling throughout your body. That's the Spirit being with you.

Through attending the temple I hope our family will be together forever. Exaltation is being privileged to live with God for eternity after you're dead, to be raised to experience resurrection as Christ did and then live with God forever as a family, with your wife and children. (See Doctrine and Covenants Section 76) To be truly exalted is to have all of that family relationship and to have that ability to continue as a family. If we are alone and have no family there's still hope for us. Jesus said we're blessed based on our righteous desires. If you are living worthily you will given that opportunity after this life to be in a family to have that relationship. There's only going to be so many people that turn out worthy enough to live with God. They're going to then receive additional blessings by having additional family relationships.

Christ made this all possible through the Atonement. I described earlier my feelings of repentance. That gift is provided to us by the Atonement of Christ. He suffered for the sins of all men, all that ever were and ever will be. I can't imagine the suffering he went through. I've gone through individual repentance and it is suffering we have to experience. It is anguish of mind and regret for the mistakes we've made and knowing that we can receive forgiveness for what we do, as it is God's will. It just keeps me going. It makes life worth while. If you make a mistake you don't have to carry that burden forever.

Christ suffered for all men. You have to go through repentance in your life to put that to use. His resurrection is a free gift to all men.

We are saved from death by that and that will happen to all but the most wicked of people. We are also saved by our works. They are most definitely necessary to be saved. Christ had a follower come to him who was a rich man who basically professed his faith in Christ and wanted to follow him. He asked "What do I have to do?" Jesus told him to sell all that he had and to follow him. This young man couldn't do that. He loved the things that he had more. That was a real tragedy for him, but it is a good example that we have to do more than just profess to believe. We actually have to follow and do the things that he says. The scriptures help us to do that.

Both Abraham and Moses, in The Pearl of Great Price, described the experience of Adam and Eve in the Garden and it explains to me pretty well the Creation. It's explained in The Book of Mormon in various parts and in the Doctrine and Covenants we have also the full Plan of Salvation, as we call it in the Church, which really describes the purpose for us being here and the tests that we'll be going through. The reason we're here is for our growth to prove ourselves and to gain an eternal reward—we must be able to prove worthy to live with God.

I don't think that merely saying that you believe in Christ proves anything. My children, many times, they'll have a squabble. I say "Apologize." You can tell whether it's sincere or not. It's the same thing as following Christ. Just by saying that you believe in Christ is not enough. If you really believe in Christ you'll want to follow him, to do what he has said, to follow his example. And his example is doing good works to help others. He didn't care for himself. He cared for others. It says in the scriptures that when you lose yourself you'll find yourself. That's exactly what Christ did. He was defined by his service to others.

He was made greater by the service he gave. He said "No greater love hath man than to lay down his life for his friends." (John 15:13) That is what Christ did. We also must be willing to do the same thing. I think that applies to all of us. We have to be as Christ, to try to follow him. To merely say that you are saved by only professing belief is not enough. We are saved to an extent as a free gift, without doing anything. Past that, you've got to earn it. What you earn is the right to live with God. And to live with God you've got to strive to be as righteous as God is. Those who are not clean and pure cannot tolerate his presence. You've got to prove that and as you do that, you change your way of thinking. Your whole way of feeling changes as you give service. That's absolutely necessary.

Things are not easy on our own. I know God will be there for me as He has while I went through a mission. Something I said earlier: On my own I wouldn't have done it, I couldn't have done it, yet I knew that I had to do it. It was expected of me and I was able to help some people and to bring them the Gospel, the joy that it is and as it is with all things, I now have current responsibilities. I have to speak in the Church often. That is something I could never have done alone. When I was a youth—to get up and speak at all was an amazing difficulty. But I don't even give it a thought now. I'm strengthened by it, supported by it. It's the Spirit.

I have been asked if I would be willing to die for what I believe in. I would like to say "Yes," but you never know until you're faced with that. That's not something I would look forward to doing because I know there's a lot here to live for. But it's more than me— my family depends on me, but I would be willing to do that if it had to be done. Life is respected and it's not something that God would have us treat lightly. I think the best example of that is Abraham with his son, Isaac. He was asked of God to sacrifice his son to prove that he would. And then the requirement was taken back. He didn't have to suffer that anymore. That's the lesson to us, also. Our Father in Heaven had to sacrifice Jesus Christ and he had to go through the suffering and pain. God loved him as any father loves his son.

I know and accept the truth of the miracle of the birth of Jesus Christ. The way I know that it is true is again through my testimony, the prayers I have had. It has been witnessed to me that Christ is the Son of God and I know that he came to the earth for our benefit. The witness again is a strong feeling plus the words in my mind. It is almost like a whisper of a voice telling me the truth of things, answering my prayers.

My essential testimony is that God lives, that He really wants us to succeed, and by succeeding, he really wants us to live with Him. That's really what it's all about, to be worthy to live with Him and to learn those lessons we need to know. He's provided us our Savior, He's provided us our Church, all these things to help. And prayer. Prayer has been with humanity from the beginning of time. So he has never left us on our own. If we would just exercise prayer. I know that God lives, that Jesus Christ is our Savior and that he loves us. I know that we can receive the strength from the Holy Ghost. The Church of Jesus Christ of Latter-day Saints is the Church of Jesus Christ on the earth today. It is restored and has the fullness of the gospel therein. This I give in the name of Jesus Christ, amen.

And we talk of Christ,
We rejoice in Christ,
We preach of Christ,
We prophesy of Christ

And we write according to our prophecies,

That our children may know
To what source they may look
For a remission of their sins.

2Ne25:26

JOHN T's STORY

Born: Anderson, South Carolina	Married with children
Family:Only son of three living children	Lifelong Christian
Profession: Aerospace Engineer	Age: 47

FROM MY EARLIEST CHILDHOOD MEMORIES, I have believed in Jesus Christ. My mom was converted to the Church of Jesus Christ of Latter-day Saints when she was fourteen, and so she took us kids to Church. I don't recall much about Church experiences from those times, except just a few incidents; like Mom singing little songs to us in the car, like "I love you, a bushel and a peck, you bet your pretty neck I do..." And I dimly recall being left in the nursery or primary, and feeling great anxiety at being left by my mom. We lived near Columbia, South Carolina at the time.

When I was three or four, I remember my mom kneeling beside me at bedtime to teach me to say my prayers. She taught me the little children's prayer, "Now I lay me down to sleep, I pray thee, Lord my soul to keep; if I should die before I wake, I pray thee, Lord, my soul to take. Amen." From that day till now, I could probably count on one hand the number of nights I may have missed my bedtime prayer. When I got a little older, I started adding my own words onto the end of that little recited prayer, and soon dropped the recitation altogether and replaced it with my own words.

My dad is non-LDS, and was not at all cooperative with my mom about Church. He criticized her Church activity and tried to pressure her into quitting. He was raised as a Baptist, and felt prejudice and animosity towards the Mormon Church, even though he himself had very little if any religious beliefs. He is basically an agnostic, very worldly and secular in his outlook on life. Before my parents were married, he feigned interest in the Church and pretended kindly regards toward the missionaries, but just about as soon as the wedding was over, his true feelings came out. In my adult life I've seen several other marriages take the same turn, where faithful Church members think their future spouse will share their religion, only to learn the sad pretense after the wedding.

When I was about eight years old, we lived in Greenwood and attended Church in Abbeville, South Carolina. And I remember one particular Church conference meeting there, where Brother Ginn came down from Gaffney and spoke. I don't recall what he said, but I clearly remember feeling very spiritually excited and invigorated by his talk. I clearly understood and felt thrilled with the message. I know the Holy Spirit touched me that day.

At that age, I should have been eligible for baptism into the Church; but my dad said no. I was disappointed, but resigned myself to wait till I was old enough to get baptized on my own.

I have a cousin from Montana who was called to serve a mission for the Church in South Carolina while I was in high school. This fulfilled a promise given in his patriarchal blessing. Mormon kids, when they are in their late teens, can go to a patriarch of the Church, a man who is specially ordained for this calling, who places his hands on their heads and by inspiration gives them a patriarchal blessing, which gives them guidance for their lives. My cousin Anthony's patriarchal blessing had prophetically told him that he would be called on a mission to serve among his kindred in the land of his family ancestry, which was South Carolina. In those days the President of the Church prayed for inspiration as to where to send each missionary, and then issued a calling according to that inspiration. Now I'm pretty certain that President McKay, when he called cousin Anthony, did not have access to that patriarchal blessing, yet he called him to serve in South Carolina just as that blessing had prophesied.

After a year or so on his mission, Anthony was assigned as a District Leader over the missionaries in my home town. Whenever he came over to visit them, he would also come over to my house and ask me if I wanted to get baptized into the Church. I told him that I did, but I was sure that my dad would not let me, and then Anthony would needle me to ask my dad for permission. I'd say something like, "Well, maybe I'll ask him later." Each time he visited, Anthony would ask me, "Did you ask your dad yet?" I'd answer.

"Well, no." I was very much afraid of my dad because he was capricious and drank a lot, and for no clearly defined reason that a kid could figure out, he'd get mad and give me a spanking. So I didn't want to approach him about anything in the way of decision making or requests for permission for anything. But finally, after a bit of pressure from my cousin, I worked up the nerve. I walked into his bedroom where he was resting on the bed, and timidly asked my dad for permission to get baptized. I expected him to yell at me or something, but he just quietly said Well if that's what you really wanna do, then go ahead. I was very relieved and very happy. This was right after I graduated from high school, and I was about three months short of my eighteenth birthday. A few days later my cousin Anthony baptized me in a lake, and I was confirmed and given the gift of the Holy Ghost by my maternal grandfather, Papa Smith, whom I dearly loved and admired. My dad was not present.

When I was growing up, a very large percentage of the kids around me, with whom I associated in my neighborhoods and schools, seemed to be what you might call bad boys. They talked about and did all kinds of things contrary to Gospel principles. My experiences with them affirm to me the correctness of the Church doctrine that the age of accountability for children arrives at age eight. Before age eight, it was as though the Lord was shielding me from all knowledge of evil and temptations. But the moment I turned eight, bad little boys in my neighborhood began teaching me every imaginable wrong thing and urging me to participate in them all. It was as though the devil had finally been unleashed upon me to do his worst. Those boys were a bad influence on me in a big way, but somehow I managed to disengage myself from their influences, to steer away from that and to follow a course that seemed like it was ingrained into my soul from the very beginning. The older I got, the more I felt the need to distance myself from those kinds of peers and follow the Lord. My conscience spoke to me very strongly, not in words and not with guilty feelings, but almost like the electronic navigation system that guides a spacecraft in flight to a distant planet, it guided me towards a better way.

Christian people often speak of a testimony of Jesus Christ. I would like to express what I think a testimony is. To me, having a testimony means that you can testify, as a sworn witness. I liken it to a court of law where a witness gives a testimony of something he has seen and knows. In the Gospel sense, a testimony is similar in that if you have a testimony, you can stand as a witness and testify of Gospel truths that you know. The way you can do this is that the Holy Ghost or Holy Spirit has testified to you, and that you have had spiritual or religious experiences by which you know that the Gospel is true. With that knowledge you can then testify that you do know. He reveals these Gospel truths to you in ways that are beyond the five senses; it is not seeing, hearing, tasting, smelling, or tactile feeling. It goes beyond that. It's a warm, loving, sweet feeling that enters your mind and heart and clearly and powerfully tells you that Jesus Christ is the Savior, the Redeemer, the Messiah, the divine Son of God. It testifies that he has risen from the dead and he qualifies to be worshipped and called God, the everlasting Father, the Prince of Peace. When the Holy Spirit has born witness of these things to us, then we can also testify of them. I can so testify of Jesus Christ and his Gospel.

The testimony that I have came on gradually, from my first exposure to the Gospel as my mom took me to Church as a very little child. I can't point to any one event or any one occasion where my testimony suddenly formed, as in the manner of some Christians who say that they were saved on such and such a date. Rather, it's like I have always had a testimony of Jesus Christ, to some extent. It has been growing throughout my life. Of course, certain events in my life have added to it, like taking a big step up some stairs. But I almost feel as though I was born with a testimony. To me, it seems that everything I ever heard about the Gospel and about Christ and such when I was a child, I just felt Of course! This is true, it's gotta be true; it's the real thing. It's just innately infused into my being. It's like it struck a resonant chord within me. I just always felt that it was true.

Not that I never had any doubts, though. Occasionally doubts have arisen, and I've contemplated whether the things that I believe might possibly be untrue. I've occasionally wondered Is there really a God and is there really a Jesus Christ, His Son? And I've wondered Was Joseph Smith really a prophet and is there really life after this life? Those doubts have crossed my mind: what if it isn't true, then what would happen? But even though I've contemplated doubts here and there, still I have always felt the firm conviction that the Gospel is true, that there never has been really substantive doubt on that. I've doubted my own self and my own worthiness much more than the truthfulness of the Gospel. Whenever doubts have arisen, I haven't had too much of a dilemma because I would always think back on experiences that I have had, spiritual experiences that have affirmed to me that my beliefs are valid, as I remembered that this or that spiritual experience happened, and so what's the problem, where is this doubt coming from?

Now, I don't claim to have lived a perfect sinless life. Not by a long shot. Only Jesus has ever done that, and there will never be anyone else that will be able to do it. I've done plenty of foolish and shameful sins. But I always have felt a desire to be righteous, and to follow the Lord and keep his commandments. Whenever I have done wrong, I have always felt that I wished I had not done it, and that I intended to do better, and I longed and hungered for more strength to rise above temptations. The main core of myself has always been consistent in returning to doing the right thing. From the earliest awakenings of my conscience as a child, I have always wanted to do the right thing. To me that has always been a higher priority than peer acceptance or having fun, or whatnot. Knowing the Gospel teachings, knowing that everyone is born with a conscience, the light of Christ, has clarified to me why I am that way, and has motivated me to culti-vate that in my life and to do better. My belief in Jesus is the driving force in strengthening my allegiance to principles of right.

Since my family life was a bit rocky during my childhood, I didn't feel really able to relate to God or Jesus as Father images in my youth. My limited perception of Fatherhood did not help me to relate to the love of God the Father and His Son, Jesus all that much. I had not consciously tried to model myself after any personage, not Christ or any man, till I became more mature. I had few if any heroes in my life, since I had felt let down and disappointed by my relationships with several adults. But there were a few influential people who helped my spiritual growth quite a bit. My mom, her parents, and a few special teachers and leaders at Church really helped build my testimony a lot, and I admired and appreciated them all. But as I was making decisions about my life and responding to experiences of my youth, I was not consciously setting Jesus Christ as my role model or father figure, although I definitely did believe in him and tried to keep his commandments. Whether due to my experiences or just my own nature, I tended to respond more to principles than to personages. When I learned Gospel principles, something inside my soul said Yes! That principle is valid, it really makes sense. Later, as I matured more and started to think about it as I read the scriptures and learned more of Christ, the man, and Christ the God, the Savior, I learned to think more about him as an individual; His thoughts, his feelings, his emotions, and his example. In that gradual maturing process I felt that I was drawing closer to him as years went by.

After I was baptized and received the gift of the Holy Ghost, I felt a definite, manifest difference in my life. I found that it gave me noticeably greater strength to resist temptations. And I found that I had more spiritual energy to rise above spiritual laziness and lethargy. I distinctly noticed it and felt grateful for it.

After high school I wanted to go to BYU or Ricks College (a Church-owned junior college in Idaho). My Dad wanted me to go to Clemson, where he had gone, and tried to prevail upon me to do that. But I knew that there were very few Latter-day Saints at Clemson, and I wanted to mingle with as many of them as possible in college. At Ricks College I was cousin Anthony's roommate, and I got a job on campus as a part-time janitor, cleaning toilets and mopping floors to pay as much of my expenses as I could, and my mom worked and sent me money too.

After that first year at Ricks, I came home to South Carolina, and decided to serve a mission for the Church. It was a tough decision because I had a girlfriend from Idaho that I wanted to see again at Ricks, thinking I would like to marry her. But I knew I should serve, and so I went. My dad was not at all pleased with this decision, and I remember his exact words to me as he tried to dissuade me. He said it was a foolish waste of time and money. But I went and served the Lord on a mission.

During the first two weeks of my mission, I remember starting to feel distinctly inadequate for the job. I had always admired missionaries as these wonderful guys who were nearly perfect, and there I was, just regular old John T., masquerading as a missionary by wearing a suit and tie and holding scriptures in my hand. And I wondered to myself, Am I fit to be doing this? Am I good enough for this? I had some really discouraging thoughts. One night I went to bed thinking about those things, and I felt some presence come to me, almost seeming to whisper in my ear, saying things like John, you're no good; you can't succeed at this. You aren't important at all; you won't make a difference. If you were to just drop off the face of the earth right now, nobody would really miss you. You're just an insignificant one of many billions of unimportant little people that even Heavenly Father wouldn't even miss. A melancholy, sad feeling seemed to sweep over me, and I cried myself to sleep.

But then, within a day or two, I had a very special spiritual experience that swept all that aside. I prayed a humble prayer in behalf of a lady who was investigating the Church, and as I concluded the prayer, it was answered immediately, while the words were still fresh on my lips. I felt this very powerful, extremely wonderful and sweet and loving feeling flood into my heart and my mind as though the Lord had opened up the door to my heart and poured it straight in there. It was a pure love, a pure, clean, peaceful, exciting, exhilarating feeling that powerfully communicated to me the presence of the Holy Ghost and the love that the Lord has for me. I felt almost as if I were lifting off the floor with this feeling, I felt so happy and so wonderful. It was the first time in my life that I had ever felt that feeling and it was very, very strong. Since then I have had it again on several different occasions, sometimes even stronger, but often not as strong. Now I get it to some extent almost every time I read the scriptures, especially The Book of Mormon. That's one thing I really wanted to say about the Holy Ghost; by those experiences I know his presence is real. I know it. I have experienced it. It transcends the five senses.

I had many other wonderful and growing experiences on my mission, and I proved to myself that my Dad's words to me about it being a foolish waste of time and money couldn't have been further from the truth. I cherish my missionary experiences, even though there was a lot of trial and difficulty and struggle too. I may not have been personally adequate for the job, but I had a firm testimony to share with the world, and with Jesus and the Holy Ghost on my side, I succeeded.

After my mission, I returned to Ricks College, and right after I graduated from there, my parents got divorced. My Mom moved out to Utah and within about a year or two remarried. My Dad has had two additional marriages and two additional divorces.

I went to BYU and majored in mechanical engineering, but I didn't go straight through because I lacked the money. I dropped out and worked for awhile, then went back, and dropped out and worked again, then went back, etc. I was a rather poor student because I had a rather daydreamy mind, low self esteem and severe shyness, and poor study habits. And depression. This was despite the fact that I had served my mission with some degree of boldness as I met strangers and taught them the Gospel of Jesus Christ.

It's really tough to discuss the emotional trials and tribulations I've had. My parent's divorce was emotionally very tough on me, even though I was twenty-three when it happened, and I realized that their entire marriage had been a divorce waiting to happen. I somehow felt cast adrift, without a home (not the home consisting of four walls and a roof, but the home consisting of a loving family and a place of belonging). And in my formative years, my home life had been a bit tumultuous. I vividly remember several fearful incidents where my dad spanked me and/or my next-younger sister without my realizing what wrong I had done. The only rule I could under-stand was not to annoy The Dad, because I might get sternly scolded and spanked. There never seemed to be any clearly defined rules. What was okay one day might be wrong the next, because it might annoy The Dad tomorrow, though it didn't annoy him today. So I grew up under a fearful emotional state where I always felt insecure, that I was teetering on the brink of upsetting The Dad, and walking on eggshells, so to speak. I grew up with a lot of anxieties and feel-ings of inadequacy, wondering how people might respond to me, fearing that they might reject me. This stifled my social development and caused me to be somewhat of a very shy loner.

This brings up a point about the Atonement of Christ and about the role of the Holy Ghost that is important to me. I think most Christians realize that Jesus took upon him the penalty and punish-ment for all our sins, so that we may be forgiven and spared that punishment if we do what he asks. But I m not sure that very many people realize that he also suffered all the pains of all mankind and that he knows and empathizes with all the troubles of every human heart. His atonement also has power to heal the scarred and wounded psyche. Those who don't understand this sometimes believe that emotional and psychic damage done to a child can't be reversed in later life, that he's doomed to remain emotionally or socially crippled, like the physical crippling that results from vitamin D deprivation, known as rickets. But part of the good news of the Gospel of Christ is that this is not so. It may be a long and difficult struggle, but Jesus can heal the wounded and scarred heart. He does it largely through the Holy Ghost, which works a mighty change on the mind and heart.

For me this has taken quite a long time, but it has happened and is happening still. The Bible gives one important key to what we must do to experience this kind of healing. It says "He that findeth his life shall lose it: and he that loseth his life for my sake shall find it." (Matthew 10:39) To me, one main meaning of this is that if we absorb ourselves into concerns for our own selves, we actually lose the fulfillment and the power of Christ in our lives that we need to be healed, but if we forget about our own selves and just put our effort into serving our fellow men and women and thereby serving Jesus, then the healing power and influence of Christ through the Holy Ghost will just naturally flow into our lives, changing us and enabling us to find joy, happiness, and fulfillment. Over the years, I have felt this influence gradually refining and purifying and developing my mind, heart, and spirit. He can gradually remold an entire character and personality if we make the right choices with our lives and take the right steps, and work at it.

When I was in my twenties I felt an anxiety attack whenever I came in contact with an eligible woman whom I found attractive and thought I would like to get to know. This problem persisted for years, blocking my ability to get married and start a family. Over the years I suffered a lot because of complications and embarrassments associated with this. But, finally, the Lord provided me a fine, sweet wife, and I am happily married.

But it took work and struggle on my part. That's one thing that is really fundamental to life. A lot of Christians miss the point on this. They read the scripture that says "That if thou shalt confess with thy mouth the Lord Jesus, and shalt believe in thine heart that God hath raised him from the dead, thou shalt be saved." (Romans 10:9) and then they think that that is literally all you have to do to be saved. They miss the point that this was written to the Romans, who risked being fed to the lions in the Coliseum, or at least severe persecution, if their discipleship were publicly known. This would be a severe test of faith, whereas in today's world it would be no test of faith at all, because most people would simply say "That's nice," whenever someone confesses Christ with their lips. The mentality of simply believe and confess Jesus and be saved not only contradicts many other scriptures in the New Testament, but it also defies common sense and misses a fundamental point about the way the cosmos works, about human nature and the laws of the universe. Getting something for nothing doesn't work. People only appreciate what they work for. The only true victory is a victory that is won with an actual battle. If you don't have a struggle there is no achievement. We will always have trials and struggles in this life. That is part of life's purpose, because the mastery of ourselves and strong, pure character cannot be achieved in any other way. That is part of God's plan for our journey through mortal life. Jesus tells us in the Bible To him that overcometh will I grant to sit with me in my throne, even as I also overcame, and am set down with my Father in his throne. (Revelation 3:21)

The true doctrine of how Christ's atonement absolves us of sins is this:

First, we must have faith in Jesus Christ, and believe that he is actually the divine Son of God and our personal Savior. That faith is put into effect by the actions we take, or our good works. In the Bible, James said "Even so faith, if it hath not works, is dead, being alone. Yea, a man may say, Thou hast faith, and I have works: shew me thy faith without thy works, and I will shew thee my faith by my works." (James 2:17-18)

Then we must repent of our sins, which means to feel sorry for them, to confess to God and to any injured party and apologize and ask their forgiveness, to make the fullest restitution we possibly can, to completely stop doing the sin, to forgive those who injure us, and to devote our lives to Christian service to God and our fellow men.

Next we must make a covenant with Jesus Christ, to take upon ourselves his name and become his disciples and to keep his commandments, and this covenant must be done in the way he has appointed. The only way he has established for this covenant to be made is by being baptized by immersion, by someone who is a duly authorized representative or agent for the Lord, who holds his priesthood.

Then we must receive the Holy Ghost, which brings about the baptism of fire and the rebirth of the spirit spoken of in the scriptures. The only way the Lord has established for us to receive the Holy Ghost is by having someone who holds his priesthood lay his hands upon our head and confirm us a member of Jesus Church, and by his priesthood power, confer upon us the gift of the Holy Ghost, as was done in the New Testament (see Acts 8:14-20).

Then we must fill our hearts with charity, which is the pure love of Christ. Jesus expressed this when he told us the greatest commandments: And he answering said, Thou shalt love the Lord thy God with all thy heart, and with all thy soul, and with all thy strength, and with all thy mind; and thy neighbour as thyself. (Luke 10:27) That is one of the major purposes of mortal life. Charity should be the fundamental feature of the human heart and soul. The Bible is full of other scriptures which tell us that.

And finally, we must endure to the end in devoting our lives as true disciples of Jesus, and continue to repent and strive to keep his commandments.

When we follow this course, then and only then will gain that blessed state that the scriptures call eternal life.

> *He that overcometh shall inherit all things; and I will be his God, and he shall be my son.*

> *Revelation 21:7*

One very important thing in the formation of my testimony of Jesus Christ has been The Book of Mormon. I have been acquainted with Christians who fear and loathe it as they would a snake, without ever having even looked at what it says. To me that is strange, but it fulfills a prophecy given in The Book of Mormon that many would scorn it and reject it without even looking at it, saying that the Bible is all the word of God that mankind could possibly have or need. Yet there are several references in the Bible to books of scripture written by various prophets, which are not found in the Bible. If the Bible itself is the only way people can have the word of God, then what did Adam and Eve do for scriptures before it was written? What did disciples of Jesus in Corinth and Galatia and Rome and various places do before the New Testament was written? In the New Testament there is a verse that says:

> *And there are also many other things which Jesus did, the which, if they should be written every one, I suppose that even the world itself could not contain the books that should be written. Amen.*

> *John 21:25*

From this we learn that there is much more of the word of God that we do not now have, yet the scriptures tell us:

...and Man shall not live by bread alone, but by every word that proceedeth out of the mouth of God.

Matthew 4:4

Also the Bible tells us that and the testimony of Jesus is the spirit of prophecy.

Revelation 19:10

So if anyone in our day has the testimony of Jesus, there should also be latter day prophecy. That is how we got The Book of Mormon, through latter day prophecy, in which the Lord revealed to Joseph Smith an ancient book of scripture and gave him power to translate it.

And yet people say, "Oh, no! There can't be any more than just the Bible." That's so confined, you know. How can they presume to dictate to the Lord that he can only speak one set of scriptures, or only one book? What evidence can they present that the Lord never intended to have more written down prophecy and revelation? How can they say to the Lord, Oh, no, you can't give me any more book than this one book, because I won't believe that you are willing to provide another book, or that we need it?

To me, I don't fear investigating new knowledge. I want to know all I can about important and interesting matters. I don't fear investigating other people's religions. I have read pamphlets from Jehovah's Witnesses, and I've even read parts of the Koran, just for the sake of new knowledge and understanding, even though the Holy Ghost testified to me that they are not the true word of God.

To me, The Book of Mormon is a wonderful thing. It testifies of Jesus Christ as the Son of God, the Savior and Redeemer. It is a very Christian book. Yet some Christians say "You're going to hell for reading The Book of Mormon and believing in it." They seem to think that by believing in The Book of Mormon that we are not orthodox Christians, and of course if we are not orthodox, then we believe in heresy. Since they think we believe in heresy then they think we are damned. Yet most of them also say that all you have to do is believe in Jesus and he will forgive your sins and save you. We Mormons believe in Jesus. If The Book of Mormon is a heresy, why will Jesus not save Mormons who believe in Him and commit this so-called heresy, yet save other Christians who believe in Him and commit other sins equally as bad as heresy? Where is the logical consistency in that attitude?

I know that The Book of Mormon is true. I have read it many times and the Holy Ghost testifies to me that it is the word of God. It motivates me to be a Christian and follow Jesus and serve him and my fellow man.

I would like to say a few things about the mission Jesus has accomplished. To me, it is fabulous. He created this earth. Before the earth was created he and his Father agreed to a plan whereby Christ promised to take upon himself the penalty, the burden and the punishment for the sins of all mankind. That was his promise, and He was completely trustworthy. In the Bible we read In the beginning was the Word, and the Word was with God, and the Word was God. The same was in the beginning with God. (John 1:1-2)

I've contemplated how Jesus was the Word. I don't know if this is totally the correct interpretation, but one that came to me was that He gave His word to his Father; he said something like "Yes, I promise that I will go down upon the earth and take upon myself the penalties of the sins of all mankind." Once He gave His word, His word was perfect. You have heard people say "My word is my bond." With Jesus, it really was so much so that his Father could rest the foundation of the entire Plan of Salvation upon that word. Once Jesus had given his word, Heavenly Father, his Father, trusted that promise so much that the fate of all mankind hung in the balance.

And Jesus fulfilled that mission. He has gone through all we've gone through; a mortal experience, being born onto this earth, being subjected to physical difficulties, temptations, trials, pains, and sufferings of all kinds, like anyone else, with two major differences: First, he was perfect and never committed even the tiniest infraction or sin. And second, he took upon himself the penalty, weight, burden, and punishment for all our sins. He wrought the infinite atonement. In suffering that, he bled from every pore. He thereby purchased us with his blood (Acts 20:28), so because of that he became eligible to set the terms and conditions for our salvation. He is also the one to whom we will answer for our lives and he is our judge. As he has purchased our souls, he has thereby become our Father in that sense, as Isaiah called him

...the mighty God, the Everlasting Father, the Prince of Peace.

Isaiah 9:6

So in that sense, we have two immortal Fathers. We started out, of course, with Heavenly Father, the Father of our spirits (Hebrews 12:9), who also is the Father of Jesus. But our Heavenly Father has committed the keys of this earth and all of our salvation into the hands of His only begotten Son, Jesus Christ (We are Heavenly Father's sons and daughters too, but not begotten, as Jesus was.) So in a sense he was our elder brother, but now he is our Father, in that we are adopted to him because of his atoning sacrifice.

For Jesus to be able to take all this upon himself, he had to be more intelligent than the sum total of all the rest of us. He had to have more love and compassion and empathy than all the rest of mankind. He is the perfect embodiment of love, kindness, compassion, and mercy, but he's also the one who has the responsibility to execute justice and judgment upon us. He knows the end, and how things will turn out, even from the very beginning. He has even shown some of the prophets visions of the future that he himself knew, right down to the minutest detail of what was going to happen. Not that he predestined it to happen. Our freedom to choose has always been a sacred principle to Jesus. But he had foreknowledge of how the sum total of all the choices of all mankind would blend together to unfold history, before it ever happened. This even extends to knowing exactly what choices each of us will make long before we make them.

I feel that it is important for us that know and believe in Jesus Christ, to testify of him. There are so many people whose lives need him as their Savior. In The Book of Mormon, there were some missionaries who cared for the souls of their fellow man. It says:

> Now they were desirous that salvation should be declared to every creature, for they could not bear that any human soul should perish; yea, even the very thoughts that any soul should endure endless torment did cause them to quake and tremble.
>
> *Mosiah 28:3*

Jesus loves those people who don't know him, and wants us to help him reach them. He wants them to find eternal joy and happiness, and receive salvation.

In the New Testament there is a scripture that says "My sheep hear my voice, and I know them, and they follow me:" (John 10:27)

And how is his voice heard? In my mind his voice is partially heard through our testimonies. Once they hear our testimonies, the Holy Ghost can work with that message in their hearts and work a transformation that can bring them to know Christ also. It may occur while we are speaking to them, or it may happen a few days or even years later. But it is important that they hear the message.

We who love Jesus are the light of the world and the salt of the earth. Our example is constantly on display.

One great Book of Mormon prophet expressed his desire to help save others this way:

> *O that I were an angel, and could have the wish of mine heart, that I might go forth and speak with the trump of God, with a voice to shake the earth, and cry repentance unto every people! Yea, I would declare unto every soul, as with the voice of thunder, repentance and the plan of redemption, that they should repent and come unto our God, that there might not be more sorrow upon all the face of the earth.*

> *Alma 29:1-2*

The God to whom he wanted to bring them is Jesus Christ. And I know, as he stated, that if all mankind would come unto Jesus, there would be no more sorrow upon the earth, nor wars, nor famines.

I can testify and know with a deep conviction that Jesus Christ is the Son of God, the Savior and Redeemer. I know that he was born of a virgin as described in the New Testament and also in The Book of Mormon. I know that he took upon himself our sins, on the conditions he has set, as I stated earlier.

That's one element of my testimony. Another element is that lip service to Christ is inadequate. If we are to receive him, we must receive his servants, and we must receive his words, and not refuse to even read them or listen to them, as some do who reject The Book of Mormon without ever even knowing what it contains. If we follow Christ we seek with an open mind and open ourselves up to the messages he offers us. We confirm his words by the power of the Holy Ghost testifying to us that they are true, and by living the principles we learn.

Another thing that I do know is that there was a Great Apostasy in which the principles of Christianity were indeed perverted and darkened, many of them were lost, and the authority and power for man to act in behalf of Christ was taken from the earth. But a great light has pierced the darkness of that apostasy. There has been an even greater restoration, in which Christ has restored and re-established his Church on the earth. And just as his earthly ministry was not implemented through the accepted channels of the established religious order, neither was the latter day restoration. The restoration means that there are living prophets once again on this earth who are fully authorized and endowed with power to act in behalf of Jesus. This power and authority is His priesthood. That priesthood power has been restored through the Prophet Joseph Smith who actually saw God, the Eternal Father, and His Son, Jesus Christ, as two separate and distinct individual beings who actually appeared to him. I have a firm testimony and conviction and knowledge that this is true, that it did happen.

After Heavenly Father and Jesus Christ appeared to Joseph Smith, I have a testimony that other heavenly messengers, angels, appeared to him also. I know The Book of Mormon was revealed to Joseph Smith by God and translated by him through the gift and power of God, and that it contains many great and essential elements of truth for our salvation which had been hidden from the world until it came forth. These things had been hidden because of the blindness and hardness of the hearts of men who would not receive the word of God when it was given to them. I have a testimony that The Book of Mormon is truly the word of God and is entirely consistent with the Bible. I know that the Bible is also the word of God as far as it is translated correctly.

I know that The Church of Jesus Christ of Latter-day Saints is actually the true Church of Jesus Christ. It is not a denomination, sect, or cult, but is Jesus' own true Church, which he restored and re-established in the latter days. I know it is the repository of all the authority of Christ on the earth. It is the institution in which Christ has invested his authority and the Holy Spirit in the latter days. It is his organization and his Church, he established it. It was not founded and established by Joseph Smith, but rather was founded and established by Jesus Christ. This Church has living power that has continued through the more than 150 years since it was restored to the earth.

I have a testimony that the man who currently presides over this Church is a true prophet of God and is vested with all the power and authority and keys of this priesthood that God sees fit that mankind should have in these days. President Hinkley today is a prophet, seer, and revelator, just as great as the ancient prophets in the Old and New testaments. Every president of the Church from the time of Joseph Smith to this present day has been likewise.

I know that joy and happiness are found by accepting the Gospel of Jesus Christ by all the steps I have mentioned previously, including faith in Jesus Christ, repentance, baptism into this the true Church of Jesus Christ, and receiving the gift of the Holy Ghost and abiding by the precepts that we hold dear. Without that knowledge and without that discipline of one of Jesus disciples, life is pretty bland, meaningless, and empty. It is a barren wasteland.

I hope to be able to remain true and faithful and to endure to the end, and become perfected in Christ and have him say to me when he brings me home, Well done, thou good and faithful servant, as He gives me a warm welcoming embrace. I testify to the truth of these things, as the Holy Ghost has testified to me, in the name of Jesus Christ, amen.

Amazing Grace, how sweet the sound that saved a wretch like me.
I once was lost, but now I'm found, was blind, but now I see.

T'was grace that taught my heart to fear; and grace my fears relieved;
How precious did that grace appear the hour I first believed!

Thru many dangers, toils and snares I have already come;
This grace hath bro't me safe thus far and grace will lead me home.

Words and music by John Newton

MARLENA'S STORY

Born: Canton, Ohio   Divorced, no children
Parents: Russian Jewish, deceased. Younger brother   Christian since 1988
Occupation: Medical Secretary, author   Age: 50's

I WAS BORN INTO A FAMILY OF JEWS, descendants of Russian and western European stock who, in the early years of this century left their homeland and traveled with great hope in their hearts to this wondrous land of America, there to make a new life for themselves and their heirs.

Growing up, I heard of the wonders of God; how he had saved our people from Egyptian, Assyrian, Babylonian, Roman, German and Russian tyranny, bringing them through the anguish of slavery, through their great wanderings in the deserts of Judea and out of the shivering darkness of the shtetls of western Europe. I heard in the prayers of the elders of the synagogue their gratitude for deliverance from the hands of ancient mortal enemies. I heard Elohim praised for remembering the Jews in their dispersion throughout the world, and for His great mercy during their awful trials at the hands of Hitler and his legions. I was taught that the greatest events in human history were the creation of man by God and then the freeing of the Hebrew people from Egyptian and Babylonian rule. Through the prayers of the faithful I learned to love and to fear our immortal Father who lives in Heaven and who, I was taught, we cannot really know.

In a broad sense a congregation is missionary to its members. I was easily converted to the knowledge that my heritage was special above all others. My mother told me to be proud that I was the latest in my family of a long line of Hebrew women, part of the eternal covenant God made with Abraham, Isaac and Jacob that the Jewish people were special to Him because of their willingness to live His Law. I was not learned in scripture but I read with great interest the Old Testament's first five books and the book of Judges, together making up the text of the sacred Pentateuch or Torah.

The Talmud, a collection of complex commentaries of the learned rabbis of past ages, was also a part of my study. Since Jews do not read the New Testament or believe that a Savior and Redeemer named Jesus Christ has come to them, I knew nothing of the Christ. My Lord was God, and my promised land was Israel. But I loved and believed in the stories of the prophets. These wondrous men were heroes to me because of their passionate relationship with God and their religious fervor to learn and to spread the word of God among their followers. All of them prophesied and testified of the *Mashiach* who would one day save the Jewish people and return them to their homeland of Israel. Prophets could always be counted upon to speak the truth and in those times many of them were sent by God to counsel the masses who were stiffnecked even then.

But there was no prophet in my life and times. We were all adrift to wander as the wind moved us, tribes of Jews torn away from their precious homeland and still at odds in a new society, we became pioneers of private destinies. It seemed a long and lonely road, but any desires I had about a personal God who would help me with the increasing complexity of my life I hid away within my deepest self. With the rest of my people I waited and watched for the *Mashiach* to arrive.

As I grew to be a woman, however, my feelings about my religion became more conflicting. Though I loved to hear the cantor sing during services, listening to the ritualized prayers offered by the rabbi increasingly left me with feelings of abandonment and loneliness. Friday night services and Sunday School were times of friendship and feeling part of a special congregation, but at the same time many of the services were of ancient origin, unchanging, impersonalized. I felt overlooked, uninspired, unfulfilled. There was more to know, I was sure, before I could give my full heart to God or begin to understand His design for me. Somehow, that was of prime importance even in my youth. I began to resent the People Israel concept that was a subject of reverence in every synagogue because little emphasis was placed upon situations of the present time and the conflicts which weave themselves inextricably into our lives.

Eventually, by the time I had turned fourteen I wandered away from the services, feeling that something was wrong, untrue, not right, though I could not then name the doubts that pulled at my mind. I understand now that I was seeking a way to know for sure that which I suspected… my spirit longed to know its Maker and to be at peace. I wanted to know of life before life and after death, for that would give me clues as to the purposes of God concerning the human soul. I wanted God to speak to me alone as His child, separate from Israel. But I didn't know how to bring that about. Prayer, my only recourse, seemed without fruit. It took most of half a century before I was made aware that the truth was all around me, waiting only for my discovery.

That wondrous time came unexpectedly after many years of unhappy living and as much soul searching. During that time I was to be married and divorced but never blessed with children. My childhood had been abusive, my teenage years were spent trying to disprove many of the lessons on morality my strict Jewish parents had taught me. I was quite unready for the responsibilities of adulthood and marriage. Personal unhappiness caused job failures. Lack of a healthy self respect caused me to make poorly thought out decisions regarding a marriage partner. I seemed headed for mental breakdown at times and had to seek counseling more than once. Eventually, career relocations, readjustments after divorce and a few liaisons resulted in serious personality problems. There were many moves through many states, once even to Mexico for a year where I nearly died of a virus I contracted after drinking a single glass of contaminated water. I arrived in my forties a much sadder and quieter woman, sure of very little and longing for more than I could understand.

And he humbled thee, and suffered thee to hunger…that he might make thee know that man doth not live by bread only, but by every word that proceedeth out of the mouth of the Lord doth man live.

Deuteronomy 8:3

It was not really by accident that I first experienced Christian doctrine. My brother had been the first of our Jewish family to join The Church of Jesus Christ of Latter-day Saints shortly after marrying a Tongan woman who was strong in that Church. On a rare visit he presented me with a Book of Mormon, thereby laying the groundwork for visits by Mormon missionaries in the months to come. Though I did not comprehend the beauty of The Book of Mormon then or feel that I was able to accept Jesus Christ, I was moved by the things they taught me. Their information about the pre-mortal existence of mankind, about humanity's purpose on earth and especially revealed doctrine concerning eternal life and exaltation through Jesus Christ fascinated me. They taught me a lot I could never have learned through my Jewish experience. I attended church with them after Sunday services on two occasions, out of curiosity, really, to learn what I would feel in that rarified air. I was amazed to discover myself touched so strongly by emotions I did not understand that I broke into tears touching the chapel door! But when, eventually, the missionaries wanted me to be baptized I told them honestly that I couldn't, because I had to be true to Judaic teachings which forbade baptism in the name of, or in any way associated with Jesus Christ. Though I was no longer active in my faith I retained strong loyalties to the past.

On my own, I did find my way back into that chapel from time to time after everyone had left the Sunday service there. Something told me I would be listened to. I would enter the chapel on Sunday afternoons after everyone else was gone so as not to be recognized as a Jew attending a Christian church. It sounds silly now, but I actually thought I would be ostracized and made to leave if I were found in a church!

With great reservation and not a little fear, I sat in the pews and prayed. So many times I strongly felt a presence close behind me, but when I turned around I could see no one. It was mystifying, a new experience, a beginning. Even stranger, after every prayer I offered I found within the following week true relief and help. Soon it became a regular practice. I attended Friday night services in the local synagogue, and on Sunday afternoons when the Church chapel was empty I stole my way in to ask God for help. Unfailingly, time after time my needs were met! I didn't understand, but it was great. I was on a roll!

The Lord wanted me in his flock, I believe, because fate again caused me to move, this time to Oregon where my brother lived with his family. His wife, just thirty-four and sick now with cancer, was dying. Their four sweet children were frightened for her. I came to help in any way I could and once there found the kindness of the

Latter-day Saint community something I could not ignore. They did not try to change me. They loved and cared for me more than my own people had done in many years. I came to respect them for the intensity of their love for Jesus Christ and their watchful care of and service to others.

The Lord is my shepherd; I shall not want...He restoreth my soul: he leadeth me in the paths of righteousness for his name's sake.

Psalm 23:1,3

Eventually, I became close to some stake missionaries who told me again that the Gospel of Jesus Christ was true. To test that concept I would have to have faith in God. They said that I would not have to give up anything I already knew was true, but only add to what I knew. They told me that all people on the earth today were descendants of the twelve original tribes or families of ancient Israel through the biblical Joseph who, in the Old Testament, was the owner of the coat of many colors. Joseph was the son of Jacob, son of Isaac, son of the great prophet Abraham. (Through a blessing after joining the Church I later learned that I was a descendant of the ancient tribe of Judah.)

The stake missionaries were descendents of another of Joseph's sons, Ephraim, as are a great many gentiles (people of non-Israelite lineage and those without the Gospel), entitled to the ancient blessings which he received from his father. I looked up the references they gave me in Genesis 48, where it states that the seed of Ephraim will become a multitude of nations, again in Genesis 49, when the sons of Joseph are blessed, Judah among them, as the lineage which would welcome the Savior's return in glory. These promises were made by our Father in Heaven who loves the Jewish people as His first chosen. He will not let them perish but one day will bring them together again, ready for the Savior's appearance in their midst. I was overcome by this knowledge. What a great joy to know that the Jews will be restored to Israel to again occupy their homeland! In 2Nephi in The Book of Mormon God reveals His plan to gather the Jewish remnants to Israel where they will live in peace with their *Mashiach*. This prophecy is the fulfillment of the dream of all generations of displaced Jews throughout the world. How grateful I am for this great gift!

The missionaries had taught me that this Joseph of the coat of many colors was a "fruitful bough...by a well whose branches run over the wall," (Gen 49:22). He was blessed that through his loins would come a modern prophet into a new country across the wall and well of the sea whose name would be as his and through whose unselfish and tireless efforts the waiting world would hear the true and full Gospel of Jesus Christ restored to the earth after many hundreds of years of spiritual darkness. This marvelous prediction was made a couple of thousand years before its occurrence in 1830 when the boy Joseph Smith was led to the golden plates that through revelation from God became The Book of Mormon, so that we in these last days can have the truth restored to us.

> ...the Prophet Joseph Smith said: "I told the brethren that the Book of Mormon was the most correct of any book on earth, and the keystone of our religion, and a man would get nearer to God by abiding by its precepts, than by any other book.

> *Introduction, Book of Mormon*

Through all the many lonely years of my life, hearing and reading these things gradually had a profound impact on me. I listened. I wanted to hear more, though years earlier the young missionaries had told me the same things. Not being ready to hear their message then, I had forgotten much, but hearing it now my soul was stirred. I found myself taking it in. There were many conflicts between what I remembered from my past and what I was now being told. Why do we need a Savior? Could the Jews have been wrong about Christ's divinity all these years? Isn't our Heavenly Father enough to save us? Is it true that Christ saved us from sin and the terror of spiritual death and also wants us to have exaltation in the kingdom of God? If there is a Holy Ghost, where is the biblical Old Testament reference to him and to the divinity of Christ? I knew nothing of Jesus Christ or Christianity. Christianity was a concept I had always thought was inferior to Judaism, an entirely secular world that was confusing (and unnecessary).

I also had many questions about the story of the buried golden plates of early American prophets and the coming forth of The Book of Mormon through the Prophet Joseph Smith. Was he really a latter day prophet of God? How important is revelation? How could I know for sure if this Christian faith was more correct than all others? Why was it important enough to study?

The most important question, as I look back, was how it all fit together in my mind and heart.

Eventually, working part time as a nurse aide I offered to help my new found friends build a room on their barn so I could move into it. "I will study your books and my books," I told them. "And I will stay in that room, except for work, until I solve this problem." I was forty, divorced, childless, not knowing how to further map my course. What did I have to lose?

We built the room in a month and I moved most of my belongings into their barn loft. I moved myself beneath it in my new room, just across from the goats. (They made sweet but restless and noisy neighbors.) My new sanctuary had no toilet and no running water but the main house was only twenty five feet away. I had electric lights, a bed, my television, my typewriter, The Book of Mormon, the Doctrine and Covenants, the Pearl of Great Price, the Torah and the Talmud. As if to keep me literally on my toes or on my bed, a family of field mice took up shelter beneath the bed frame. I could hear their chirping and chewing while I read. It made me shudder. I remember praying to God to keep them from jumping into bed with me while I slept! In self defense I sometimes read aloud to them from the scriptures while they scurried and mewed beneath me.

Finally I set traps for the mice and for the following five months I worked, read, studied and prayed that the knowledge I sought be revealed to me through the scriptures. I prayed for a harvest, and like a desperate detective I hunted among the thin pages of ancient knowledge hoping to excavate the great truths that waited there. I spread out the volumes on my bed like the precious fragments of recorded time they are and let my mind and heart scan the centuries, from Genesis through the Exodus, from the Davidic kings through the advent of Christ to the prophecies of John in Revelations. Concentrating especially on the prophets I came to understand their great missions and how they always could be counted on to speak the truth.

In that little room I read, prayed, slept, read some more. I was starved to know everything those books could teach me. After a long time, I began to discern the ways of God as separate from mankind, to see how His mighty hand adjudicated in the affairs of men. From Old Testament writings to the life mission, death and resurrection of Jesus, from the Revelations to the ancient record of the forerunners of the Indians of America, where Christ appeared after his resurrection to visit his "other sheep" to establish His Church among the earliest ancestors of this continent. I discovered that The Book of Mormon is a marvelous record of that visit and of those early civilizations. Inscribed on gold plates during the period from 600 B.C. through A.D. 421, it truly is a companion to the Bible, giving further prophecy of Jesus as the Savior of the world. I found it to be an undeniable second witness of Christ.

I learned of Joseph Smith, chosen to bring about the Gospel's restoration after many hundreds of years when no one holding that sacred priesthood authority was on the earth. He told all who would hearken that he had been called of God to restore that ancient authority, that he was a modern mouthpiece for the Almighty. He came as a servant, a conduit for the word of God to bring that enlightenment promised in the scriptural canon, to support and augment what the Bible teaches.

I began to believe that the Doctrine and Covenants, a book of the revelations of Christ to the Prophet Joseph Smith and others, was an inspired record revealing in present day language the ways of God among men, instructing through revelation the building up of the restored Church of Jesus Christ upon the earth, outlining "the purpose of mortality, the necessity for obedience, the need for repentance, the workings of the Holy Spirit, the ordinances and performances that pertain to salvation, the destiny of the earth, the future condition of man after the resurrection..." (See Explanatory Introduction, the Doctrine and Covenants) and many other wondrous ideas that no man or group of men could have conceived. I realized that no human intelligence could be so profound or boast such broad scope as I found in those pages. This truly was the work of that great author, the Word of God.

And also those to whom these commandments were given, might have power to lay the foundation of this church, and to bring it forth out of obscurity and out of darkness, the only true and living church upon the face of the whole earth, with which I, the Lord, am well pleased.

Doctrine and Covenants 1:30

But the fundamental problem begged solving. I prayed to know how all of this could all be true if Jesus was not the Christ. The blinders I wore came from centuries of secular programming. Should I erase that from my past? Could I actually make the change? My very identity had always seemed to depend upon my allegiance to the teachings of the Torah and the rabbis in the synagogue. I was a Jew. Jews do not believe that the *Mashiach* has come. For a Jew to say that Jesus is the Christ is to declare oneself as dead to Judaism. Jewish families have held funerals for members who crossed to that side of the barbed wire. They were turncoats. They became amongst fellow Jews a hiss and a byword, unwelcome in the streets and in synagogues. They were unwelcome even in their own homes.

Though I was now faced with evidence I could no longer deny, where would permission come from so that I might finally accept the fact that long ago in Palestine there was a man who came to speak to those from whose loins all modern Jews have descended. Carrying that banner of the covenant with Abraham this humble, gentle and loving man truly was and is the Messiah of this world, through his own choice he had come to lead humankind toward their eternal home and inheritance: eternal life leading to exaltation in the Kingdom of God.

One day I was driving alone into town. At a stop sign a voice went through my mind: Jesus Christ is the Savior of the world. I started. What was that? Again the same words came to me. I remember staring at the red light, watching it turn green and red again. No cars were behind me, so I just sat there trying to understand what I had heard. The voice was still, but I was amazed at its message, amazed that I had heard something that didn't come from myself. I began to think about those words. Slowly I reasoned that if Jesus were just some teacher of long ago there would be no churches erected to his name, nor would he be worshipped as the Messiah throughout all these centuries. If he were the Messiah, then of course it made sense that Christians would follow him and look forward to his Millennial reign, as they have done since his resurrection. Without any warning, without any emotion, it was like a problem solved. It made sense.

That Sunday I attended the Sacrament meeting at the local LDS Church and stayed for classes afterward. There the Plan of Salvation was clearly and simply explained to me, as I had heard it years before but now it bore its truth to me. Now I opened my heart to that great message. If this was all true, then I wanted for the rest of my life to follow the Savior. I vowed to seriously consider baptism. I prayed to be led and to know the truth. It wasn't until later that I discovered that somewhere beneath my own knowing I had, since my first encounter with the missionaries, been building a new infra-structure inside the old barricades, a lighter, cleaner spirituality, in half-conscious anticipation of a newly emerging self.

When I was reminded that Jesus Christ died for me that I might be free of death and sin, that through my faithfulness and works I could realize my spiritual potential, I didn't know what to feel. I wondered why God would do that for us, and why He would send His son to be sacrificed. I knew I was unworthy of such an act, even genuinely embarrassed by it. But gradually, as though I had always suspected it I realized that Jesus, if he were the *Mashiach*, was the Jews' truest hero; the mightiest, bravest of them all and merciful beyond human understanding, someone who, through his supreme act was able to save not only the Jewish people from physical and spiritual bondage, but even all mankind. His gracious and profound message to those he saved, his wondrous miracles and great courage among those who were enemies, his love for all of us proved that he could do anything he chose to do.

> *Behold, I am Jesus Christ, the Son of the living God, who created the heavens and the earth, a light which cannot be hid in darkness;*

> Doctrine and Covenants 14:9

Growing within me now was a new feeling, gentle but insistent, a discovery that seemed to have finally persuaded my body's every cell of the answer to my lonely quest: Here at long last was a flesh and blood gift from God to each mortal soul. My Father in Heaven had shown His great love for me in a way I could not any longer ignore. I was becoming sure that I could also gladly serve and adore His Son. Here at last, I felt, was someone who truly understood my deepest need for love and acceptance. Here was a Perfect One through whom I could realize my potential for faith and trust in God and learn His plan for my sojourn on earth and throughout eternity. I was rapidly learning that in Christ I had found the one for whom I would willingly give up my sins, even my life.

And then a funny thing happened. I waited. And waited. I attended Church but didn't ask for the missionary discussions, which must precede baptism. I worked and thought about what I had discovered but did nothing about it. When my Mormon friends asked me for a commitment, I demurred. It was as if the knowledge was itself enough, but in my most private moments I knew I was still afraid to make through baptism the essential Christian covenant: to follow Christ, to live the full gospel.

Soon after my discovery I was chosen to meet a friend at the hospital and bring her home following a minor surgery. I was late and hurriedly left my little room in the barn. Standing outside it I adjusted my coat. No one else was on the property.

Suddenly there was a Presence at my right side. He was taller than I, though I didn't see him with my natural eyes. I saw him with spiritual eyes. I know he had a definite body because I felt it was there, felt the weight of it next to me. I was aware of the perimeters of his body. He said only "You need to understand that it's all in how you look at it. This is God's Church." Profound words from an angel of God.

How can I describe my reaction? He had simply imparted a bit of knowledge to me, but it hit me like an explosion! It was as if the thought came from *me!* I looked upward as he spoke. The sky was suddenly a vast, gateless field of air. It seemed to expand for me and I realized that now for the first time I was *free*. Truly, completely, without apology, free! I felt wonderful, a prisoner released. As if the words he uttered had been my thoughts! Aloud I said suddenly "If that is true I want to become a Mormon." It was the release of an unrealized wish. That's when a miracle happened.

Sometimes in a life it is as though all moments meet, all hours suddenly account for their time and direction. It was so then and there. My heart swelled and pounded until I felt it was bursting! My body was tingling from bottom to top. I felt joyous for the first time in my life. In that moment I was changed forever. I felt a new certainty. With sudden and great force of heart and mind, I knew—standing there filling full of light—that Jesus *is* the Christ and that The Church of Jesus Christ of Latter-day Saints *is* the restored Church of Jesus Christ on the earth and that there is a living prophet of God on the earth today. I knew of the power of revelation. I knew that every prayer I had begged an answer for was at that moment being answered. God has never stopped speaking to us. All the roads of my life coalesced at that moment of perfect unity. I was free to choose and I had just received heavenly permission. *It is all true.* And it was all mine.

I was baptized April 6, 1988 a member of The Church of Jesus Christ of Latter-day Saints, a happy Jewish woman from the ancient tribe of Judah, certain for the first time in my life of what I was doing.

To be baptized in the name of Jesus Christ is no small thing for one who has followed only the teachings of Torah and Talmud to the exclusion of all further light and knowledge. That moment in the water was truly the burial of my sins, the cleansing of my soul, the lifting of the terrible weights of conscience that life had brought me. I received the second baptism; the laying on of hands for the reception of the gift of the Holy Ghost, in accordance with the revelation given the Prophet Joseph Smith. The LDS Church is the only one which baptizes in this way, following Christ's example.

Is it crazy to say that the conversion of a Jewish soul is the culmination of the wanderings of ancient Jews who followed Abraham and Moses out of hellish Egypt? My own family's ancestors lived as hunted animals in the wartime ghettos of Europe. They came looking for freedom but ended being herded like cattle across Germany in the killing boxcars. They endured bravely the stuffy, overloaded boats that bore them on the last leg of their Diaspora and brought them to a waiting America that they might worship in freedom.

They came here also for me, that I, too, might worship in freedom. I carried with me their darkness, their unrelieved yearning for the light the full Gospel brings. My future would now be filled with the bright light of Christ and the further assurance that I was finally in his Church. In the sacred moments of baptism by one having true authority, then the laying on of hands for the reception of the gift of the Holy Ghost, it was made known to me that I had learned the ways of God at Jesus' feet! As a new Christian I would be required to follow him in all things as one of the many thousands of missionaries of the Restoration, to progress in my life's journey until that day when I should hopefully meet him again at that Bar of eternal judgment.

> Ask, and it shall be given unto you; seek, and ye shall find; knock, and it shall be opened unto you.
>
> For everyone that asketh receiveth; and he that seeketh, findeth; and to him that knocketh, it shall be opened.
>
> 3Ne 14:7-8

A year after my baptism I received a cherished Recommend permitting me to enter one of the temples of the Lord. These holy houses of the Lord have been reestablished in these latter days throughout the world in increasing numbers of countries. (At this writing there are nearly seventy operating, under construction and in planning stages in more than thirty countries.) I participated in temple ordinances and blessings which are authorized by the sacred sealing and binding power of that Melchizedek priesthood which Jesus and his apostles held. It has been my great joy to be a part of these saving administrations for the living and the dead which Jesus instituted (1Cor 15:22-58), that my family, indeed that each of us, may be forever together, not only with our present but also our ancestral families through eternal and sacred covenants, if we prove our faithfulness through righteous living.

I know that marriage can be forever. Families separated in life can be reunited after their earthly sojourns have ended. Grieving for the departed does not have to be traumatic because of the revelation to latter day prophets that we have always lived and will continue throughout eternity to live, to be further taught those sacred truths that will help us to progress in our understanding of God's kingdom. Knowing the full Gospel of Jesus Christ truly has made me see how perfect is the Plan of Salvation of our Heavenly Father. He wants us to return to Him, to continue to progress toward perfection after our time on earth. He has promised His children that they can eventually inherit all He has and realize their spiritual potential. How truly grateful I am for this great knowledge.

How I love my Savior! When I read the marvelous revelations given by him to the Prophet Joseph Smith I am filled with awe at Christ's great love for mankind. I am humbled by his love for me. Through latter day scripture which tells of his visit to the American continent where he reestablished his Gospel following his resurrection I found a great treasure of knowledge and wisdom. I eagerly listen to his unceasing communication through his living prophets today. I know that God's mercy toward us is unfailing. I know that after my death, if I am worthy I shall see Him again and renew our friendship.

Jesus the Christ is my example of all things good. He is my brother. He helps me to leave a legacy to all the world through my testimony that he is the Christ who shed his blood for us that death and sin would be forever overcome. Through him I have learned that baptism by one having proper authority is the gateway to eternal life through the ancient covenant between God and His great prophets Adam, Abraham, Isaac, Moses, Noah, Isaiah, Jeremiah, John the Baptist, Jesus

Christ, Joseph Smith, and those who have come after him.

I have, finally, the knowledge of where I came from, why I am here and where I am going. Our Heavenly Father and our Redeemer have prepared many blessings and gifts of the spirit for each of us. If we will but come to Him with a humble heart, a repentant spirit and a love of discovery we can all find those bestowals waiting for us to claim.

There are souls who love the Lord with only a part of their being, seemingly in little need of spiritual nourishment. But to a Jew who loves God more than life and longs for the saving grace of a personal Savior and the guiding ministrations of the great Comforter, even the Holy Spirit, The Church of Jesus Christ of Latter-day Saints is the coming home, the bringing forward out of silent darkness into brilliant light truths that are saving and eternal. To me, this is the fulfillment of any life. The full Gospel contains all that anyone needs to know of Christ and his truth at the current time because Christ is its living head. It is a table spread before the faithful searcher, filled with survival food for the soul. It is, simply, the perfect feast.

> *Wherefore, ye must press forward with a steadfastness in Christ, having a perfect brightness of hope, and a love of God and of all men. Wherefore, if ye shall press forward, feasting upon the word of Christ, and endure to the end, behold, thus saith the Father: Ye shall have eternal life.*

> 2NE 31:20

I know that my Savior lives, that he sits on the right hand of the Father, and that the Holy Ghost teaches and testifies of all truth. I know by the power of the Holy Ghost that Joseph Smith was and is a prophet of God and that The Church of Jesus Christ of Latter-day Saints is the restored Church of Christ upon the earth today and that we have a living prophet, Gordon B. Hinckley, who receives revelation for all mankind. He is President of that Church. I solemnly testify by the power of the Holy Ghost that these things are true, in the sacred name of Jesus Christ, amen.

For I am not ashamed of the gospel of Christ:
for it is the power of God unto salvation to
every one that believeth; to the Jew first, also
to the Greek

Romans 1:16

BIBLIOGRAPHY
THE FIRST FOUR CHAPTERS

A New Witness for the Articles of Faith
Bruce R. McConkie
Deseret Book
Salt Lake City, Utah 1985

The Archko Volume
or the Archaeological Writings of the Sanhadrim & Talmuds of the Jews
Translated by Drs. McIntosh & Twyman
Unabridged Edition
Keats Publishing Company, Connecticut 1975

The Articles of Faith
James E. Talmage
The Church of Jesus Christ of Latter day-Saints
Salt Lake City, Utah 1982

Biblical Archaeology Review
January-February 1998
Volume 24:1
The Enigma of Qumran, pp. 24-37

The Book of Mormon, Another Testament of Jesus Christ
The Doctrine and Covenants
The Pearl of Great Price
The Church of Jesus Christ of Latter-day Saints
Salt Lake City, Utah 1987

The Complete Works of Josephus
Flavius Josephus
Translated by Wm Whiston
Kregel Publications
Grand Rapids, Michigan 1981

The Day Christ Died
Jim Bishop
Harper Bros.
New York, New York 1951

Halley's Bible Handbook
Revised Edition
Henry H. Halley
Regency Reference Library
Zondervan Publishing House
Michigan 1965

History of Jesus Christ
R. L. Bruckberger
Viking Press
New York 1965

The Holy Bible, King James Version
The Church of Jesus Christ of Latter-day Saints
Salt Lake City, Utah 1987

Invitation To The Talmud, A Teaching Book
Jacob Neusser
Harper & Row
New York, New York 1973

Jerusalem The Eternal City
David B. Galbraith, D. Kelly Ogden, Andrew C. Skinner
Deseret Book Company
Salt Lake City, Utah 1996

Jesus in the First Three Gospels
Millar Burrows
Abingdon Press
Nashville, Tennessee 1977

Jesus of Nazareth, The Hidden Years
Robert Aron
William Morrow & Co.
New York, New York 1962

Jesus the Christ
James E. Talmage
The Church of Jesus Christ of Latter-day Saints
Salt Lake City, Utah 1981

Jewish Wisdom
Rabbi Joseph Telushkin
William Morrow and Company, Inc.
New York, New York 1994

The Life and Teachings of Jesus and His Apostles
Course Manual, Second Edition
The Church of Jesus Christ of Latter-day Saints
Salt Lake City, Utah 1979

The Random House Dictionary of the English Language
Unabridged
Jess Stern, Editor
Random House
New York, New York 1971

The Union Prayer Book for Jewish Worship
The Central Conference of American Rabbis
Revised, Part II
Cincinnati, Ohio 1950

The Temple, Its Ministry and Services
Updated Edition
Alfred Edersheim
Hendrickson Publishers, Inc.
Peabody, Massachusetts 1994

ABOUT THE AUTHOR

MARLENA TANYA MUCHNICK IS A JEWISH convert to
The Church of Jesus Christ of Latter-day Saints of
ten years. A longtime resident of the Pacific Northwest, Marlena
writes as an inspired avocation. This volume is the product of two
years of interviews and research into the spiritual lives of those to
whom the Spirit has led her and is a result of inspired promptings.
Her personal and moving testimony has been published under the
title *Notes of a Jewish Convert to the LDS Church, Conversion of a Soul*. A
story for children is in the works.

The author invites all who are moved by these stories to communicate with her and the other contributors through her email
address: *myambra@hotmail.com* or: http://*www.jewishconvert-lds.com*.
Letters may be addressed to Marlena Yambra, P.O. Box 16701,
Seattle, WA 98116.